Culture and Development Series
No. 1

General Editor
Kapila Vatsyayan

Interface of
Cultural Identity and Development

Interface of Cultural Identity and Development

Edited by
Baidyanath Saraswati

Indira Gandhi National Centre for the Arts
New Delhi

D. K. Printworld (P) Ltd.
New Delhi

Cataloging in Publication Data — DK

Interface of cultural identity and development /
edited by Baidyanath Saraswati.
(Culture and development series; no. 1).
Includes bibliographical references.

1. Culture and development. I. Saraswati,
Baidyanath, 1932- II. Series : Culture and
development series; no. 1.

ISBN 81-246-0054-6

First Published in India in 1996

Publishers
Indira Gandhi National Centre for the Arts
Central Vista Mess, Janpath, New Delhi - 110001

D.K. Printworld (P) Ltd.
Regd. office : 'Sri Kunj', F-52, Bali Nagar, New Delhi - 110015

Foreword

Kapila Vatsyayan

One of the major programmes of the Indira Gandhi National Centre for the Arts is the lifestyle studies which aim at exploring all fields of cultural knowledge with a view to understanding the functioning of various communities in their totality. In 1989, an international Workshop on "Cross-cultural Lifestyle Studies with Multimedia Computerizable Documentation", was organized under the aegis of Unesco. The proceedings of the Workshop have been published in two volumes. The deliberations on general concepts, theories, and methods, were followed by a series of pilot studies of various cohesive communities in different parts of rural India. Each of these studies pointed out not only the processes of inevitable change but the pace and speed of change. All societies undergo change, adopt, assimilate and reject influence. However, trauma on the individuals and societal psyche occurs when pace is artificially accelerated or there is only an external impetus. Identity crisis is sense of loss of what is most precious in a human being. It is a matter of gratification that Unesco responded again to this concern of the IGNCA and facilitated a Meeting of Experts in April 1993, to examine the question of cultural identity, and to think about issues revolving around that other crucial word 'development'.

The broad area of cultural identity is, indeed, complex since it requires one to ask, initially, questions about the 'self' and the 'other'. It means covering a whole range of variables and definitions; the notions about the self — individual and collective — and the cultural 'other' in terms of whether one is referring to economic, social or cultural dimensions. These debates are very active in the West, and elsewhere, wherever the idea of 'development' and 'progress' has taken roots.

Closely linked with the crisis of cultural identity, are developmental issues which seem to take for granted the primacy of socio-economic man, and that, too, within the context of nation-state notions. But in doing so, it, in its very logic, tends to sow the seed of fragmentation, conflict, and crisis. This is so because it implies a confrontation between several interests, especially, between the individual self and society — the 'other' — at many levels.

The area of cultural identity in this seminar, brought to the fore, the basic distinctions that exist between two world-views; one, the anthropocentric approach, and the other, the cosmocentric viewpoint. It seemed that cultures could be defined in these terms, as seen in their lifestyle within the content of the ecological environment. For example, cultures of the cohesive traditional communities, and those of the modern world, are clearly distinguishable. The attributes of the former, often referred to as preliterate, preindustrial societies, are characterised by the whole gamut of variables attributable to oral traditions; viz., a lifestyle discernible in their dress and food habits, music and dance, habitat, rites-de-passage and above all, in these cultures, the distinction between the individual and society is not only blurred but it is not one of confrontation as is the case in modern society. It does not mean that uniqueness and diversity are absent; it means that there is great deal of interdependence within the cohesive community. On the other hand, in modern societies while great emphasis is given to the individual personality, yet, at the same time, he/she has to conform to the other — society — in terms of some impersonally imposed standardization and homogenization that arises out of a monolithic world-view. Briefly, then, these are some of the problems which as well confront the developing world today.

Clearly, one sees that today there cannot be just one universal model of development that can be applied to all cultures everywhere. The diverse nature of humanity, and the ecological environment which is essentially linked to this world-view, has to be taken into account by the 'developing' world. We are all well aware of the disastrous consequences of a homogenized global village, and, consequently, the increasing violent demand for cultural autonomy in many parts of the world. Not only are alternate paradigms needed to be evolved, but a reconsideration of the instrumentalities — ranging from policies and programmes, industry and technology — has to be urgently taken up. Of course, focus on the convergence of mystical ancient insights and modern science has to be noted in seeking alternatives for the crisis of cultural identity and development.

Bearing the above preamble in mind, the Experts in their meeting discussed and reflected on what constituted culture and development not *per se*, but as an integral holistic notion of, say, culture and lifestyle, culture and development and, culture as identity, specifically in its attributes of language which plays a very important role in the emergence of regional identities; that there is an equation between culture, language and ecological regions. This is why various linguistic groups demand national or sub-national autonomy — as is the case in India, and elsewhere.

The seminar also highlighted the close linkages that exist between religion and culture. It was, naturally, hotly debated. It was pointed out that religion has to be given due cognizance at a cultural level and not politicised by viewing it only from the institutional level. This meant that the entire issue has to be contextualised within a cosmology — the nature of the universe, the fundamental debate on the role of man within the interplay of the macro-micro levels. In short, due recognition of the vertical or spiritual dimension of human existence, seemed to be the consensus.

The questions of diverse regional socio-economic and social structures, along with the disparities, were also discussed. There was a great concern for those smaller communities who are on the verge of being swallowed by the dominant world-view and nation-state complexes. The application of a universal yardstick of 'national' development to all communities was questioned, especially from the viewpoint of human rights, as well.

The crucial dimension of what constituted technology was a controversial issue; it covered the entire range — from the beginnings of technology in prehistoric times to modern times, and also the technology of the human brain-mind, thought, and so on. Associated with this, was the idea of culture and industry and industrialisation. What does one understand by it? Is one ushering a monopolistic market for the entire globe without distinction between developed nations and developing nations? The aspects of "small is beautiful", the question of self-reliance, of self-dependence, of interdependence, were also raised.

Finally, the whole debate boiled down to a very interesting discussion on what constitutes modelling of societies, how a society is to be modelled. In short, are we looking at adopting derived global models based on linearity, or in terms of looking at models which arise from specific culture-historical situations? Therefore, distinctions about civilizational approaches to building culturally endogenous models within the context of development, becomes significant if the results are to be in terms of qualitative optimum growth of the total being of man, rather than just for maximising consumeristic quantifiable results. I am indebted to Unesco, the delegates for support and participation.

I thank my colleagues Prof. B.N. Saraswati and his team for organising the conference and deeply appreciate Prof. B.N. Saraswati and Prof. S.C. Malik's assistance and help during the conference.

Prologue

Francis Childe

Unesco, as you may know, is the lead agency for the World Decade for Cultural Development which was launched on January 21, 1988, and will run through 1997. The Decade has four major objectives:

(i) to strengthen awareness of the cultural dimension of development;
(ii) to affirm and enrich cultural identities;
(iii) to broaden participation in cultural life;
(iv) to promote international cultural cooperation.

Just over five years after its inception, we are now at the mid-point of the World Decade. So this is an opportune moment to reflect on where we have come from, what has been accomplished thus far, and what still lies ahead.

Background to the Decade

First, allow me to situate this World Decade for Cultural Development in context, and to consider for a moment why the Decade was originally conceived.

Most **development** theories, as opposed to **economic** theories, are fairly recent, and date essentially from the period of post-World War II decolonization. In fact, for a long time, development thinking was based on our experience of the reconstruction of Europe in the late 1940s and 1950s, and on the success of the Marshall Plan. Or, in other quarters, on the Soviet model of a centrally planned command economy. These models left little or no room for consideration of the socio-cultural context in which development might take place. Economics was reality, culture was something else. Economics was tangible, culture was intangible — and the idea that culture could make an input to development strategies would have been considered far-fetched indeed. In fact, the implicit assumption was that all development would eventually conform to one model, as if existing in a cultural vacuum or inert human environment. At the time, little did we imagine how little this might correspond to the social, cultural and geographical realities of Asia, Africa, Latin America, and the Caribbean.

In fact, for several decades — yes, even into the 1980s — mainstream development thinking seemed blind to its shortcomings, and even its failures. Not necessarily 'wilfully' blind, perhaps just 'hoping against hope'. But the fact remains that until very recently, development efforts have focused on economics, on the one dimensional abstraction of *homo economicus*, to the exclusion of all else. And the evidence is incontrovertible — such an approach not only neglects the enormous depth and breadth of our real nature as human beings, but it is also a failure in its own terms. Simply put, it makes for poor economics. And it is this missing element that is referred to in the first objective of the Decade — "strengthening the **cultural** dimension of development".

So how does the World Decade understand **culture** ? Culture, we may recall, comes from the Latin 'colere' and 'culturare', meaning "to till or cultivate" the land. At the same time, these words carried the sense of worship. Culture, then, is something elaborated by humankind: expressions of our creativity, including our language, architecture, literature, music and art. But past this, it is also the way we live, the way we think, the way we see the world: our beliefs, attitudes, customs, and social relations. Culture transmits to us its own intrinsic understanding of the way the world works, as well as to lead us to see what is important within that world — in a word, our values.

It is in this context that the World Decade for Cultural Development was conceived, and that led Federico Mayor, Director-General of Unesco, to say at its launching at Unesco House in Paris, in January 1988:

> The experience of the last two decades has shown that culture cannot be dissociated from development in any society, whatever its level of economic growth or its political and economic orientation... Wherever a country has set itself the target of economic growth without reference to its cultural environment, grave economic and cultural imbalances have resulted and its creative potential has been seriously weakened. Genuine development must be based on the best possible use of the human resources and material wealth of a

community. Thus, in the final analysis, the priorities, motivations and objectives of development must be found in culture.

So culture, long regarded by policy-makers as something of an ornament or even a luxury, may now be said to have a place at the top of the political agenda of the international community. During the general policy debate at the last session of the Unesco General Conference, the heads of many delegations referred in their statements to the multifarious ways in which culture exercises a key influence in the contemporary world. Many examples were cited. Inter-ethnic relations, whether in times of strife or of peaceful co-existence, are clearly rooted essentially in culture. The worldwide movement towards greater democratization and freedom of political expression is at once universal but also culture-specific, differing in its form from continent to continent and from one society to another. To take a third example, the relationship between society and nature, or, if you will, between culture and environment, is at the very forefront of world concerns today. For while there are certainly important technical and political questions to be resolved as regards the environment, the issue is clearly not only a scientific or even a political one. More than anything else, the state of the planet's environment is a reflection of our values and our attitudes — and any changes in our relationship with the Earth's environment will necessarily entail a revolution in our attitudes, values and behaviour. In a word, the state of the environment is to an important extent a reflection of the state of our culture.

The Decade Thus Far

The first part of my address has been to situate the World Decade in the context in which it was conceived, but I ask you now to reflect for a moment on the enormous, almost unimaginable changes which have taken place in the world since the Decade was launched in 1988. Consider the situation then and now: in Eastern Europe and the former Soviet Union; in large parts of Africa, including, of course, South Africa; in Chile and Paraguay; in Afghanistan and Cambodia. In 1988, the Berlin Wall was still standing, and Mr. Vaclav Havel was still a political prisoner in the country of which he was to become President. Nelson Mandela was also a prisoner, and his country still firmly under the sway of apartheid. The terrible threat of a nuclear war between the two superpowers was omnipresent. In nations all over the globe, totalitarian regimes that had ruled for decades were about to fall, to be swept away by the winds of freedom.

This new-found freedom has unleashed enormous potential — both for good and for evil. And nowhere more so than between neighbouring people of different religions or ethnicity. Old scores and rivalries, simmering for so long, are now being settled. . . and, moreover, new problems are emerging. Are we, the human race, willing to take up the challenge of living **by choice** in pluralistic societies? Are we willing to accept, and even to embrace, those of different colour, different religion, different language, and different culture — and not just in the country next door, but even in the house next door? The question is as crucial right here in Asia as it is in South Africa, in the former Soviet Union as in Latin America. How can we create a genuine culture of peace? But the culture of peace will not thrive without equity, freedom and justice. It will not grow if people are unable to express their distinctive creative faculties, if their hopes and the force of their spirit are not pooled in the quest for a common future.

On another front, ladies and gentlemen, think of what we have learned in the last few years of our natural environment, and specifically of the ozone layer in the earth's atmosphere. Five years ago, the first reports of a then mysterious hole in the ozone layer over Antarctica were appearing. It is now clear that refrigerators, air-conditioning, aerosols, jet travel, as well as rockets and space shuttles are combining to tear a hole in our collective sun-screen, and that another hole has opened in the atmosphere over the Northern Hemisphere. While a moment's reflection on the list of contributory factors leaves no doubt as to the cultural connection, it is only very recently that we have begun to face the implications.

I could go on at some length, but I am sure that my point is clear — the world we live in today is not the same as it was when the World Decade for Cultural Development was launched in 1988. Moreover, not only are events still unfolding, they are also clearly speeding up, and the radical shift in the world situation is far from accomplished.

Future Prospects

It is for these reasons that I referred earlier to this mid-point of the Decade as being "an opportune moment for reflection". In one sense, the launching of the Decade was an almost prophetic act that foresaw the forces at work in the world even before the world at large became conscious of them. In another sense, events have already overtaken us, and we must now take fresh stock of where we are.

It is on this account that, in consultation with United Nations Secretary-

General Boutros Ghali, Unesco Director-General, Mr. Federico Mayor, has recently appointed Mr. Javier Pérez de Cuéllar to chair the newly created World Commission on Culture and Development. And in consultation with Mr. Pérez de Cuéllar, Mr. Mayor has recently announced the appointment of the other members of this Commission, including, from Asia, Ms. Chie Nakane from Japan, Mr. Mahbub ul Haq from Pakistan, and among the honorary members, Ms. Aung San Suu Kyi, the Nobel Peace Prize winner from Myanmar. The Commission's members are all highly respected and eminent persons, with a wealth of experience indispensable for the implementation of such an undertaking. Several Member States of Unesco have already pledged to contribute substantial sums to the financing of the Commission, and within the past few weeks, the Commission has begun its work in earnest — the task of preparing "a policy-oriented World Report on Culture and Development based on the collection and analysis of information from all regions and diverse sources". There is no doubt that this World Commission on Culture and Development will give new impetus to the Decade during its second half, and will strengthen our understanding of the crucial role that culture plays in the profound changes taking place throughout the world, and in the development process, wherever it may be observed.

At the same time, ladies and gentlemen, while many of us may recognize the role culture plays in the development of societies, we have not yet convinced the decision-makers — whether they be desk or field officers in the major bilateral or multi-lateral development agencies, or Ministers of Planning, Development, or Finance — at this realization **must** be put to practical use. It is not enough, then, for us to proclaim the need to take account of culture in the development process. We must also progress on the scientific and theoretical level, in order to be able to identify and, to the extent possible, to quantify those factors which are instrumental to the outcome of development strategies or projects. In a word, we need to provide the practical tools — a methodology, if you will — whereby socio-cultural factors can be integrated into development planning and project implementation.

This task is among the most important practical contributions Unesco can make in this area, and we have set ourselves a plan of work whereby over the next two years a tentative methodology, including specific guidelines, will be developed. We are working and consulting with several other actors in this effort — in Africa, for example, we are working closely with UNICEF and the World Bank (and I would say as an aside, if we can convince the bankers, we will surely carry the day!); in Asia, with national planning authorities and research institutes; and at our head office in Paris, a series of consultations has already taken place, and has included representatives from US AID, British ODA, Canadian CIDA, la Coopération Française, the PANOS Institute in London, UNDP, OECD, the EEC, the ILO, and many grass roots NGOs both from the North and the South, among others.

Once this methodology has been elaborated, the next step will be to field test it, working in close cooperation with our sister agencies of the United Nations system, as well as with national authorities in the developing countries. This will have the dual effect of refining the methodology, and of already introducing its use into the major donor and implementing agencies in the UN system, as well as into a number of national development planning agencies. In other words, while we are refining the theory, we shall also be introducing the **practice**.

The third implement we have envisioned to help us carry through the Decade in its second half has been to institute a "World Day for Cultural Development", to be celebrated annually on May 21. Each year's celebration will centre around a specific contemporary theme linked to the Decade's objectives. In 1992, for example, we chose the theme "Culture and Environment", as a particular contribution to the run up to the Earth Summit in Rio de Janeiro.

In the years to come, we plan to continue this approach. This year, in 1993, we will explore the theme of "Culture, Education and Work"; in 1994, "Culture and Development"; in 1995, "Culture and Agriculture"; in 1996, "Culture and Health"; and in 1997, "Culture and Technology: Arts, Science and Communication".

In looking back, we must admit that this World Decade for Cultural Development has taken time to be understood, and to take root. In its first few years, "cultural development" was understood — misunderstood — to relate to culture as the arts, music, sculpture, painting, and the like. Many of the activities undertaken by Unesco's Member States, or proposed by Unesco's traditional partners, were of this rather narrow nature. And to be frank, our sister agencies in the UN system, understanding the Decade in the same fashion, were lukewarm at best. Now, however, we begin to see a perceptible shift in the kinds of activities being undertaken, and in the interest elsewhere in the United Nations, especially among agencies like the UNDP, UNICEF, FAO, and the World Bank, all in the front line of development work.

In this world of imbalances, contradictions and absurdities, as the North continues to consume more than it needs while the South is still trying so desperately to obtain the basic necessities, only one resource is shared equally —

and what a wonderful one it is — the resource of culture and of human wisdom and understanding. For there is no culture in the North or South that has not preserved the most sparkling reflections — on life and how it is best lived — of individual thinkers among its ancestors, of the sages, village story-tellers, and wise men and women who began it all. It is this wealth and diversity of culture and of understanding that UNESCO is determined to make better known and place at the service of human development. In order to do this, UNESCO needs the help of all its Member States, not only at government level but at all levels of civil society. It has already done much to promote dialogue, but we still have a long way to go to persuade our world's leaders that although culture is at the root of many of our conflicts, it also offers our only possibility of reconciliation.

Contents

Introduction

Baidyanath Saraswati

CAN a particular life-style be superior to, or more satisfying than, another? Can the life-style of another culture (in its widest anthropological sense) be adopted without disturbing one's own cultural identity? Can a people's cultural identity remain absolute, independent and eternally valid? Can a true assessment of the human world be made without examining its internal realities? If the answer to all these is in the negative, then there emerges the need and possibility of a paradigm shift in development ideology.

The twenty-two essays collected here are based on a Unesco-sponsored meeting of experts on 'Interface of Cultural Identity and Development' held at the Indira Gandhi National Centre for the Arts, New Delhi, on 19-23 April 1993. The meeting aimed at: (a) *rethinking* universality in modern sciences and the mutually differentiating epistemologies or world-views; (b) *examining* cultural identity, touching upon aspects from grassroots sociology and cosmology to the philosophers' metaphysics; (c) *evaluating* development ideologies and the crises of creative individuals in a changing techno-cultural order, arising from the imposition of alien paradigms on social reality; (d) *identifying* development processes, forms of modernisation and methods of restoration of the moral order in relation to ecology, economy and society; and (e) *considering* endogenic development models, mainly with reference to traditional visions of one's own cultures.

Rethinking Universality

Can human imagination grasp the technical mystery of the universe?

Yes, by employing meditation, mathematics, and geometry as an unfailing guide.

How?

The key feature of Upanisadic thinking concerns the Universe of Brahman.

What is Brahman?

Brahman is the universal Self.

Is Brahman the creator of the universe?

Brahman itself is the universe.

How did the universe start?

The universe did not start at any particular time. It is set in eternal cycles of creation, existence and dissolution.

How can the universe change and yet remain eternal?

Although space and time have beginning and end, both continue for ever through a cosmological scheme that repeats itself endlessly.

Is the universe a machine called Brahman?

Not, in the Newtonian sense of a deterministic machine.

To what extent does the Upanisadic concept of the universe relate itself to other traditions?

This picture of the universe is different from that of the Semitic traditions. But it does not seem to be much at variance with modern theories in science.

The Upanisadic sages have shown that 'One is many and many are One', that every part of the universe contains the whole and the whole all the parts. In such a world-view there is no place for the notion of a universality that claims to be *exclusive*, *unique* and *chosen*.

The concept of universality is not universal. The universality of Western science and civilisation is not a *factual consensus* of opinion. Yet, as S.C. Malik in his paper on 'Interface of Science Consciousness and Identity' points out, what is considered universal today usually implies a dominant Western world-view — whatever way one may define it — and all other categories have to be subsumed within it in the name of universalism. The questioning of the Western notion of universality is exemplified by the essay of Anisuzzaman. It contends that whatever the West has produced in the last five hundred years is universal and modern, the thing to emulate, that other world-views are traditional as opposed to the modern and thus obsolete, and that the Western world-view is not only the dominant one but also the only universal one.

We are concerned here with the problem of a universal doctrine of development. The development strategies which have so long been framed by the Western world need to be modified and indigenised. Happily, the possibility of building endogenic models of development has increased with the redefinition of 'culture' and 'development' adopted at the 1982 Mexico Conference and followed by Unesco's World Decade for Cultural Development. Taking cultural factors into development does not mean that development is restricted to cultural products. Unesco's endeavour has been to make culture and development compatible. However, our problem still remains.

There are many forms of culture, each valid in its own framework, but no single *chosen* culture can claim universality. Regrettably, most developing countries, rich in cultural heritage, aspire for the type of universality which Western cultures claim. If the traditional vision were to work, every culture would develop a sense of self-identity, and collectively all cultures would realise that any *chosen universality* is neither a right nor a justification but simply a way of understanding one's own identity.

Examining Cultural Identity

Rarely the identity- question is raised in as straightforward a manner as in the following example.

> Once upon a time Satyakama Jabala addressed his mother Jabala: 'Mother! I desire to live the life of a student of sacred knowledge. Of what family, pray, am I?
>
> Then she said to him: 'I do not know this, my dear — of what family you are. In my youth, when I went about a great deal serving as a maid, I got you. So I do not know of what family you are. However, I am Jabala by name; you are Satyakama by name. So you may speak of yourself as Satyakama Jabala'.
>
> Then he went to Haridrumata Gautama and said, 'I will live the life of a student of sacred knowledge. I will become a pupil of yours, sir'.
>
> He was asked: 'Of what family, pray, are you, my dear'?

> Then he said: 'I do not know sir, of what family I am. I asked my mother. She answered me: "In my youth, when I went about a great deal serving as a maid, I got you. So I do not know this, of what family you are. However, I am Jabala by name; you are Satyakama by name". So I am Satyakama Jabala, sir'.
>
> To him he then said: 'A non-Brahman would not be able to explain it thus. Bring the fuel, my dear. I will receive you as a pupil. You have not deviated from the truth.
>
> *Chandogya Upanisad*, 4.4.1 – 5

This is how identity with the infinite Real was the ultimate identity. Satyakama Jabala later became famous as one of the Upanisadic sages.

Identity with the Self. What is suggested in this example of Satyakama Jabala is the essential oneness of the individual self and the universal Self. The sages asked questions at the dawn of human consciousness.

'What is this'?

'This is One'.

'Who is this One'?

'This He is'.

'Who is He'?

'He is the Self'.

'What am I'?

'I am all this'.

'Who am I'?

'I am the Self'.

'Who are you'?

'I am you'.

An Upanisad describes the beginning of identity in these terms:

> In the beginning this was the Self alone, in the form of a Man. Looking around he saw nothing whatever except himself. He said in

> the beginning: 'I am' and hence arose the name 'I'. So even today when a Man is addressed, he says in the beginning, 'It is I', and then adds any other name he may have.
>
> *Brhadaranyaka Upanisad,* I.4.1

The unitary principle has been explained:

> As the one wind has entered the world
> And becomes corresponding in form to every form,
> So the one Inner Self of all things
> Is corresponding in form to every form
> And yet is outside.
>
> *Katha Upanisad,* 5.10

Here in the *Upanisads* are set forth the theory of the *absolute* dimension of the Self, which claims that it is precisely the primordial oneness that makes differentiation intrinsically possible. It shows that the individual self is also valuable as itself, because all generic and ontic differences are included in One, the universal Self.

As Malik explains, the inner psyche is still looking for 'Who am I'? but in the present trance-like conditioning one continues to grope in the hope of 'tomorrow and tomorrow', little realizing that mirages continuously recede and the goal will never be realized. In his paper on 'Identity, Tribesman and Development', Mrinal Miri also mentions the question 'Who am I'? or 'What am I'? but does not pursue it further because, in his opinion, it is not about the mundane or the earthly but about the metaphysical or the transcendent and its answer is something that is ultimately a matter of mystical realisation. He, however, clarifies his position, saying that it is not because he thinks the mystical is erroneous or illusory but simply because he feels more at home with the non-mystical mode of thinking.

Multiple identities. Moving on to the mundane approach to the question of the human sense of identity, it is soon realised that one lives in the world of others. It is in relation to 'others' — to the society and the environment in which one lives — that one's own identity is formed. Generally, identity is characterised by function — husband, wife, parent, child, teacher, student and so on — in a relative way. There are other relative characterisations, dependent and temporal, such as rich and poor, tall and short, male and female, foreigner and national — each having a counterpart.

From both mystical and mundane approaches, Man is not an isolated being but a constitutive relationship. He is related not only with the universal Self but with the selves of his fellow-men. He is not an individual but a person. Considering this relatedness, personal identity may be defined as a shared totality — an awareness that one is connected with others at various levels of interaction. In short, each person plays multiple roles in multiple ways in multiple contexts, and thus each individual self has multiple identities. Problems arise when any single identity is focused to the exclusion of the others.

Identity with space. Leah Lui of Australia illustrates how the open ocean is central to her sense of identity, having determined her way of life, subsistence practices, ceremonies, songs and stories. Otgonbayar of Mongolia describes the early history of Central Asia that bears witness to the formation of nomadic identity of the tribes of Mongol and Turk origin and their coexistence and struggle for dominance over the region. The question of 'national identity', which also relates to space and draws considerable attention in recent years, has been raised at some length in respect of Turkey (Bozkurt Guvenc), Indonesia (S. Buddhisantoso), Nepal (D.R. Dahal), India (A.R. Momin), and Bangladesh (Anisuzzaman).

Religious identity. One of the essential and existential enigmas of modern nations is religion. Wit Wisadavet considers Buddhism as one of the pillars of Thai cultural identity, and equates Thainess with Buddhism. Otgonbayar points out that Buddhism has become one of the most important criteria of Mongolian nomadic identity. Guvenc has observed that while well educated and well-to-do citizens with status may lean towards Turkish national identity and see themselves as Turks, private citizens of varied ethnic origins may prefer their Muslim heritage. This basic dichotomy, he points out, brews two intermediary identities like Muslim Turks and Turkish Muslims. Momin draws attention to the *Hindutva* syndrome in contemporary India and its misplaced identification between Hinduism and nationalism.

Ethnic identity. Lui defines her aboriginal sense of identity in terms of her extended families, within which respect for elders is preserved, obligations to kin are met, resources are shared, and emotional and spiritual support is given. Also what makes her a Torres Strait Islander are her language, her dances, her songs, her myths and legends and ceremonies. Miri refers to tribal identity in the sense of its being determined by 'strong evaluation' — evaluation in terms of a value such as 'allegiance to the tribe' — such that this value overrides other values in a fundamental way. Although L.M. Khubchandani finds apparent ambiguities in defining the concept of mother tongue, post-Independence India reorganized its territories on the basis of language and linguistic identities continues to be strong in the political context.

Identity crisis. Dahal cites several examples of ethnic tensions in Nepal, arising between hillmen and plainsmen, between high-caste Hindu groups and the so-called indigenous groups, and even between the Brahman and the Newar. Ethnic problems in India are far more complex and violent. Miri's philosophical explanation of ethnic violence is noteworthy. He argues that violence to oneself as well as to another is the result of darkness and fragmentation rather than motivated by the illumination and integration of successful 'strong evaluation'. In his view, terrorism in the cause of tribal identity may quite likely be an expression of a profound sense of emptiness and impending moral fragmentation rather than a genuine part of the articulation of tribal identity.

Identity in time. It may be said that the concept of identity changes and, perhaps, yet does not change. Modern thinking about *relativity* appears opposed to the Upanisadic vision at first, because it does not see the Self established in his own glory. The contributors to this volume have tried to capture the various expressions of identity which may be taken as relative descriptions of the absolute reality of another kind. Here the reality is seen in terms of Man as material, as a thing. The essential point in modern thinking is that Man exists in his own glory and *absoluteness*, and holds literally to the dictum 'Man is the measure of all'.

Evaluating Development Ideology

The attitude of the Vedic sages towards the world was essentially a religious one.

> O God, grant us of boons the best,
> a mind to think and a smiling love,
> increase of wealth, a healthy body,
> speech that is winsome and days that are fair.
>
> *Rgveda* II, 21

> Peaceful be heaven, peaceful the earth,
> peaceful the broad space between.
> Peaceful for us be the running waters,
> peaceful the plants and herbs!

Peaceful to us be the signs of the future,
peaceful what is done and undone,
Peaceful to us be what is and what will be.
May all to us be gracious!

Atharvaveda, XIX.9, 1-2

The ancient people *lived* in the agricultural golden age of human civilization. They *glorified* the forest and lived in positive symbiosis with the animal world. They *built* houses by worship, *prayed* for increase of wealth and the joy of fearlessness, and *desired* to attain the span of a hundred winters. They *knew* that human fullness is incomplete without peace.

This is true even today for most traditional societies which build a structure of ideology around and in relation to peace and harmony. Wisadavet demonstrates in his short paper that the Thai Buddhists do not have a negative attitude towards science and technology and there is little or no conflict between the modern way of development and the Buddhist cultural identity. Otgonbayer gives another example of the Buddhist way of developing a nomadic Mongolian society with distinct characteristics. Dawa Norbu's paper on 'Cultural Preconditions for Development' also brings into relief how and why Buddhism, Confucianism and Hinduism have provided some of the necessary favourable cultural preconditions for development in most of the industrialising Asian societies.

Nevertheless, in a very real sense virtually all developing countries to varying degrees feel a deep sense of loss. This is often expressed in such terms as: 'development is a trap designed by Western powers to perpetuate colonialism', 'development as transformative interventions', 'the evangelists of development secularizing the message of salvation', 'development ruining the intellectual landscape' (Khubchandani); 'thrusting Western ideology of capitalism', 'loss of right to control one's own means of production' (Lui), and so forth. Khubchandani specifically refers to the 'imposition of metropolitan values' of affluent countries leading to the 'homogenization of cultures'. He points out further how development planning in India has constructed change as the 'replacement of values', instead of as an increment in the existing order. Paying little regard to the language assets in traditional speech communities, equating traditional knowledge with primitiveness and backwardness, and the elitist orientation of Indian academia are examples. In her paper on 'Popular Culture and Arabesque Music in Turkey', Meral Ozbek speaks of the 'aesthetic crisis' created by high culture. All such expressions are perception of facts, not figments of imagination.

Now an increasing number of thinkers in both East and West are coming to realise the inner contradictions and limits of development. If development is a human project, then surely the one-pointed concern for the material self is not enough. There is the primordial human aspiration — the realisation of the social and the spiritual selves — the neglect of which entails struggle, strife and antagonistic dynamisms. Modern epistemology that determines development ideology has certain fundamental features that separate it from most of the traditional systems of knowledge to an extent that makes holistic thinking highly problematic. Its domination has now been called into question. Unesco's role in rethinking the development ideology has been pervasively influential.

Identifying Development Process

Becoming and destruction —
He who this pair conjointly knows,
With destruction passing over death,
With becoming wins the immortal.

Isa Upanisad, 14

The concept of development is bound up with a number of key terms such as modernisation, nationalisation, pluralisation, Westernisation, globalisation, and so forth. These terms epitomise a certain positive force of becoming. Cultural destruction is another important aspect that figures in the contemporary discourse on development.

Anisuzzaman challenges the definition of modernisation as the process of social change whereby less developed societies acquire characteristics common to more developed societies. His contention is that this definition is heavily loaded in favour of the cultural dimension of the Western world and this is where modernisation and development become synonymous with Westernisation. Otgonbayer points out that modernisation with the increasing effect of Westernisation or Europeanisation has eroded traditional values in many eastern societies. Premasiri refers to the production of modern science and technology having the veritable effect of dehumanising development. On the interface between tradition and modernity, Norbu claims that nowhere in the Third World does modernisation bring all societies to a level of cultural homogeneity washing their cultural identities. Contrary to this claim, Olga Gostin presents a case of Australia. Examining the aspects of aboriginal Australian experience in tertiary education, she draws attention to the fact that the threat of homogenisation and Westernisation of distinctive aboriginal programmes is very real in Australia today.

There appears to exist a deep dilemma over the transfer of modern Western science and technology to traditional non-Western societies. As Norbu has observed, there is today hardly any country in world that does not want to embrace science and technology for their *sheer utility*, even though many have serious reservations about 'modernising' the superstructure of their societies. Appropriate technology has often been suggested as the middle path. Examining the case of tribal society, Miri realises that the epistemological and moral assumptions implicit in the contemporary discourse on appropriate technology is far from being self-luminously valid. In his essay on 'Technology, Man and Spirituality', Mohammed Reza Rikhtegaran pleads for a union between the technocentric West and the spiritual East, and stresses the point that the world today requires a different kind of spirituality which is not purely Eastern. He sounds a somewhat optimistic note concerning the emergence of a new culture of technology. In his opinion, mastery of technology today has taken such a shape that Being has unconcealed a new spirituality, and hence 'sanctifying technology through sacrifice' is of crucial importance. Fatemah Farahani also takes a positive attitude toward the 'culture of technology'. Arguing that technology is a means in the service of a superior objective that is the better recognition of nature and a more suitable utilisation of nature, she claims that the best technology is not the most modern technology.

Today we are witnessing in many parts of Asia, Africa, and Europe the prominent upsurge of a number of ethno-nationalist movement as a reaction against the excessive or centralising and homogenising policies of the nation or nation-state. As Dahal points out, it becomes an immensely difficult task to define a national culture or the cultural identity of a nation, especially when a nation is composed of diverse ethnic/caste groups with differences in race, language, religion and culture. However, in considering the present changing socio-political context, he suggests that the govenment must adopt cultural policies to develop Nepal as a multi-cultural nation. Examining the interface of development and cultural identity in the Indian context, Momin points out that it has two interrelated dimensions: pan-Indian civilizational on the one hand, and regional culture on the other. At both the macro and micro levels, he thinks, the development process needs to be informed and guided by the pluralistic and composite ethos of Indian society. On Turkish national unity or historical diversities and continuities, Guvenc concludes that the unity – diversity paradigm has been one of the guidelines of Western democracies and also one of the landmarks of Eastern wisdom. Ravindra K. Jain, in his paper on 'Civilizations and Settlement Societies', deals with the decentralised paradigm of unity in diversity. He recalls the issues raised in the process of nation-building (namely, clash and diversity of religion with its twin faces of communalism and the partition of the country into India and Pakistan) and the cultural problems in the functioning of a federal state structure (namely, the formation of linguistic states) in India. Khubchandani looks at the Indian reality differently. He refers to India's *organic pluralism* by which different groups attempt to retain and preserve their *unique* cultural attributes (language or religion) while developing common institutional participation at the national level. Such a situation, he says, can be regarded as being quite distinct from the *structural pluralism* found in some European countries.

We live in an age of nationalism. Experience shows that the achievement of true cultural pluralism and of national integration is particularly problematic. The problem looms large with the acceleration of the technocentric process which creates conditions of homogeneity within culural units. To maintain a monolithic national identity, it is almost inevitable to have one kind of culture, one style of communication, and a centralised educational system. The emphasis of the developing nations, therefore, has been largely on the unconditional adoption of a development process based on technology transfer and mass industrialisation.

Considering Endogenic Development

While evaluating the modern idea of development in social, economic, political, religious, aesthetic or yet other terms, one is struck by the thrust toward uniformisation of cultural groups. There is something about this phenomenon that needs explanation. Combative arguments of several authors of this volume are that the fundamental ideology of development is based on a particular world-view claiming to possess a universally acceptable message, ignoring all other world-views or taking only a part of the whole. The basic assumption in this theory is that only a certain type of nationality or a certain order of life is relevant, and if something is not addressed from this viewpoint, it is not really valid. There is a challenge to this notion of universality. If a particular order of thought and behaviour is not acceptable or intelligible to people outside the modern milieu, how can it be universal? Why should rationality of other kinds and other world-views be necessarily false? Must all cultures be reduced to a single pattern of development to suit a particular culture's claim to universality?

Uniformity versus unity, homogenisation versus heterogenisation, universality versus specificity, centralisation versus decentralisation are the discordant voices of human traditions. Do we reduce them to a single voice? Despite the implications of the modern milieu, there is a search for inner harmony from within. The most critical and contentious challenge is posed by the Third World countries.

Drawing attention to the increasing dependence on the West, Anisuzzaman makes a clarion call: We would like to be universal, but not uniform; we would like to develop our specificity without restricting ourselves to narrow fields or ideas. However, the problem does not end by doing away with Western thought. The crucial factors involved in the re-making of the multicultural Third World countries are: (a) centralised control, (b) national identity, and (c) technocentric culture. Consider the illusive democracy and bureaucratisation of development policies, with a distinction between the power-holders and the common man. Consider the dominance of monolithic national identity as opposed to multicultural identities. Consider the tyranny of technocentric culture demanding standardised technical education, mass media of communication and uniform life-styles. Consider the transition from a rural culture to a modern urban one being treated as the inevitable destiny of all Third World nations. Nationalism has done much of its work in the making of a national industrial high culture. The role of the national bureaucracy in people's welfare has been questioned in bold, powerful, and creative ways.

In his paper on 'Secular Sovereign and Artha', Parthasarthi Banerjee takes the position that welfare is not possible without a sovereign. Theories of development, he says, very often either deny or disregard such a supremacy of the sovereign authority in development. He goes further to show that the secularisation of development is not only misconceived but also that an autonomous development is actually in a certain sense morally purposive. Drawing upon India's exegetic tradition he takes care to point out that this supremacy of the sovereign should not be confounded with secularism as is done by Western interpreters of Indian society. It is obvious from B.D. Sharma's case study of a tribal village in Central India that the problems of development are far more complex than theoretical frameworks with which to address development ideology and process. In his paper on 'Taming Structural Transformation', he presents the story of the people's struggle against an authoritarian State and insidious money-power. As a social activist he presents the experiential reality of development, pointing out the myriad difficulties facing a non-violent people with the greatest natural resources.

Bunker Roy, another social activist, reflects upon the fluorescence of 'Development Activism: The Importance of Being Voluntary'. Major issues that he highlights in his paper are 'development has to be slow', 'literate Man the most formidable obstacle to development', 'looking down on one's own culture', 'lack of space for individual growth', 'lack of self-respect', and so forth. All these flaws in the development process, he points out, are linked to flaws in the human beings implementing the programmes in the field. Obviously the solution lies in integral action. Baidyanath Saraswati's paper on 'Freedom to Grow and Growing into One' prepares the ground for a *swadeshi* (endogenic) model of development. He brings into focus the insight of the great genial master and *mahatma*, Mohandas Karamchand Gandhi. To evolve a *swadeshi* model, he suggests, a five-fold programme must begin with redefining 'development' as a human project, rethinking universality in terms of the cosmological principle, restrengthening *swadeshi* with the eternal rule of life, resanctifying human creativity and interpersonal relationships, and rededicating oneself to the laws of moral advancement with minimum material.

To conclude,

> *I do not want my house to be walled on all sides and my windows to be stuffed. I want the cultures of all lands to be blown about my house as freely as possible. But I refuse to be blown off my feet by any. I refuse to live in other people's houses as an interloper, a beggar or a slave.*
>
> (M.K. Gandhi, 1921)

1

Interface of Science Consciousness and Identity

S. C. Malik

In the light of the preamble circulated by the organizers, several interrelated issues may be raised, especially in the context of certain unexamined philosophical assumptions and presuppositions, and their obsolescence in the context of humankind's predicament — not merely of the non-Western world. These are as follows:

(i) Issues of survival, due to the threat of nuclear, ecological, population and other disasters that face humankind.

(ii) Reassessing notions of tradition, development, modernity and post-modernity; values inherent in these words having arisen due to an impact of science and technology.

(iii) The need to remove the substandard existence of fellow human beings, since values of egalitarianism, social justice and so on have widespread acceptance — hence cannot be ignored.

(iv) The specific problem of Indian cultural variation, its socio-cultural and psychic maintenance — problems applicable perhaps to most of the developing world.

In the light of the title of the paper, not all of the issues are dealt with, except to emphasise the fact that cultural transformations are possible within the context of contemporary knowledge wherein lie the philosophical assumptions which have governed the ideas of tradition, development and modernity. Just as until recently social scientific understanding of cultural phenomenon was based on developments in science, the new vision of scientific knowledge needs to be taken into account as it is converging towards certain perennial philosophical statements, often stated in traditional wisdom, especially in the context of the nature of Consciousness. It is within this framework that ideas are outlined below, so that the implications with regard to the interface of cultural identity and development are implicit.

The Background

Some time after World War II, there was a great deal of assurance for humankind for the practical dimensions of the notion of 'progress' on a global scale, equated with high technology. But the same mood has not only led to a crisis of confidence but also to unprecedented barbaric inhumanities everywhere. The reason being that the dictates of applied science and technology continue to be governed by an intellectual comprehension of the material world which is viewed as composed of separate objects or particles. Without going into details, it is clear that Western thought has consistently modelled those world-views which have generated ontological gaps that run across the whole domain of experience. For example, human and other organisms, in spite of the fact that they share the same cosmic niche, are considered to be literally worlds apart. This dualism is one of the fundamental, often tacit tenets of Western metaphysics, epistemology and ethics. Dualist conceptions of human beings themselves are rooted in this deep-seated anthropocentrism (Malik 1968; 1969; 1972; 1975; 1989a, b; 1990a, b; 1992; 1993a, b).

This dominant world-view has even assimilated evolutionary theory, by historicising the ontological gap. All religious or secular-teleological perspectives construe the variety of life forms as the result of a process leading to the advent of humankind. *Homo sapiens* is not seen as a stage in an indefinite flux of change, but as an end, the glorious result of a history of trial and error. Is there any difference between this view and that of creationism? The dichotomy between humans and non-humans was frequently extended to other races, often treated as slaves and even women were not exactly placed in the same category as evolved humans — this was especially the case with many nineteenth-century Darwinians. Social differences within Europe itself were classified in this line of thought (Bouissac 1991).

Of course, in contemporary terms these systems may seem aberrant. Nevertheless, many of the biases continue covertly. For example, what is considered universal today usually implies a dominant Western world-view — whatever way one may define it — and all other categories have to be subsumed within it in the name of universalism. In this one may include the idea of linear time, progress towards a certain state. But this makes these approaches flexible, as against those cultures which see evolutionary developments in terms of cyclical times wherein catastrophes are part of nature and reality and, further, encompassed within a larger context. And so on.

Thus, modern science and technology — Scientific Revolution — took place within a specific historical-philosophical climate of Western Europe during the sixteenth-seventeenth centuries. It is worth our while to recapitulate certain of these fundamental philosophical presuppositions that are termed as essentially Western, which dominate contemporary times in general. The background against which science arose, historically, is as follows, briefly:

The tensions between the church and science in Western culture around the seventeenth century formed the basic ontological and epistemological assumptions that underlie modern science. By the eighteenth century it had adopted an ontological assumption of separateness: observer from the observed, man from nature, mind from matter, science from religion, of fundamental particles from each other, of the different parts of an organism from each other, specialization of different scientific disciplines and, finally, the psychological fall out — the competition among scientists, of domination and subordination, etc. In short, humankind could pursue its objectives, irrespective of taking the earth and its creatures into account for its benefit. The reductionist explanations, which social science and humanities borrowed wholesale, are what led to the ethics of competition. It emphasizes the localization of causes, excluding action at a distance, especially since the sole epistemological assumption is one of empirical evidence, i.e., data arising from our physical senses. But the middle of this century these two metaphysical assumptions, of separateness and empiricism, became intrinsic to science.

Most of what has been summarised above is well-known. It is also known that these points are radically different to other presuppositions available in non-Western traditions. Of course, many a Western poet and mystic have felt at odds with cultural implications of modern science and technology. Recent advances in science are beyond these early assumptions, especially in physics. But in general there has been no serious challenge to these assumptions from many quarters and have a hegemony which remains unchallenged by and large. It has widely spread like a surgical transplant, such as in India, subverting all that is there in the indigenous and inherent to Indian traditions in a deep sense.

Science and Consciousness

Of course, the notion of the earth as a complex system within which organisms interact with each other and with geophysical and chemical processes in a predictable manner is at the root of modern science. It permeates Western and Westernised cultures and prevails across the spectrum, beginning with elementary textbooks. But the interrelatedness is still in terms of a mechanical interpretation, a one to one cause-effect relationship. For instance, earthquakes have geophysical causes since we know that the earth is made up of inert matter explainable locally and regionally rather than in any global systemic terms. No notion of an independent variable — say a god in heaven — would suffice, for an explanation of the earthquake.

The belief of inert components of the earth has also led to the passive exploitation of the resources. The belief of the Navaho, who treat the earth as mother and have sacred places, would consider coal mining as digging into mother's body — a heinous crime; or other groups of the non-Western world who apologize to the tree before cutting it. Both are equally compelling truths within the boundaries of their world-views. The holistic view perhaps helps in a sustainable development for a long time, while the exploitation of maximum resources for development and progress is a short time approach even in the historical-evolutionary terms.

Today, no longer can one describe earth and life in terms of mere laws of physics and chemistry; that life just happened by chance on earth. Shifting world-views within the Western tradition is reflected by not only the developments in physics, chemistry and biology but also of the Gaia hypothesis; this particular world-view that is both holistic and multi-centered developed within the scientific tradition of the West — in the framework of evolutionary biology (Lovelock: 1979, 1988). It is congruent with many Eastern world-views, and if such convergences are possible, it is also imperative, if humankind is to survive, provided that the idea of interrelatedness within the framework of Consciousness is taken seriously. The prevailing world-view in terms of the humanistic psychology of the modern man contrasts with the traditional world-views all over the world; i.e., nature is unfriendly and confrontational, therefore the need for control, hence, the feeling of alienation and separation. Hence, the necessity to provide orderliness, protection and predictability for its members through structure, property rights, laws, enforcement agencies and a central hierarchy of authority. And so on.

The transformational world-view, which the new science and ancient insights suggests, is that of a friendly universe, to be accepted, experienced and celebrated; space and time are relative — infinitely small or large units. Nature is an evolving eco-system of which you and me, the human species, are a part. Therefore by enhancing nature we enhance ourselves. Life is a matter of contributing through myself and others to the universe. The purpose of human society is to increase the service of its members to other human beings and to themselves. To do this, I must realise my fullest potential of body, mind, and spirit. To do this requires an environment that supports and encourages self-actualization and self-responsibility. I am unique, but I am also one with the human species.

In other words, the quest is for seeking a unified field in science and in other areas of a unity in nature and man. But it all begins with a personal yearning. Throughout human history in every endeavour human beings have searched for connections, for ways to make a harmonious whole out of parts.

Contemplating in this manner creates problems since the social system one lives in feels threatened by these manifest expressions and statements, for these go against the old generalizations of most nineteenth-century notions, ideas to which most of the social sciences and even proper science in many parts of the world, where it is equated to technology and scientism, continue to cling to. Not all of the current state of science, perhaps, accepts this notion of an ocean of Intelligence, of a universal energy or a unified field. If it is so, it has not penetrated to the larger society of scientists or society at large. It also speaks of an attributeless, nameless and formless energy. The body-brain instrument which in its subtler aspects is a light and sound vibration speaking in material terms, while the universe is a Play of Consciousness. . .

The movement from a religious metaphor guiding the ancient past to a scientific metaphor of the modern times continues endlessly since the latter is increasingly being recognized as incomplete to tell us about the various contemporary issues, such as the crisis of environmental pollution, ecological imbalances, and so on. The modern movement marked a departure from the old dynamics of life when humankind lived closer to nature, sustained and motivated by an understanding of our higher nature — an understanding that came easily and naturally to them. The confidence of the modern era wishes to achieve better living conditions, through progress in terms of the conquest of nature — introducing both physical and psychological new parameters, separating man from nature, from the universe and hence not being responsible for an overall harmony by being subservient to the cosmos, but pretending itself to be the dominant force. Thus being good and bad became mere matters of technical feasibility, since moral, spiritual and other dimensions had little to do with the material solid practicality of material comforts. Now, all this is outdated, in view of some ideas ahead of the times, this reductionistic paradigm which alienated man from the cosmos. It is in this context that scientists are moving in both the inner and outer dimensions, science and religion, between matter and consciousness, even if physics and chemistry are inadequate to deal with such problems, since, so far, science has no moral dimensions to it, albeit scientific and ethical values are not inseparable.

The suggestion is that it is important to live in an open-ended system, as a human-being and not merely as a good scientist or scholar; for example, molecular biologists think that the whole of nature or life can be comprehended in terms of molecular biology — it is a mechanistic way of thinking that this is what science is about and that is all that matter (Mayr 1991). Thus, the open-mindedness of science is limited within established ideas or paradigms — just as many religions also say the same thing, or social scientists who think that the framework or content one is examining is the whole thing itself. Although the rational approach is very useful in many productive ways, it has ignored psychological and spiritual dimensions, especially in the area of consciousness — areas often relegated to a waste of time or stupidity. This narrow vision, extreme specialization — at the same time claiming open-endedness — is very neurotic and hence destructive, consequences that weigh heavily upon us in this century. For example, even the role of intuition is not recognized in the work of the scientist himself, or his own creative process of which little is known — not to speak of knowing oneself before knowing the universe (Gandhi 1990, Harris 1991).

The philosophy of science rests largely on empirical methodology and involves formulating one's hypothesis, subjecting it to empirical experiment via carefully collected data that verify or falsify the hypothesis, in order to draw conclusions that will become a theory or perhaps a law, using equations and mathematics which is its handmaiden. Science is thus concerned with concrete details and abstract reasoning, between inductive and deductive ways; it has a very sophisticated structure. However, unless the thing at hand, under study, is both itself and something beyond itself, it loses meaning or becomes destructive in the long run as we see between science and technology — scientism and empiricism. Scientific details only acquire meaning when they glow with another metascientific reality. The collections of sense data about data is not a mere collection but depicts, not describes, like poetry and art does, a single reality of grandeur and beauty which may be experienced on multiple levels — only a handful of scientists like Einstein express it publicly. Feeling and experiencing this oneness is, if it must be defined, mysticism. Science, originating from philosophical searches, also arises from the idea of wonder and awe; there is both an ethical as well as aesthetic side to it. Perhaps now it explains the mystery of being, while mysticism experiences it; the former is limited while the latter is unbounded. Nevertheless, both seek unity, a unified field of existence which forms the link, the substratum. What is this, and how is it tied to the existence of the scientist-scholar and itself? It is possible that now one is speaking of a realm that is beyond language — schema-symbols, too feeble to translate that ineffable domain, and of Silence. Nevertheless, it is knowable, communicable even if whatever one says about it becomes an untruth. Like in physics, there can be only approximations of the statements one makes (Weber 1986).

Holistic Approach

Perhaps, one may call science and the inner exploration outer empiricism and inner empiricism, and the common ground is unity — linking the microcosm and the macrocosm, nature and man, the observer and the observed. Max Planck acknowledged it well, "Science cannot solve the ultimate mystery of nature. . . because in the last analysis we are ourselves part of nature, and, therefore, part of the mystery that we are trying to solve".

The view of this paper has been to emphasize the fact that there is an urgent need to change the basic paradigm globally, from a mechanistic one to holistic one in the physio-psychic realm. The split-dualism is built into the very texture of the scientific study of matter, of thought, is seen in all walks life; its limitations have to be seen because a unified mode is available, as has been shown by particle physics and extra-galactic cosmology through post-Einsteinian physics by Heisenberg and others, of the dissolution of solid matter into waves of probability. The shift indicates that Consciousness is not an epi-phenomenon of matter but the very matrix, the Context of all contexts within which everything functions, i.e., it is the way of perception itself (Smith 1975, Stiskin 1972).

Now, the organism, the body-brain mechanism, itself is being hard put to understand all these goings on; it is struggling to know this state of affairs of utter conflict and contradiction since in its very depth of being it knows it is made up of all the elements of the universe. It is in fact in all of its activities trying to relate and communicate by its surroundings — the environment. But this conditioning is so deep-rooted, as a separate self, or an identity, that obviously it causes agony and alienation as well, since it seems to give an empty feeling about one's identity. This so-called separate self cannot really discover unconsciously any solid, stable 'me' or an answer to 'who am I?' In normal life, all one does is to play the various social roles that are based on a reaction-reaction system within the relatedness to the other, functionally given. Without the other, there is no separate identity even at the social level.

Nevertheless, since the conditioning is so strong, the brain struggles to search for its real identity, and not finding one in what it has learnt within that limited dimension, it is thoroughly exasperated, it goes beserk despite trying to maintain some semblance to sanity, it becomes frantic, and it is in despair totally alienated both within and without. One may ask, since the separate self has always been there, why is the turmoil so great today? Earlier, perhaps by and large individuals functioned within certain stable social setups that were not governed by rapid changes and one's position in society was relatively secure in terms of who's who and what was one's position. This gave a certain kind of stability within the given world-views which were accepted as one's context of existence in the universe. The same has no longer been true since the beginning of the modern era in the seventeenth century with the rapid growth of industrialization, urbanization and philosophy of crass consumerism that has become the global way of life, barring some minor exceptions. All socio-cultural boundaries have been eroded quickly and there is no certitude even in any world-view, unless it is a reversion to fundamentalism for a last ditch battle. The brain has no time to adjust to changes occurring externally in all walks of life, not excluding the environmental changes. A new order based on intrinsic equality is a long way off, just like is the case in terms of socio-political and economic equality. The different parts are not co-ordinated, especially psychologically, since thought itself is based as yet on hierarchy and domination and subordination principles.

Identity and Unity

The inner psyche is still looking for 'who am I?', who one is, and no amount of external solutions in the absence of the overarching umbrella of Consciousness will bring about any lasting peace or contentment. The organism somehow knows its true nature, or at least that what is given is not so. But in the present trance-like conditioning one continues to grope in the hope of 'tomorrow and tomorrow', little realizing that mirages continuously recede and will never materialize. The first signs of the awakening of Consciousness is to be aware of this false image, the false changes, this hope against hope, this untruth. This is the first step towards a new dimension which, without being stated, may bring about the 180 degrees transformation that is so imperative in bringing about the shift in Global Consciousness in all walks of life.

Thus nothing is clear even externally in this age of transition when even the views of the cosmos are far from clear and the old ones no longer provide any adequate answers. Perhaps, these are phase changes, like what Prigogine (1980, 1984) speaks of the time of dissipative structures. One can imagine the state of affairs in the brain, given the enormity of the problem briefly stated above. This is the uncertainty, and the cause of violence, upheavals, since every aspect of life is destabilized into several contending problems, their solutions, theories, etc. Despite the weight one gives to creating artificial identities, old or new formulations, these are still not one's natural or spontaneous creations. These formulations are made more out of a sense of insecurity, clinging to a so-called reinterpreted past. These are reactive attempts which do not create security since it is a reaction to the others who also are against it — mutually dependent enemies.

Correlating consciousness with matter, as a subject of science, has been a long-standing puzzle. Recent developments since 1970 in cognitive science have somewhat attempted to unravel this puzzle. Especially the developments of quantum physics and chaos theory have shown us that in any strict sense, science cannot always predict and control. Some say that after a certain point in time, in evolution, consciousness comes into play which is qualitatively different from the reductionist causes of science. May be the hypothesis of an all-pervasive energetic field of quantum zero-point energy is the all-pervasive field, which Consciousness of the esoteric traditions too talk about.

However, all recent attempts basically retain the old tested approach of science, which wants to understand it as down-upwards causation. First one must understand this, and then reverse this approach and direct it towards an all inclusive holistic one, an up-downwards causation. Implying thereby that the basic stuff of the universe to study is the physical energy, matter, even if it is in terms of the fundamental particles and their associated interrelationships. It has been a mistake of modern science to assume that ultimately reductionistic scientific causes are explanations of everything. It is not an adequate world-view, since it has resulted in gaining control through manipulation of the physical environment — and thereby the psychological-cultural implications albeit within that context everything seems to work well. It is leading to conflicts, confrontational dualities between science and religion, free will versus determinism, you versus me, and so on.

Of course, these foundational assumptions have been modified with the advent of quantum physics, particularly by the indeterminacy principle and the inherent statistical nature of measurement of the very small. Agreement is spreading among the few that science must develop the ability to look at things, particularly living things, more holistically. There is evidence that everything physical and mental that is experienced is part of an intercommunicating unity, a oneness, and there is no justification of the assumption of separateness. However, within specific contexts, isolating parts from the whole, the ordinary concepts of scientific causation do also apply.

In other words, if we include both ways, inner and outer, into account then we know that one reality is to be known in two ways that are not separate but interlinked. The epistemological issue involves: is our encountering of reality limited to being aware of, and giving meaning, to the messages from our physical senses (objective), or does it not also include a subjective aspect in an intuitive, aesthetic, spiritual, noetic and mystical sense? In any case, in normal science ethics and aesthetics (elegance) enters in various ways. In a restructuring of our view of science, of matter, inner explorers may be included. In doing so, science would be more inclusive and this is not to invalidate any of the physical and biological sciences. One may thus be both distancing oneself and be also participatory in being one with the subject.

Conclusion

The point of the above discussion is to point out new directions of holistic science, of oneness — Consciousness — as the new foundations and metaphysics, when whole new vistas are open before us. Many anomalies, paranormal phenomena, will begin to fit in this framework, that does not insist on fitting everything into a reductionistic science and we humans are here solely through random causes, in a meaningless universe; nor that our consciousness is merely the chemical and physical processes of the brain.

Few scientists are willing to question the philosophical issues underlying their work that they are part of the underlying definition of science — say the objectivist, positivistic, determinist, and reductionist assumptions of logical empiricism. Not that these have not served science and technological development well, however less so in biology even though the new gospel is molecular biology; but when the social scientist has aped these approaches it is a disaster.

Most scientists would assert that science has moved away from all this for over half a century ago. But it is not clear towards what; and consciousness has not yet come into the picture even though major paradoxes are today facing science, namely:

(i) The fundamental nature of things does not appear to be convergent — more and more of fundamental particles are appearing — reductionism is in fact pointing to a wholeness, and in their separation these are connected.

(ii) The fundamental organizing force in living systems from the largest to the smallest is unexplained by physical principles (homeostasis; intricate flower patterns, butterfly wings, etc.; healing, regeneration, ontogenesis, etc.).

(iii) The problem of action at a distance, or non-local causality, is appearing in the far reaches of quantum physics e.g., meaningful coincidences or connections, or Jungian Synchronicity — called paranormal, telepathic, clairvoyant communication; a host of others.

(iv) The knowledge of the universe is incomplete since there is no place for the consciousness of the observer, as if he is not in it (the notion of free will, volition and other characteristics of consciousness). Going from physio-chemical to the consciousness does not work; it is the movement from higher, subtle, to the lower or gross which will take many of these aspects into account.

(v) For the notion of the self the concept is not clear and not taken into account even though it is involved in the act of observation.

(vi) What are altered states of consciousness, which mystics and others know of but indicated in ordinary mundane lives also and sought after by one and all in aesthetic experience and so on? If atom and other splitting cause the release of unforeseen energy, the splitting of the ego releases another dimension of consciousness little known in everyday living in a sleep-dreamlike state.

Given the above puzzles, researchers are moving into new areas to understand matter and consciousness, unthinkable a couple of decades ago. It requires a restructuring of the approach towards a oneness picture, a wholeness science as some would like to call it. This is to say one experiences the world from inside as consciousness, which is also the whole, since the outside experienced by the senses is its external manifestation. Speaking evolutionarily, evolution is the manifestation of consciousness, not just a single track of separate evolution from times immemorial. Consciousness — thus becomes an agency — in the relevant data which we desire to create for our images and pictures of reality.

This approach thus implies a sensitization of the observer, whereby he/she is altered and — willing to be transformed in an ongoing dialogue — with whatsoever — which is the essence of creation and not any rigid stand of authority, expertise that leads to entropy. This transformation happens, if it is true for the anthropologist, psychotherapist, and so would be for the scientist who wishes to study meditation and altered states of consciousness. May be the movement is up and down, like an hour glass or a spiral. This process of conscious awareness involves unconscious processes, volition and the concept of the self and so on. In scale, depending on the level, where one is placed, that matter becomes consciousness and consciousness matter. It all is real or unreal — whatever suits one's terminology.

Naturally, in the new approach (e.g., not that bodies have consciousness, but consciousness has bodies) the questions asked will radically change: how does separateness arise, if all is one? does the brain act as a filtering and reductive mechanism? No longer will one think, how to integrate the universe but how it feels separate; how to explain the interconnections — but not through linear processes of the big-bang; of seeking a unified theory involving many different fields (gravitational, electromagnetic, morphogenetic, string theory, etc.), the various energies. Once, following Einstein who took light velocity to be basic, consciousness becomes the base line and different explanations will follow — a quantum jump! It will serve us well in individual and societal development as well. Openness to alternative theories in this scheme, explanations and healthy scepticism remains a part and parcel of it. In short, the new approach of the research scientific endeavours include both the direct experience of the inner senses and the outer physical ones as a unity of consciousness; and is not based on any principle of exclusion to any human experience.

References

Bouissac, Paul, 1990. "Semiotics and the Gaia Hypothesis: Towards the Restructuring of Western Thought", In *Philosophy and the Future of Humanity*, Vol. 1, 2. pp. 168-84.

Gandhi, Kishore (ed.), 1990. *The Odyssey of Science, Culture and Consciousness*, New Delhi.

Harris, Errol E., 1991. *Cosmos and Anthropos — A Philosophical Interpretation of the Anthropic Principle*; London.

Lovelock, James, 1979. *A New Look at Life on Earth*, Oxford.

Lovelock, James, 1988. *The Ages of Gaia*, London.

Malik, S.C., 1968. *Indian Civilization; the Formative Period — A Study of Archaeology as Anthropology*, Shimla. (reprinted, 1987).

———, 1969. "Culture Areas, Ecology and Regionalism", In *Language Culture and Society*, Shimla.

———, 1972. "Human Evolution: Some Reflections on its Philosophy", In *Eastern Anthropologist*, Lucknow.

———, 1975. *Understanding Indian Civilization — A Framework of Enquiry*, Shimla.

———, 1989a. *Modern Civilization — A Crisis of Fragmentation*, New Delhi.

———, 1989b. "Intellectuals, Traditions and Ethnographic Studies — Some Basic Questions", In *Man in India*, Ranchi.

———, 1990a. "Holism and Lifestyle Studies — the Civilization Context", In *Eastern Anthropologist*, Lucknow.

———, 1990b. "Alternative Futures: Towards an Integral Universe", In *NMML Occasional Papers*, New Delhi. Mimeographed.

———, 1992. "Matter and Consciousness", In *The Nature of Matter Seminar*, Pune. Mimeographed.

———, 1993a. "Holistic Science and Consciousness", In *Nature and Man — An Integral Vision Seminar*, New Delhi. Mimeographed.

———, 1993b. "A Question of Consciousness", In *Future of the Mind — Mind of the Future Seminar*, New Delhi. Mimeographed.

Mayr, Ernest, 1991. *Towards a New Philosophy of Biology: Observations of an Evolutionist*, Harvard.

Prigogine, I., 1980. *From Being to Becoming*, San Fransisco.

———, 1984. *Order Out of Chaos*, New York.

Smith, Lester, 1975. *Intelligence Came First*, Illinois.

Stitskin, Mahur, 1972. *The Looking Glass God*, Canada.

Weber, Renee, 1986. *Dialogue with Sages and Scientists*, New York.

2

Humanization of Development

A Theravada Buddhist Perspective

P. D. Premasiri

In accordance with an important logical distinction to which contemporary philosophers have drawn our attention it is reasonable to affirm that the term development is the one primary meaning which is evaluative rather than descriptive. The term development implies the growth of something, but when used in the sense of a goal to be pursued by communities and nations the intended growth must be desirable and worthwhile. Just as the term 'reform' logically involves the effecting of a change which is desirable and worthwhile the term development too logically involves a process of change which is desirable and worthwhile. Questions regarding what is desirable and worthwhile cannot be decided purely on the basis of descriptive criteria. They are not questions of empirical science but questions of value involving primarily moral criteria. It is a common assumption that evaluate judgements are culture-relative. It is true to a great extent that this is so. But today it appears to be the case that there is a tendency towards the establishment of a global culture or a universal culture and the dominant elements of this global culture appear to be supplied by the Western model. The cultural values of the West are an intermixture of the traditional theistic religious values derived from the Judeo-Christian faith and its more modern materialist values springing from the consideration that the source of all human knowledge is modern science and the source of all power is the technology derived from the applications of scientific knowledge. The evaluative assumptions underlying the contemporary Western concept of development are being blindly adopted by other civilizations of the world without a sufficient critique of the very contradictions evidently involved in the practical implications of such a concept. It is an urgent requirement in the context of the contemporary human predicament to point out that there is profound wisdom concealed in the cultural heritage of the non-Western civilizations which could be utilized as a corrective to some of the ill-conceived evaluative assumptions of the Western concept of development which is increasingly leading to a dehumanization of man. It might, of course be contended that judgements of value are non-rational and therefore cannot be established as universally valid judgements. However, many contemporary philosophers have drawn attention to the possibility of finding a rational basis for value judgements including those in the field of morality although such a basis might not accord fully with the inductive and/or deductive rationality found in the other sciences. If such a possibility is admitted the search for some degree of universality in our value judgements would not be in vain. In order to do this all authority has to be suspended, and values imposed on people by new forms of cultural imperialism have to be boldly subjected to criticism. This approach seems extremely relevant in the discussion of the concept of development.

The term 'development' is used today with a characteristically materialist bias. This is evident when one considers the basis on which countries are described as developed or underdeveloped. The principal criteria adopted for determining whether a nation is developed are the quantity of goods produced and consumed, the gross national product and the per capita income of the people. All these criteria are monetary or material. Surely, if in any community people die due to starvation, poor health facilities, lack of proper clothing and shelter it would not be proper to call such a community developed. There are certain basic material needs without the fulfilment of which the quality of life of a human being can in no way be conceived as satisfactory. The admission of this fact need not commit us to a purely materialistic conception of development. For such a concept of development can be said to be based on an inadequate and unexamined evaluative assumption. If people die of starvation in a particular community we will not be inclined to call that community developed. But what if people face the threat of being robbed at gunpoint in the most modernized cities of the world, or of being shot in broad daylight in a market square, or if a young lady is not safe from being molested and raped by sex criminals, or if people attempt to overcome their discontentment with life with large doses of debilitating drugs and alcohol which create immense misery within their families and households, and if more and more people have to seek the help of sedatives or psychiatric treatment to overcome their mental distress and above all if we face the constant threat of being annihilated by nuclear war between superpowers who incessantly compete for a bigger share of the world's resources? Under such circumstances can we boast of any genuine development?

When development is used in the context of human notions it is possible to speak of numerous spheres of development such as economic, technological, political, educational, social, cultural, moral, spiritual and so on, which, though separately conceivable are causally interrelated. Like in Plato's doctrine of the soul according to which justice is established by each part of the soul fulfilling its appropriate function, development can be said to occur when an appropriate development has occurred in each of the above spheres. Therefore, when development is thought of in general it would be necessary to take into account a desirable harmony and integration of several different areas of human concern. Among these different areas some may seem to have a priority as well as an overriding claim over others. A sound development policy needs to pay adequate attention to these priorities in order to make the development effort meaningful in the human context. Some spheres in which development may be effected could adversely affect others resulting in lopsided development. This is likely to lead to a process of development which is ultimately self-defeating. The contradictions and dilemmas that have arisen in connection with the lives of people living in the so-called developed or affluent world makes it imperative that we should consider development in terms of a holistic vision. Such a holistic vision demands a moral foundation for development. It is in connection with such a holistic vision and a moral foundation for development that the teachings of Theravada Buddhism seem to have something very significant to offer.

A process of growth which is not conducive to or which is detrimental to the well-being of man cannot properly be called development just as any action or pattern of behaviour which is not conducive to the well-being of the agent and those affected by such actions or patterns of behaviour cannot be called moral. The current trends of development policy which seem to be becoming gradually universalized compel right thinking men to pause and ask the question 'Is man for development or is development for man?' What is becoming increasingly evident is that the former alternative is becoming the order of the day. The natural consequence of this is that man is getting more and more alienated, and is being reduced merely to a cogwheel in a machine, created by powers and authorities beyond his/her control, depriving him/her of the opportunity to develop the real human spiritual potential. It is this spiritual potential in man which developed to its fullness makes him/her ultimately satisfied, contented and happy. In brief development appears to be dehumanizing man increasingly. The time has reached to reassess this trend and to think of ways and means of humanizing development.

Mankind has already begun to feel the effects of the development policy pursued by the so-called developed nations of the present century. The effects of industrialization on the natural environment is drawing the attention of ecologists. The problem of industrial wastes polluting the water resources, factory fumes and other gases emitted by modern machinery polluting the atmosphere, the damage done to the ozone layer, the poisons introduced in the form of modern agricultural technology affecting all forms of life on earth including human, and numerous other ecological problems are the visible effects of the current development policy which is universally advocated. The effects of competition for the limited resources available for human consumption in accordance with the affluent life-styles of nations who call themselves developed have produced the paradoxical consequence of allocating nearly three-fourths of the world's economic resources for the creation of weapons destructive of both human life and the natural environment. The unrestrained pursuit of material wealth and the immoderate urge for the gratification of the senses have only led to a complete obliteration of a reasonable distinction between mankind's needs and wants. The naturally unlimited and insatiable wants are being converted into needs under the extremely unwise and unwarranted assumption that there are enough resources in the world to satisfy all the needs that are being artificially created. Such newly created needs can be satisfied only by disregarding the delicate balance between man and his natural environment. The modern city which is a creation of the current concept of development is described by some writers as a product of a new form of terrorism in the guise of development. All that is beautiful in nature is destroyed to create an artificial environment consisting of concrete forests in which human beings are crowded like animals in a zoo. At this point it is necessary to pause and question the unexamined belief in the omnipotence of material science and technology and recognize the potency of a science (*vijja*) which has for a long time been ignored even by those people who were the traditional inheritors of it. It is the science of spiritual discipline, the science of self-development which is advocated in the philosophy of life and the philosophy of development implicit in Buddhism. It may be argued that in this 'science' is to be found a viable solution to the contradictions and paradoxes of the currently dominant concept of development.

Buddhism uses the term *bhavana* which in meaning is very proximate to the English term development. Since the term has been used primarily in the context of the development of the self or the mind or the spiritual potential of man, the term has usually been rendered into English as 'meditation'. This rendering has obscured the fact that the spiritual discipline promoted by means of *bhavana* is a kind of self-development. In the Buddhist context development is believed to be desirable first and foremost of man himself, who serves as the very instrument of other forms of development. It is men themselves who formulate development policy and it is men themselves who implement such policy. The nature of the influence of the moral character of the supreme agent or instrument of all development activity on the nature of the development achieved has often been overlooked. It is here that the question of the moral quality of the development achieved arises. Should development be geared to the production of what Mill once called 'satisfied pigs'. According to Buddhism, development basically stands for the development of man, his/her character, his/her personality and his/her humaneness. In Buddhism one who has a developed or cultivated personality is referred to as *bhavitatta*. In the full sense of the term it is a person who is fully enlightened and liberated from the miseries of existence, who is perfectly happy and at ease and who can truly be characterized as a developed personality. According to Buddhism the foremost of such developed beings is a Buddha whose personality represents the highest development of great compassion (*mahakaruna*) and great wisdom (*mahapanna*). The greatness as well as the quality of the life of a human being depends, according to Buddhism, on the wisdom and morality that is perfected in him/her. The conquest of oneself is better than conquering thousands of men in battle.[1] There is no power in this world that can take away the victory of the person who has conquered himself/herself through self-development.[2] Self-development involves the elimination of the unwholesome traits of mind, the roots of evil behaviour (*akusalamula*), greed, hatred and confusion of mind. The prescribed method for such development is presented as the eightfold path or the threefold moral training consisting of the cultivation of wholesome patterns of behaviour in terms of observing certain norms of conduct (*sila*), attaining composure of the mind and developing the wisdom which results in a total self-transformation leading to the elimination of all unwholesome traits of mind.

The Buddhist position is that if men are wise they would give priority to self-development over and above all other development. Self-development should serve as the basis for other kinds of development. As the *Dhammapada* says: "Irrigators divert water. Fletchers shape the arrow shaft. Carpenters shape wood. The wise ones tame themselves."[3] Any development that is effected outside ourselves, that is in man's material environment, must be directed and controlled by persons with cultivated minds. If what moves them to decisions and actions are the roots of unwholesome behaviour, greed, hatred and confusion, the consequence of development attempts are likely to be self-defeating.

The Buddhist concept of self-development is believed to be a hindrance to development by the advocates of the Western concept. It is believed to be incompatible with the goals of development as conceived by them. The self-development advocated in Buddhism, it is believed, is intended for the liberation of the individual. It is said to lack any social concern. It is argued that the "aim of Buddhism is not to shape life in the world, but to teach liberation, release from the world."[4] The Buddhist attempt to attain inner peace (*nibbana*) through self-development is understood as "an absolutely personal performance of the single individual".[5] This is a gross misrepresentation of the Buddhist position suggesting that the Buddhist ideal of self-development is incompatible with real social and material development. This is extremely unfortunate, for what is required in the context of the contemporary human predicament appears to be precisely a sound moral basis for material and social development. Buddhism does not consider self-development in its sense of the full flowering of the spiritual potential of man as an absolutely personal attainment of a single individual. The enlightenment attained by each individual is an event of great cosmic significance. The Buddhist tradition appears to have indicated this figuratively in its canonical account of the preaching of the first sermon of the Buddha, the supremely enlightened one. According to this account the great news of the first sermon of the Buddha reaches even the high heavens in the cosmos, inhabited by sentient beings of superhuman excellence.[5] This shows that the liberation doctrine of Buddhism which insists on the importance of self-development is of universal and cosmic significance.

Buddhism does not see an absolute separation between a concern with the affairs of the world and a concern with liberation in a more ideal and spiritual sense. In fact, the highest liberation is something to be won here and now (*dittheva dhamme*) not in a life after death. Degeneration in the affairs of the world is closely linked to the absence of a sound moral ideal as well as the scarcity of those who dedicate themselves solely to the pursuit of moral and spiritual perfection. Buddhism does not place its trust entirely in politicians. Politicians are dependable only when their actions are governed by righteousness (*dhamma*). Guidance in righteousness has to come from the spiritual community, or from persons who are in the real sense of the term awakened to truth (*sambuddha*). In the Buddhist tradition it is held that there are two persons who are born for the welfare of all rational beings. First and foremost it is a fully enlightened Buddha who gives direction on the path of righteousness. Secondly it is a Universal Ruler (*cakkavattiraja*) who establishes a just social and political order.

The Buddhist ideal of *Nibbana* has been wrongly interpreted as an other-worldly ideal. On the contrary it could be viewed as the kind of ideal that is necessary for the promotion of a harmonious world-order. The spiritual community referred to in Buddhism as *samanabrahmana* are those who pursue the goal of moral perfection. They are expected to perform a social role of no mean significance. The enlightened sage wanders in the community like the bee that produces fruit by taking the essence of the flower.[6] The ideal ruler (*cakkavatti*) preserves, protects and extends due patronage to the spiritual community as part of his cardinal duties. It is also customary for a ruler of that stature to approach the spiritual community and get moral advice and direction.[7] The Buddha mentions as one of the principles that prevented the degeneration (*aparihaniya dhamma*) of the Vajjian community and their care and concern for the spiritual community.[8] There is a tendency today, specially among those who believe in the omnipotence of material science, to be cynical about a way of life which gives priority to spiritual discipline. Buddhism sees a social order which disregards the importance of spiritual discipline, devalues persons engaged in such a pursuit, and gives no active encouragement to it treading a path of development which is in the end self-defeating.

The common belief is that the contemplative life of the spiritual seeker involves a negation of action. This belief has led to a tendency to contrast it with the active life. This attitude is to be seen among those advocates of current notions of development who believe the contemplative life of the spiritual seeker to be a hindrance to development as envisaged by them. In the Buddha's own day there are instances in which such criticism was directed against Buddhism. Some critics of the life of the Buddhist recluses saw their lifestyle as one given to inaction and laziness (*akammakama alasa*). The Buddhist response to this was that those who engaged themselves in self-development were engaged in the performance of the highest form of work (*kammasetthassa karaka*).[9] For they were supposed to be engaged in an endeavour involving the elimination of greed and hatred. The Buddha himself is said to have met with a similar response when he once went on his usual round of alms-begging. In this instance he points out that he is not a mere idler, but one who like a farmer, is engaged in cultivating his self the produce of which is the fruit of immortality (*amatapphala*).[10] It is difficult to comprehend these Buddhist attitudes on a purely materialist approach to values. What is important is to judge whether when we suspend materialist presuppositions and fit the Buddhist ideal into a more holistic perception of the nature of the human predicament it has something very meaningful to offer. Buddhism envisages a society in which a distinctive role is assigned to the life of the recluse who cultivates total detachment and provides moral inspiration to the lesser moral beings in order that they could themselves gradually progress towards the most desirable goal of final liberation from unwholesome passions. The close tie that has traditionally existed (which is today getting fast eroded) in Buddhist societies between the lay community and the community of *bhikkhus* can be viewed as a devise of promoting the material development of a community on the basis of moral and spiritual values. Those who have failed to understand the dynamics of such a social order have interpreted the relationship as a dichotomous separation into "this worldliness" and "other-worldliness".

This mistake is evident in observations made by anthropologists like Spiro who introduce a somewhat artificial dichotomy between what is called "kammatic Buddhism" and "Nibbanic Buddhism". It is my contention that there is only one type of Buddhism, and that is both 'Nibbanic' and 'kammatic'. Commenting on the Buddhist goal of liberation Spiro says:

> Ideationally, its conception of salvation is indeed a radical one, entailing the transcendence of the entire physico-temporal world. Sociologically, its character for a soteriological community is equally radical: in order to transcend the physico-temporal world, it is necessary to abandon the socio-political world. But physical retreat from the world is not sufficient; it is merely a necessary condition for yet another psychologically radical act: having abandoned the world, one must sever all ties to it and withdraw cathexes from it. Salvation can only be achieved by a total and radical rejection of the world in all its aspects.[11]

It need not be denied that such aberrations of the Buddhist ideal have sometimes occurred in its historical development and that there have been and are representatives of the kind of ideology which Spiro describes. But neither the Buddha nor his most accomplished disciples subscribed to a way of life which accords with such a description. Such descriptions have overlooked the role of Nibbanic persons in the world as it is conceived in the teachings of Buddhism and traditionally understood by Buddhist societies. Enlightened, Nibbanic beings who have accomplished the task of self-development are born out of the world, grow in the world and live in the world without being tainted by the ways of the world (*loke jato loke samvaddho loka accuggamma titthati anupalitto lokena*). They are the most capable of providing the much needed good sense and moral illumination to the world. They are like the beautiful lotus that grows in the mud but remains in the mud without being tainted by the muddy water.

Insofar as development is conceived as a change in the course of things effected by human intervention, planning, deliberation and effort as a means of overcoming human misery and of promoting human well-being, the proper starting point for such a process of change should be the hearts and minds of men. However, with the growth of the mechanistic view of the world that has taken root along with the developments in the natural sciences since the seventeenth century the belief that human behaviour is totally determined by the external stimuli came to be widely accepted. This belief has been further promoted by the developments in behaviourist psychology of the twentieth century, and by socio-political doctrines like Marxism. The consequence of this belief has been that all attempts at overcoming unhappiness and misery through self-discipline have been considered to be unrealistic. There is no doubt that material conditions of life affect people's moral consciousness. Buddhism, to be sure, has recognized this. Moral degeneration and social disharmony are sometimes traceable to unjust socio-economic structures. But the process involving morally degenerate men and unjust socio-economic structures is a viciously circular process. The question is, how we could break into the vicious circle and put an end to it. The key to it lies in a change of heart especially among those who assume the role of leadership, political authority and social responsibility. Those persons in whose hands the responsibility of giving direction to a social change lies, are required to possess, if not in full, at least to a considerable degree, the kind of self-development that is envisaged in Buddhism. A noticeable weakening of the unwholesome dispositions, greed, hatred and delusion which can be identified as the roots of evil behaviour which generate suffering not only to the possessors of these traits but also to the community at large becomes an urgent requirement. When a change in the course of events is to take place in accordance with human plans and intentions, human beings themselves become operative links in the process of change. The original source of the intended change is ultimately a network of human decisions and actions. What if this source is itself intensely corrupt due to the influence of the deep-rooted unwholesome dispositions and attitudes? What if those at the source do not care to be guided by moral ideals, by notions of justice, by kindness, compassion and universal fellow feeling? Under such circumstances neatly formulated social and political theories fail miserably, as has been amply demonstrated in the recent history of mankind.

The dominant belief today which has taken root along with the materialist and mechanistic world-view is that the use of science and technology is the solution to all our problems. Questions about the cultivation of man's inner nature are considered as irrelevancies indulged in by those accustomed to outmoded and obscurantist modes of thinking. The widespread belief is that scientific rationality and technical competence is sufficient to solve all of mankind's problems. Insistence on moral virtues serves no purpose, for according to their view they will never be acquired by mankind. Buddhism, on the other hand insists on the comprehension of the inner sources of human wickedness, evil, tensions and miseries. According to Buddhism it is a psychological fact that there is no point at which man can reach fulfilment in the satisfaction of desires (*kamesu loke na hi atthi titti*). A point of fulfilment can be reached not by permitting human needs to keep on increasing by converting the limitless wants into needs, but by a kind of spiritual development which promotes contentment (*santutthi*). Contentment, according to Buddhism, is the greatest wealth (*santutthi paramam dhanam*).[12] E. F. Schumacher recognizes this psychological truth of Buddhism and relates it to the wisdom that is required in formulating development policy thus:

> An attitude to life which seeks fulfilment in the single-minded pursuit of wealth — in short, materialism — does not fit into this world, because it contains within itself no limiting principle, while the environment in which it is placed is strictly limited.[13]

Buddhism does not discourage the production of material wealth. What Buddhism discourages is the servile dependence on consumer goods. Production of wealth should not overstep morality. The production of material wealth by righteous means without exploitation is commendable. A householder's happiness consists in having sufficient wealth (*atthisukha*), in enjoying the wealth he possesses (*bhogasukha*), being free from economic indebtedness (*ananasukha*). However, far more valuable than these sources of happiness is the happiness derived from righteous living (*anavajjasukha*). The pursuit of wealth should not drive the human being to greed, avarice, miserliness and envy. In a human being's effort to make a living sufficient care should be taken not to violate the most important factor of the eightfold path which has a relevance to the economic life of a person, namely, right means of livelihood (*samma ajiva*). The ideal lay Buddhist should live the life of a householder with the mind free from the stain of avarice (*vigatamalamacherena cetasa*), with readiness to share one's wealth with others and with his hands always in readiness to be stretched out to give to others in times of need.

Factors of the Noble Eightfold Path, the threefold scheme of moral development, the four sublime abidings (*brahmavihara*), and the four grounds of beneficence (*sangahavatthu*) could be viewed as universally valid schemes for self-development. These are not sectarian virtues, they are not the commandments of any particular God; the beneficial effects of their adoption could be universally tested. Buddhism also teaches universally testable techniques of mind culture (*bhavana*) which are effective in psychological tension reduction, in the therapy of mental illness, in the treatment of psychogenic diseases of the body, and above all in the attainment of insight into things as they are (*yathabhuatanana*) and consequently, in acquiring self-transforming wisdom and attaining inner peace and tranquillity. Buddhism believes that human beings can live in peace with their fellow human beings as well as their natural environment only if they cultivate peace within themselves.

Self-development involves the development of the various aspects of personality in a balanced way so that the total personality which is the outcome of such development is not harmful to the person himself/herself nor to others. This is the principal criterion adopted in Buddhism to distinguish between what is morally good and morally bad. *Kusala* is that which is not harmful but beneficial to the person himself/herself who cultivates a particular trait of character or pattern of behaviour, as well as to other members of the society to which that person belongs (*na attabyabadhaya samvattati na parabyabadhaya samvattati na ubhayabyabadhaya samvattati sukhudrayam sukhavipakam*).[14] It is for the development of such a personality that the Middle Way of Buddhism is prescribed. Buddhism does not advocate the negation of the importance of the body or the physical aspect of personality. The body has to be adequately nourished, and taken care of by keeping it free from diseases paying due attention to its cleanliness as well as through temperance and moderation in food habits. It is for this reason that Buddhism shuns the extremes of austerity and sensuality. This ideal of the Middle Way needs to be reflected in any development policy which is modelled on the Buddhist philosophy of development. Any attempt to create stimuli that promote over indulgence in sensuality, or the other extreme of austere living which does not promote good physical growth and healthy living is not in agreement with the ideal of good life as conceived in Buddhism.

Buddhism recognizes the importance of the body or man's physical existence as a vehicle through which man can strive for the perfection of human excellence which consists in nothing but the development of the spiritual aspect of man's being. It is in this connection that Buddhism has much to offer to modern man. Buddhism insists on the importance of self-reliance and human effort and initiative, in the development of the moral and spiritual aspects of man instead of relying on superior powers which according to Buddhism could be seen as creations of man's own imagination. There is great inner spiritual wealth which a person can develop within himself. Such wealth is considered in Buddhism as Noble Wealth (*ariyadhana*). Noble Wealth consists of confidence (*saddha*), good conduct (*sila*), sense of shame and fear to do wrong (*hiri, ottappa*), learning (*suta*), generosity (*caga*) and wisdom (*panna*).[15]

The spiritual qualities to be developed in self-development involve no mystery or metaphysical concepts. They are obviously wholesome psychological qualities. These psychological qualities have a great utility not only in realizing the supreme goal of Buddhism, but also anything worthwhile in a man's life which is even lesser than the supreme goal. Thus the cultivation of *sila* at least to the extent that is required of the Buddhist layperson, produces a law abiding and useful member of any civilized society. The development of mental composure produces persons whose minds are not scattered and confused, persons who are both mentally and physically relaxed, and persons whose mental hindrances that obstruct the proper functioning of the mind in achieving any intended goal are eliminated. The mental hindrances which are supposed to be eliminated in attaining mental composure (*samadhi*) are disturbing desires for sensuous enjoyment (*kamacchanda*), hatred or ill-will (*vyapada*), restlessness and worry (*uddhaccakukkucca*), drowsiness and laziness (*thinamiddha*) and vacillation of mind due to doubt and diffidence (*vicikiccha*). These are obviously hindrances that obstruct the proper performance of any task. The Four Bases of Psychic Power (*cattaro iddhipada*) are according to the teachings of Buddhism essential components of self-development. It is believed that those who have developed, multiplied, cultivated and established within themselves these bases of psychic power may, if they wish to, elevate themselves even to the status of supernormal beings having the ability to control even material forces of nature. These bases of psychic power can also be understood as psychological qualities which could be utilized in the achievement of any worthwhile objective or goal. They consist of the development of a genuine interest in what one wants to achieve (*chanda*), effort (*viriya*), proper direction of focus of thought (*citta*) and proper investigation (*vimamsa*). In each case these qualities of mind should be rigorously harnessed in order to achieve one's objective. The interest (*chanda*), for instance, should be concentrated, it should be sustained with effort, and volitional force should be generated with a view to attaining one's objective (*chanda samadhi padhana sankhara samannagatam*). The cultivation of these psychological qualities are undoubtedly useful and necessary in the effective achievement of any worthwhile goal. The factors of enlightenment which are supposed to grow within the personality of one who applies oneself to the path of self-development are also wholesome psychological states. They are mindfulness (*sati*), investigation of truth (*dhammavicaya*), effort (*viriya*), joy (*piti*), tranquillity (*passaddhi*), mental composure (*samadhi*) and equanimity or a balanced and impartial mind (*upekkha*).

The essence of the Buddhist teaching on development is that all development must be guided by wisdom. For all development is first and foremost by man and for man. Wisdom can be gained only by self-development. Science and technology have provided us with knowledge, but not wisdom. The knowledge of the fool arises for his/her own ill (*yavadeva anatthaya nattam balassa jayate*). It might be contended that the development of science has put an end to superstition by enlightening man on human nature itself. It might further be contended that the moral ideals and patterns of behaviour traditionally upheld were derived largely from mythical beliefs and superstitions and that the scientific revolution has had the advantage of replacing those beliefs with empirically testable and scientifically valid beliefs about human nature. It might be argued that traditional moralities have been replaced by the more scientifically grounded morality which may be described as "scientific humanism". It might also be claimed that as a consequence of this the concern with human rights and resistance to all kinds of discrimination has come to the forefront in the ethical consciousness of contemporary man. All this may to a certain extent be granted. But the mechanistic and materialistic world-view associated with modern science which leads to an exclusive interest in changing the external factors for the attainment of happiness and well-being without the slightest concern about changing one's own inner nature seems certainly to be putting man on the path of self-destruction. This is true of a vast area of productions of modern science and technology having the veritable effect of a dehumanization of development. What is required for a humanization of development is nothing but self-development.

Notes

1. *Dhammapada* 103.
2. *Ibid.*, 105.
3. *Ibid.*, 50.
4. *The World of Buddhism*, edited by Heinz Bechert and Richard Gombrich (Thames and Hudson Ltd., London 1984) p. 7.
5. *Vinayapitaka* (Pali Text Society, London) I, 11-12.
6. *Dhammapada* 49.
7. *Dighanikaya* (Pali Text Society, London) 3.61. It is to be noted that the standard English translation of this passage occurring in the *Sacred Books of the Buddhists* series is totally erroneous. According to the original text the ruler should seek the advice of the spiritual community regarding what is right and wrong. According to the translation it is the ruler who should prescribe what is right and wrong to the spiritual community. Perhaps the translator could not imagine the Buddhist tradition recognizing the person who is spiritually elevated being of a higher status than the ruler.
8. *Dighanikaya* 2.75.
9. *Rohini Therigatha.*
10. *Suttanipata* (Pali Text Society) p. 13.
11. Melford E. Spiro, *Buddhism and Society*, (Harper and Row, 1970) p. 65.
12. *Dhammapada* 204.
13. *Small is Beautiful*, (Harper and Row, 1975) p. 30.
14. *Majjhimanikaya* (Pali Text Society) 1.415
15. *Dighanikaya* (Pali Text Society) 3.163.

3

Universal and Unique in Cross-cultural Interaction

A Paradigm Shift in Development Ideology

Lachman M. Khubchandani

In introducing the programmes of Janapada Sampada, the IGNCA points out to a general dissatisfaction amongst Indian scholars with Western methodology to explore the functioning of the society: "Until now each discipline has arrived at a totality, by aggregating or multiplying a single dimension, giving a fragmented picture of a society, failing to present a total view of life."

It reminds us of the parable of the blind men and the elephant. The blind men determined the reality from hasty examination of only one or more parts (identifying them as pillars, walls, fence, etc.) but missed the **organic** whole. In this regard, a noted philosopher has succinctly observed:

> As the intellectuals of the observed cultures have themselves internalised the Western categories and standards of intelligibility so that they observe, understand, and compare their own cultures in terms given to them by the West. To adopt a well-known expression from Sartre, all non-Western cultures have been reduced to the status of 'objects' by being observed and studied by Western scholars in terms of Western concepts and categories, which are treated not as culture-bound but as universal in character. In a deep and radical

sense, therefore, it is only the West that has arrogated to itself the status of subjecthood in the cognitive enterprise, reducing all others to the status of objects (Daya Krishna 1988).

Table 3.1

Dimensions of Language Development
(in a 'Centre - Periphery Frame Work)

Dimension	'Developed' languages	'Underdeveloped' languages
Ecological		
Utilization	Wider communication 'world' languages	Languages limited to a region (national, local languages)
Population strength	Dominant 'majority' languages	Dominated 'minorty' languages (often treated as dialects in policy-making)
Social		
Legitimization	Standard languages (acceptable to the elite)	Non-standard varieties, substandard languages (slangs, hybrids)
Domains of use	Full-fledged 'autonomous' languages	Languages with restrictive use (vernaculars in diglossia situations)
Projectional		
Graphization	Written languages	Unwritten languages
Literature	Literary languages	Colloquial 'bazaar' languages
Medium of instruction	Advanced 'cultivated' languages	Prepartory 'ethnic' languages
Technologization	Languages suitable for typing, shorthand and telecommunication purposes	Languages not extended for technological tasks

Source: Khubchandani, 1983, p. 21)

In the pursuit of knowledge, particularly in physical sciences, the isolation of a phenomenon under study by controlling its variables, *ceteris paribus* all other things being equal, has long been recognized as a legitimate means of enquiry, but when it comes to introducing drastic changes in human behaviour **deliberately**, then we must consider the issue with an **integrative** holistic approach. We cannot ignore the complex interactions between the targets of change and the rest of the universe.

Development Discourse

In the post-World War phase, the multi-faceted concept of development has evolved over the years from a materialistic base to a more people-centred perspective. The 'centre-periphery' hypothesis of politico-economic development tends to use economic indicators and other material factors to measure the quality of life (Dutta and Agrawal 1992). In this context, the author discusses elsewhere (Khubchandani 1983) certain dimensions of development that stress demarcating 'developed' languages from 'underdeveloped' languages (see Table 3.1).

Guided by such models, the languages of newly-emerged nations are considered to be **deficient** communication systems with all "the unprecedented disadvantages of the late-comers" (Fishman 1974). According to the evolutionary scale of development, it is assumed that newly-independent societies are to strive for 'secondary' modernization by trailing behind the path already taken by 'advanced' societies. Consequently, many of the transformations sought through modernization in these societies (such as the targets of language learning, language standardization, coining technical terminologies, devising new channels of communication and other human relations) are 'externally' induced, rather than 'internally' generated, unlike the classical European modernization processes stimulated during the Renaissance and the Reformation. Hence in the programmes of language development in most of the developing countries, Western norms and values are projected as a further intensification of modernization based upon both methods and substance overtly borrowed from successful models.

New networks of 'knowledge industry' and 'culture industry' are becoming key components of the twentieth century societies. A borrowed technology, acquired in a 'package' along with the imported exogamous know-how and the organizational ethos, cannot escape creating 'disturbance' in the prevailing ethos till it gets internalized in the recipient society; it runs even the risk of getting rejected in the long run. In this context, it will be relevant to draw attention to the shape and the meaning of borrowed items in a language. Their functional diversity and intensity in the target language generally determines the degree of *tadbhavization* from the original *tatsama* items in the source language. Such a process of **grass roots** adaptation signifies the cultural vitality of a plural society.

Critically assessing the development discourse of the last four decades, a radical thinking has been seeping from many scholars throughout the world that "development is a trap designed by Western powers to perpetuate colonialism in the post-Independence era". A recently published study *The Development Dictionary* (Sachs 1991), tracing back the ideological underpinnings of colonialism, calls this act of civiliszing the poor as 'transformative intervention': "The evangelists of development have inherited the missionary idea and have secularised the message of salvation". Donor-recipient relationship in the area of human resource development has further vitiated the scene.

The gap between North and South, between urban and tribal, is getting wider year by year. According to a recent survey, the existing technological gap between developing and developed countries at the present rate of development will triple by the end of the century. In this cruel illusion, the idea of development stands like a "ruin in the intellectual landscape" (Sachs, *ibid*). It debases everything it touched like pastures, with the entry of goats, turn into a desert. Many such programmes, initiated under the aegis of State or with the patronage from world bodies, have given birth to a body of experts, a class of development brahmanas, who serve the interests of ruling classes. "It has created in each state an economy profit-friendly for its mentors" (Constantino 1992). In this regard, Mahatma Gandhi has rightly cautioned: "On this planet there is enough for everyone's needs, but it is not sufficient for everyone's greed."

Concerns of 'haves' and 'have nots' pose many questions relating to issues of communication and community at the socio-political level. How to avoid lapsing into irreversible dependency in having access to global resources that are not infinite? According to this 'elite-directed' development, the term progress is applied "only to what the self-designated First world has already achieved. . . which was not yet available to the rest of the world" (Sbert, ed. Sachs 1991). This type of development thinking still continues to predominate that the developing countries should reach the same level of well-being by simply copying and adapting here and there the forms, criteria, the mechanisms through which the rich world had reached affluence (Somavia 1983). Such developing discourse has succeeded in making the hope of 'catching up' with the North, the principal aspiration of the peoples of South. In the Indian scenario, the international terminology of development associated with the North and the South can be applied to the metropolitan and the rural. In a way, such an approach to socio-cultural development depicts the futile race of trying to keep up with the Joneses.

So far the development scene in many 'poor' countries has been dominated by the global concerns of the **quality** of life (often measured in **quantitative** terms). This has resulted in the imposition of metropolitan values of affluent' countries leading to the homogenization of cultures:

> The elimination of socio-cultural heterogeneity, or at least its containment through standardization pressures in all walks of life, was considered inevitable by many forces of modernization in the process of development . . . Plural societies were stigmatized as 'primitive' and 'chaotic', unfit to look after themselves in the 'modern' world (Khubchandani 1990).

The abstract conceptual models, pronounced by the affluent society, and their distortions and delusions become the **official versions** of the happenings around the globe (as experienced from the CNN coverage of the Gulf War). The utilization of space communication for international contact (through the simultaneous beaming of programmes to cross-cultural audiences) is likely to add whole new dimension to the life and experience of the masses and radically affect their communication faculties. Worldwide dissemination of communication networks pose the risks of cultural alienation, and of growing 'drab' uniformity in human relations, erosion of cultural vitality through 'hypnotic' stereotyping. The overbearing levelling effect of mass media can threaten the quality of **variation** and pluralism in human communication. How to assert the authority of 'personal' as opposed to 'public' or general experience?

One of the dominant issues of conflict between tradition and modernity is that in most of our planning efforts we have, by and large, construed change as the **replacement** of values, instead of as an **increment** in the existing order. The programmes of language development in the Indian context will illuminate this point. Language planning theory at this stage seems to be largely concerned with language **problems**, paying little regard to the language **assets** in traditional speech communities. Many studies seem to assume the **handicap** model to achieve the determined targets of development. One general concern of language planners seems to be to adjust the speech behaviour of a community to the demands of modernization. Language studies, being heavily biased in favour of elitist written cultures, put a high premium on **highbrow** values of speech, and assume without question that characteristics like uniformity, precision, elegance, purity of form, allegiance to literary tradition, elaboration of language through coining terms from the *tatsama* stock (mainly loan translations based on Sanskrit or Perso-Arabic vocabularies), and other such standardization devices of 'sophisticated' communication are essential paths for development. No serious attempt is made to justify these elitist values in the realm of human communication.

Developments in exact sciences during the past two centuries, because of their overestimation of precision and confidence in a too rigid and narrow scientific method, have led to scepticism with regard to the concepts defined in a rather fuzzy manner in the natural language. But the reality appears to be otherwise, as is lately being realized among natural sciences as well:

> The concepts of natural language, vaguely defined as they are, seem to be more stable in the expansion of knowledge than the precise terms of scientific language, derived as an idealization from only limited groups of phenomena . . . hence we must be sceptical about any scepticism with regard to this natural language and its essential concepts (Heisenberg 1959).

Modern knowledge is uncritically equated with development and progress. Traditional knowledge, on the other hand, is associated with primitiveness and backwardness. With the result, there has been vast devastation of traditional knowledge in all parts of the world, including the Western hemisphere. The great enormity of the consequences of annihilating traditional knowledge are yet to be assessed. In our own midst the shastri tradition of Sanskrit pandits is rapidly declining. Recent controversy over the intellectual copyright is also confined to modern knowledge; the heritage of cultural wisdom is not counted as 'authentic' knowledge. Restoring traditional knowledge does not rule out the adaptation of new ideas to fit intellectual and cultural needs of contemporary societies.

Defining the Reality

Lately the champions of indigenous development, in their quest for Indianness, have been contesting this mad chase after secondary modernization. It is being advocated that the **adaptation** model which takes into account the given assets as well as handicaps in meeting the new challenges. Barring some half-hearted attempts in this regard, the nation is still guided by the Western models which do not provide meaningful answers in tackling the South Asian reality.

In re-examining the priorities of human resource development, it is necessary to focus attention on **autonomy** in defining the reality by which the so-called 'universal' concepts and categories (that are virtually drawn from Western experiences) could be made relevant to the Indian socio-political reality, such as the role of highbrow standard languages, emphasis on coining technical terminologies at the cost of communicability, imposing coersive homogeneity of communications through dominant languages, dichotomy of majority/minority languages, developed/developing languages, and so on.

Gandhiji realized the vitality of culture-bound concepts when communicating with the Indian masses and brought into currency terms from the Indian reality, such as *swadesi, satyagrah, ahimsa, Harijan, Ramrajya*. In a scientific discourse such cross-cultural distortions become more transparent: e.g. *dharma* is narrowly interpreted as 'religion', *jati, varna, gotra* as 'caste'. Similarly the notion of 'secularism' is beyond the reach of an average Indian mind, and its translations in Indian languages are not very satisfactory. The Sanskrit coinage *dharma nirpeksata* 'religious neutrality' appears to be a hollow term; a metaphor like *vasudhaiva kutumbakam* 'all universe is a family' will be better understood in the context of Indian reality. To some extent, the variation in Nehru's understanding of secularism from Gandhiji's *Ramrajya* can be accounted for in terms of the dilemma of terminology.

Due to the overwhelming political and economic pressures in the pursuits of development and the elitist orientation of Indian academia, limitations of this kind at the cognitive level have not yet been fully realized by the society at large. "A conceptual system is a coherent system of metaphorical concepts" (Lakoff and Johnson 1980). One understands or experiences reality through metaphors, by drawing upon associations and imageries in a coherent manner from one's cultural, intellectual and rhetorical traditions. It is, in a way, a metaphorical device of "relating one kind of things in terms of another". "There is a more subtle form of reality involving both time and eternity" (Prigogine and Stengers 1984). Language user internalizes these abstract concepts unique to his/her tradition. To understand a conceptual scheme through its metaphorical links is an empirical science, an anthropological exercise, **not necessarily** bound by any rational paradigm.

As an illustration, let us reflect on values associated with English terms such as **work, action, activity**. In everyday discourse, the term **work** implies an 'apparent' activity; it is related to an observable product with apparent benefits (mostly socio-economic). Whereas, the Sanskrit term *karman* (Hindi *kam*), based on Sanskrit root *kr* 'to do, to make' and its extensions *karta* 'doer, maker', *krta* 'deed, completed (task)', *kriya* 'making, doing', carries with it quite a different series of expectations.

The term *karman* can be referred as 'a thing made/done' in English; it incorporates all acts, including many sorts of thinking (i.e., mental activities). According to the Sanskrit conceptual system, every activity, apparent and not so apparent, is considered as *kriya* 'making' (Vatsyayana 1939). In English, thinking compassionate thoughts, or faithfully thinking of God are not regarded as spontaneous 'doings'. Notions such as 'seeing' and 'hearing' are regularly counted as mental acts in Sanskrit, whereas in English **I do not need to act to hear the noise** (Potter 1988).

In the metaphysical context, the Theory of *Karma* has emerged from the domain of mental acts'. *Karman* is extended to *samskara* 'traces' where something is made, someone is benefited and some purpose leads the activity to a series of constructs to satisfy expectations; the body is retained beyond one's birth for the *bhoga* 'experience' of *sukha/duhkha* 'satisfying/frustrating experience' (Potter 1988). In the light of this, the term *niskama karma*, outside the paradigm of *dharma, varna* and *punarjanma* (rebirth), can be distorted in literal translations as 'selfless act' or 'an act without expecting any fruit'.

There are problems of **indeterminacy** in translation from one culture to another which can lead to ethnocentric parochial interpretations. It will, therefore, be more rewarding that in a scientific discourse, when debating conceptual systems across cultures, the total connotation of a term is explicated by retaining it in original along with its metaphors that are shared by the society.

Self-image and Identity

Culture locates man in time; it links man with his lineage and heritage from which he picks up various primordial traits such as mother tongue, faith, customs and rituals, characteristics of social ethos. In societal terms, man shows special attachment to his 'tradition'; in mental terms, it is identified as the 'psyche' of a person or a group.

According to Toffler (1984), "Part of today's vast revolution in both science and culture is a reconsideration of time." He points out to Braudel's division of time into three scales —'geographical time', in which events occur over the course of aeons; the much shorter 'social time' scale by which economies, states, and civilizations are measured by the even shorter scale of 'individual time' — the history of human events:

> . . . cultures differ sharply in the way they conceive of time. For some, time is cyclical — history endlessly recurrent. For other cultures, our

> own included, time is a highway stretched between past and future, and people or whole societies march along it. In still other cultures, human lives are seen as stationary in time; the future advances toward us, instead of us toward it (Toffler 1984).

Each culture and each person tends to think in terms of 'time horizons'; some think only of the immediate — the now (e.g., politicians are often criticized for seeking only immediate, short-term results). Each society betrays its own characteristic 'time bias' — the degree to which it places emphasis on past, present, or future. But as today the social sciences have developed little in the way of a coherent theory of time (Toffler, *ibid*).

One notices many contradictions among different groups in projecting self-image, identity, and relationship with organized polities (such as, state *vis-à-vis* centre and the nation as a whole). These projections are realized in everyday life at different levels. Self-image originates from the concerns of an individual's perception — the self and others; it is primarily guided by the 'perceived' reality, whereas, identity belongs to the societal domains; and it is shaped on mutual consensus, a 'collective' reality. State or national is conceptualized in terms of a specific space — a 'normative' reality.

Self-image can be regarded as mostly intuitive, found through the total impression of the reality, as the illusion of bending pencil in water. It is very much like stereotypes available to individuals; it can be highly tentative. Identity acquires some permanence through cultural and communication ethos; it provided guidelines for selection, creativity, and propreity in one's behaviour in specific contexts.

Self-image can be highly individualistic and private, in a way, it comes close to being 'spiritual', finding within oneself. "When we look within ourselves, we find that the other or others are directly experienced within ourselves. I am continuously aware that others are looking at me, just as I am looking at them. My consciousness of my self, my self-image and my self-respect are inextricably bound up with the respect in which I am held by others, of which I too am conscious" (Chatterji 1989). Cultural identity is charged with primordial loyalty; it helps organizing the 'ingroup/ outgroup' notions in relating oneself to different sections of the heterogeneous society.[1]

Any definition of one's self implies, necessarily, a definition, explicit or implicit, of the other, and in a reciprocal manner. Issues concerning the 'distortions' of the image one has of the other (at home/in one's own societies) are **relative** in the geopolitical sense.[2] This phenomenon is most evident in contact zones between groups, communities, societies, cultures and civilizations.

A Mexican intellectual has aptly described culture as "man's capacity for reflection on himself. It is what makes us specifically human, rational and critically and ethically committed. Thanks to culture, we discern values and make choices. Because of it, man becomes aware of his incompleteness, he questions his own achievements, constantly seeks new meanings and creates works that are greater than himself" (Solana 1982).

Universal and Unique

The interplay between man and environment produces distinct, very often unique, imprints in different areas. Variation is intrinsic in nature, including human nature. Variation is a significant contributing factor to the richness in verbal and non-verbal skills. Speech variation in everyday settings is explicated as an instrument of an ongoing redefinition of relationships.

In the verbal repertoire of an individual or a group (namely, speech community, first language/second language speakers), there are many speech varieties identified as native speech, mother tongue, dialect, register, standard language, inter-group language for wider communication, pidgin, patois, and so on. Diverse profiles of speech communication in different countries and at different times makes us realize the futility of pursuing goals of universal order in the name of 'efficient' communication.

A pluralistic world-view and the relativist approach in interpreting heritage and culture have been characterized as the essence of oriental life. Often different roles in a setting or different identities or cultural legacies from one generation to another transmit some prominent values of interaction — ways of interpreting and sharing experiences. That common way, that sort of general framework is called 'communication ethos' (Khubchandani 1986, 1992). In a plural society, although on surface these identities may show differences, the Indian masscs through sustained interactions and common legacies have, by and large, developed a common way to interpret, to share experiences, to think. Sharing the same ethos does not mean that the existing differences are to be eliminated. Kroeber (1948) describes ethos as "the direction in which a culture is oriented, the things it aims at, prizes and endorses, and more or less achieves." Different socio-cultural traits get integrated through super-consensus in the process which contributes in the enrichment of the Indian society.

Modern languages of India belonging to four different language families (Indo-European, Dravidian, Austro-Asiatic, and Tibeto-Burman) represent a striking example of the processes of diffusion, grammatical as well as phonetic, over many contiguous areas.[3] Many speech groups in the region associate diversity of speech (styles, dialects, languages, etc.) around it with differential values in social interaction. In the context of culture, the traditional concept of region, that is *ksetra*, covers a wide spectrum of linguistic and cultural variation in everyday life performance. It helps fostering the feeling of oneness among diverse people in the region, creating in them 'a sense of collective reality'.[4]

In the context of the internal world of man, several *Upanisads*, the *Gita*, the Epics and the *Puranas* refer to such a synthesis of diverse manifestations as the 'Advaitic' visions, i.e., the non-dualistic understanding. It is like "a thread that runs through all the flowers in a garland. The flowers are all different in colour or shape, but the thread unites all of them" (Ranganathananda 1987). The socio-cultural ethos of ancient and medieval India, characterized by non-exclusive fuzziness in day-to-day milieu at the grass roots level, fluidity in verbal repertoire across languages, discontinuities in its beliefs and religious practices — a mark of syncretism (cf. Chandra 1990), and diverse world-views depict the intrinsic respect for variation and integral relation of its components in an organic whole.

Indian plural ethos is an apt illustration of **organic** pluralism by which different groups attempt to retain and preserve their unique cultural attributes while developing common institutional participation at the national level (cf. 'Plurality Square' Khubchandani 1983, 1991). Organic pluralism in the Indian subcontinent is, by and large, supported by **differentiating** characteristics of heterogeneity, federality, and so on. Some of the salient characteristics namely, relativity, hierarchy, instrumentality, out of which the edifice of linguistic plurality is built over the ages in the Indian subcontinent, are discussed in socio-linguistic accounts (see Khubchandani 1983, 1989, 1991).

Different identity groups signifying lineage, language, occupation and religion criss-cross in more than one respect. These groups are involved in a complex web of relationships with one another, presenting a kind of mosaic, and are averse to their being rigidly identified with a particular insulated group. Diverse groups, thus related to as an integral part of the whole under the label 'we' can be characterized as

(1 × 1 × 1 = 1): multiplication (×) signifying an **integral** relation.

Indian heterogeneity in speech, marked by implicit 'etiquette' and flexibility, can best be viewed within an overall organic unity of communication (Chatterji 1943). Multiple identities are strengthened by a measure of fluidity in their manifestation. These identities are simply two sides of the same coin.

In this framework India, as a socio-linguistic area, is not a collection of fragments which the State holds together, but it presents a series of mosaics — religious, linguistic, regional and covering other socio-cultural dimensions — which fit together in a whole as in a jigsaw puzzle, and no single constituent, however small numerically, is viewed as marginal (Khubchandani 1992).

Such a situation can be regarded quite distinct from the **structural** pluralism as found in some European countries, notably Switzerland, Belgium and erstwhile Soviet Union, where different linguistic groups are proportionately balanced in a structural whole sharing the same space and/or some interests, and are delimited in separate regions with marked boundaries within a political unit. Such identity groups, when combined under the umbrella of a common structure, characterize the label 'we' as

(1 + 1 + 1 = 3): addition (+) signifying a **combined** relation

In such societies, harmony among diverse groups is sought by containing their rival aspirations through safeguards provided within the parameters of equality and social justice (Gordon 1981). Pluralism in many contemporary societies is largely based upon the co-existence of different primary groups structurally separated by ethnic/ nationality boundaries insulated through traits such as colour, religion, and language territory (in the case of migrants, their ancestral languages).

In a plural society such as India, one need not share everything; you feel you are a member of a plural group if only you share a **core** of universe. Different partial 'universes' of the groups within co-exist in the region in a state of mutual accommodation. Individual identity groups in such milieu do not necessarily co-terminate within the bounds of the same religious or linguistic 'order/institution'. Often such groups operate across religion or language boundaries as delineated by the dictates of the clergy or grammarian and other custodians of these traditions. The cases of Mazhabi Sikhs (in West Punjab), Labana Sikhs (in Sindh), Sindhi-Amils and Sufis claiming Sikh, Hindu and Muslim identities as per the **relevance** of the context, brings home the point of discrete cultural groups marked by their **fuzzy** traits — a significant characteristic of plural society. Such discrete groups are conceptually different from the insular nationality groups in Europe, marked by **congruent** identities amenable to a clear-cut categorization by their convergence in the same territory. **Non-congruent** characteristics of plural society in the Indian context are elucidated elsewhere (Khubchandani 1983):

> . . .individuals joined by a single trait (say religion, speech) are generally marked by their variety, their lack of unity, and their tendency to act as fairly discrete groups relative to the pulls and pressures of time and space.

The constituents of this mosaic fit together to form an integral whole (accounts of Hindi-Urdu-Hindustani amalgam, and of Punjabi and Sindhi diasporas illustrate this point, see Khubchandani 1991). One finds inherent contradictions on the Indian language scene concerning different aspects of speech behaviour in meeting the demands of contemporary institutions: namely, patterns of language use, levels of competence, unconscious attitudes/images (that is, what people **think** they do with speech), language assertions/postures (that is, what people **claim** they do with speech).

The intricacies of language behaviour in the Indian context reveal apparent ambiguities in defining the concept of **mother tongue** itself (Khubchandani 1972). The posture toward, and the image of, a mother tongue do not necessarily claim congruity with actual usage, and these again are not rigidly identified with specific language territories, as is the case of many European nation-states.

In everyday reality one locates oneself in the midst of different socio-cultural, religious, civic, political and professional identities, making varying demands on the individual: (i) the Indian cultural ethos membership of a particular primordial identity is ascribed (i.e., given by tradition); (ii) observance of specific traits associated with the identity is generally left **fluid** (subject to the sensitivity to the group or to individual goals), such as the observance of five *kakkas* among Sikhs — *kesa, kada, kaccha, kangi,* and *kirpan*; and (iii) commitment or loyalty to a particular identity is **relative** to the context (and not **absolute**); at times, it could even be voluntary. The non-exclusive nature of primordial identities allows one simultaneously to belong to multiple identities.

When examining civic identities (such as, citizenship) on the same scale, one finds that (i) its membership is regulated by one's origin, birth or domicile and it can be renounced or newly acquired; (ii) the duties and privileges accompanying the membership are conditioned by the laws of the land, and their adherence is usually mandatory; and (iii) the demands of loyalty are **obligatory** and **exclusive**. One cannot simultaneously claim multiple national identities against the interests of a particular territory. Primordial identities, in contrast, generally transcend the bounds of political and administrative institutions, and are usually fostered through the strengths of 'diasporic' solidarity, *biradari*, such as the spread of the Jewish diaspora throughout the world.

In a plural nation primordial identities with diverse ethnic attributes are essentially cultural; these remain amorphous, illusionary, and irrational by definition. Such identities can enrich nation's creative faculties in the cultural realm, but it will be hazardous to explicit them as a legitimate political force, such as making a particular identity as a **defining** characteristic of a specific territory.

A Participation Paradigm

It is essential to work out a new paradigm to development by recognizing the principle of **diversity** within an interconnected world. A more humane and people-oriented approach to development promotes the dictum "People cannot be developed, they develop themselves." Peoples' participation is not something which can be mobilized or created from outside. "Human actions are seen as the process by which persons collectively maintain and create social reality". (Narula and Pearce 1986) It is a way of humanizing development as a total social process.

The model of redevelopment, presented by the Dag Hammarskjold Foundation, pays more attention to cultural preferences. The new approach recognizes human dignity and relates to the satisfaction of 'basic needs' of the human being who is to be properly considered as the subject, object, centre and primary beneficiary of development activities. The new concept of social development is defined as: "Change towards patterns of society that allow greater realization of human values, that allow a society greater control over its individuals to gain increased control over themselves" (Inayatullah 1982).

Such a democratic process leads to the participating people searching for solutions to their problems of development as **perceived** by them. In this context 1990 African Charter for Popular Participation in Development and Transformation (passed at Arusha, Tanzania) very eloquently proclaims: "As an instrument of development, popular participation provides the driving force for collective commitment for the determination of people-centred development processes, and willingness by the people to undertake sacrifices and expend their social energies for its execution."

Profiles of tribal cultures provide us many insights into probing questions such as, how to channelize the concerns of ethnic identity of small groups in a positive and sublime manner to enrich the nation's heritage, instead of treating them as underprivileged 'powerless' minorities and allowing 'small' cultures to submit to the pressures of assimilation within the dominant culture under the compulsions of joining the mainstream. (cf. a recent study on tribal identity, Khubchandani 1992)

Most of the developmental programmes for tribals are influenced by the perspective we inherited from the 'colonial' anthropology. With such a world-view the tribals are often looked upon as 'museum specimens' to be cherished for the exoticness and to be clinically observed and analyzed before their extinction — a sort of **pre**-mortem (instead of the **post**-mortem). Under such compulsions we ignore the sociological fact that all human conglomerations, so-called 'primitive' as well as 'contemporary', acquire a unique, space-and-time bound ethos. It is the synthesis emerging from the interaction of people that can bring the fruits of development to tribal society without causing physical, social or psychological damage.

In the context of resolving the socio-political aspirations of the tribal people, we need to consider the questions: How to gear the political system to promote the prevailing patterns of cross-cutting dynamism and fluidity in intra-group and inter-group relation and to check the growth of **insular** tendencies through which the centres of power monopolise controls over natural resources, trade and industry, mobility and domicile, communication and educational needs, and even on the socio-cultural identities of the population within the insulated bounds symbolizing the maximum distinction from the next door.

In this regard, Gandhiji rightly explains the interdependence of individual units in a society through an analogy of 'concentric circles in an ocean'; these circles keep on widening to the outer periphery but never ascending like 'a pyramid with the apex sustained by the bottom'. In such a pluralistic pattern, the 'inner circle' forms an integral unit of the 'outer oceanic circle', and will not be crushed by the overwhelming power of the outer periphery. On the other hand, each should give strength to the other (Kripalani 1958).

Traditionally science has dealt with universals (atemporal view of classical sciences) and humanities with particulars (based on time-oriented world-view). The holistic approach to science can bring a slow merger of physical sciences with social sciences and humanities (Khubchandani 1993). "The convergence of science and humanities gives us a glimpse of the road that leads from being to becoming" (Prigogine and Stengers 1984).

A convergence of perspectives that other groups of people may have a different basis from our own allows the 'openness' for all kinds of concepts (as implied by the term **glasnost** in Russian). This plurality consciousness, in the words of Heisenberg (1959), raises the hope that in the final state of unification many different cultural traditions may live together and may combine different human endeavours into a kind of balance between thought and deed, between activity and meditation. Scientific pursuits, instead of being used as tools for competition and dominance, can be utilized as devices for complementarity and cooperation.

In recent years Prigogine's work at the Brussels School has presented a comprehensive theory of change. It suggests that most of reality, instead of being orderly, stable and equilibral, is seething and bubbling with change, disorder and process. While a small part of the physical universe forms **closed** systems (which may operate like machines), most phenomena of nature are, in fact, **open** systems, exchanging energy or matter (and information) with their environment (Toffler 1984). Development, like biological and social systems, is open. Till recently most of the development experts have been evaluating in **mechanistic** terms which is doomed to a failure.

In classical sciences, basic processes of nature were considered to be deterministic and reversible; processes involving randomness or irreversibility were considered only exceptions. Today we see everywhere the role of irreversible processes, of fluctuations. In Prigoginian terms, all systems, close or open, contain subsystems that are continually 'fluctuating'. In the context of debates surrounding chance and determinism, Toffler (1984), commenting on the range of options available to the human decision-maker, remarks: "Free will downstairs operated only within the limits of a menu determined upstairs."

These debates are crucially linked with the issues of the **reconstruction** of reality and the issues concerning the **quality** of life in the rapidly changing environment. In the scientific endeavour there is an objective goal to aspire for the ideal of 'getting out of one's own skin'. In the light of this, one can hope that the transcending interest of mankind will not allow to lose sight of our cherished goals of bringing harmony through bio-diversity and cultural plurality on the regional, national, and global scene when framing development and communication policies for the future.

Notes

1. In contrast, allegiance to the State is characterized by contractual obligations and civic ethos; it is based on 'institutional' networks (constitutional, administrative rights versus duties) in a society.
2. For a detailed discussion on the changing perceptions of ethnic and socio-linguistic identities of the Punjab region divided between India and Pakistan, see Khubchandani 1989, 1991.
3. Emeneau (1956), highlighting the discussiuon over certain common linguistic traits across genetic boundaries in the South Asian sub-continent, points out: "The end result of the borrowings is that the languages of the two families, Indo-Aryan and Dravidian, seem in many respects more akin to one another than Indo-Aryan does to the other Indo-European languages."
4. The concept of *ksetra* is markedly different from the modern Western model of **region** defined as "a cohesive and homogeneous area", created by arbitrary selection of transit features such as religion, language, history. (Saraswati 1988) For a detailed discussion on Punjabi and Konkani *ksetras*, see Khubchandani 1989, 1991.

References

Chandra, Pratap, 1990. "Traditional Indian thinking and the Scientific Temper: The Factual Position", In *New Technological Civilization and Indian Society*, ed. by B.D. Nagchaudhuri. Shimla: Indian Institute of Advanced Study.

Chatterji, P C., 1989. "Identity: Personal and Group", In *Self-Images, Identity and Nationality*, ed. by P. C. Chatterji. Shimla: IIAS.

Chatterji, Suniti Kumar, 1943. *Languages and the Linguistic Problem*. London: Oxford University Press.

Constantino, Renato, 1992. "Development as Colonialism", In *Maharashtra Herald*, Pune; 17 September issue.

Daya Krishna, 1988. "Comparative Philosophy: What it is and what it ought to be", In *Interpreting Across Boundaries: New Essays in Comparative Philosophy*, ed. by G. J. Larson and E. Deutsch. Princeton: Princeton University Press.

Dutta, Amlan and M. M. Agrawal, eds. 1992. *The Quality of Life*. Shimla: IIAS.

Emeneau, Murray B., 1956. "India as a linguistic area", In *Language* 32, 3-16.

Fishman, Joshua A., 1974. "Language Modernization and Planning in Comparison with other types of National Modernization and Planning", In *Advances in Language Planning*, ed. by J. A. Fishman. Hague: Mouton.

Gordon, Milton M., 1981. "Models of Pluralism", In *The Annals of the American Academy of Political and Social Science*, 454 (March issue).

Heisenberg, Werner. 1959. *Physics and Philosophy: The Revolution in Modern Science.* London: Allen & Unwin.

Inayatullah, 1982 cf. In *Development Communication: A Resource Manual for Teaching*, ed. by C. Vollen and J. Simmons. AMIC 4. Singapore.

Khubchandani, Lachman M., 1972. "Mother tongue in multi-lingual societies", In *Economic and Socio-Cultural Dimensions of Regionalization*, ed. by A. Chandra Sekhar, Census Centenary Monograph 7. New Delhi: Registrar General of India.

———, 1974. "Fluidity in Mother-Tongue Identity", In *Applied Socio-Linguistics II*. ed. by A Verdoodt. Heidelberg: J. Gross; also in *Studies in Linguistics* by Khubchandani and others. Shimla: IIAS.

———, 1981. *Language, Education, Social Justice.* Pune: Centre for Communication Studies.

———, 1983. *Plural Languages, Plural Cultures: Communication, Identity, and Socio-Political Change in Contemporary India.* East-West Center Book, Honolulu: University of Hawaii Press.

———, 1985. "Language Modernization in the Developing World", In *Interaction Through Language: Socio-Linguistic Research, Cases and Application*, Vol. 99, *International Social Science Journal*, 36:1. UNESCO, Paris. 169-88.

———, 1986a. "Identity and Communication in Pluri-Lingual Societies: A South Asian Experience", In *Pluri-Lingualism et Communication*, ed. by F. Lo Jacomo. Seminar of UNESCO and Assoc. de Universelle d'Esperanto: Societe d'Etudes Linguistique et Anthropolog. de France.

———, 1986b. "Communication Ethos in Pluri-Lingual Societies", In Post-Congress Session of International Sociological Association, Central Institute of Indian Languages, Mysore.

———, 1989. "Self-Images, Identities of the Punjabi People: Ethnic and Linguistic Realities", In *Self-Images, Identity and Nationality*, ed. by P. C. Chatterji. Shimla: IIAS; revised version "Punjabi Diaspora", In Khubchandani, 1991.

———, 1990. "Plural Cultures and the Communication Technology: Priorities and the Framing of Policies", In *New Technological Civilization and Indian Society*, ed. by B. D. Nagchaudhuri. Shimla: IIAS.

———, 1991. *Language, Culture and Nation-Building: Challenges of Modernization.* Shimla: IIAS.

———, 1992a. *Tribal Identity: A Language and Communication Perspective.* Shimla: IIAS.

———, 1992b. "India as a Socio-Linguistic Area", In *Language Sciences*, 13: 2, Pergamon.

———, 1993a. "Reality and Scientific Construct from a Linguistic Perspective", In *Philosophy of Science*, ed. by J. V. Narlikar *et al.* Shimla: IIAS.

———, 1993b. "Reality and Scientific Construct: Methodological Pluralism in a Socio-Linguistic Perspective", In *International Journal of the Sociology of Language*, 100/101, 55-71..

Kripalani, Acharya J. B., 1958. *Collected Works of Mahatma Gandhi: All Men Are Brothers*. Ahmedabad: Navajivan.

Kroeber, Alfred, 1948. *Anthropology*. New York: Harcourt Brace.

Lakoff, George and M. Johnson, 1980. *Metaphors We Live By*. Chicago: Chicago University Press.

Narula, Uma and W. B. Pearce, 1986. *Development as Communication: A Perspective on India.* Carbondale: Southern Illinois University.

Potter, Karl H., 1988. "Metaphor as Key to Understanding the Thought of Other Speech Communities", In *Interpreting Across Boundaries: New Essays in Comparative Philosophy*, ed. by G. J. Larson and E. Deutsh. Princeton: Princeton University Press.

Prigogine, Ilya and I. Stengers, 1984. *Order Out of Chaos: Man's New Dialogue with Nature*. London: Flamingo.

Ranganathananda, Swami, 1987. *Our Cultural Heritage: Modern Orientation.* Sardar Patel Memorial Lectures. New Delhi: Publication Division, Government of India.

Sachs, Wolfgang, (ed.) 1991. *The Development Dictionary: A Guide to Knowledge as Power*. Zed Books.

Saraswati, Baidyanath, 1988. "Thinking About 'Region'", In *Social Science and Social Concern*, ed. by S.B. Chakrabarti. Felicitation Volume in Honour of Prof. B.K. Roy Burman, Delhi: Mittal Publications.

Solane, Fernando. 1982. "Closing Address", In *World Congress on Cultural Policies*, Mexico, Paris: UNESCO.

Somavia, Juan, 1983. "Information", In Latin American Institute for Trans-National Studies, Mexico.

Toffler, Alvin, 1984. "Science and Change", In Prigogine and Stengers.

UNESCO, 1983. *Regional Seminar on Cultural Implications of Communication Technology*. Centre for Communication Studies, Pune mimeo "A Report", *Socio-Linguistics*, Rotterdam (1985).

Vatsyayana, 1939. *Nyayabhasya*, tr. by Ganganath Jha, Poona Oriental Series 59. Pune: Deccan College Postgraduate Research Institute.

4

Universality, Uniformity and Specificity

A View from a Developing Country

Anisuzzaman

In the aftermath of the Second World War, most of the colonies of Western powers in Asia and Africa, and later in Latin America, gained independence and the primary goal of all these newly emerging states was taken to be 'development'. The model of development was already there, arrived at by the wisdom and experience of centuries, which the former colonizers were now offering us on a silver platter. There was hardly any doubt that they knew better than all of us. Since the days of the European renaissance they had developed a view of life, a code of values which they claimed, and we all agreed, were universal. This was also true of their development strategies. After all, they were at the centre of earth while we were at the periphery. And since they had formulated so many universal laws — from the law of gravitation to the law of the seas — they were bound to be correct.

Unfortunately, these development efforts did not take us from the world of want to the realm of freedom. We have gradually realized over a period of time that the development strategies in most Third World countries have made us a little more dependent on the West, while at home the masses of the people have not been able either to improve their quality of life or to develop their own potentials. Within our national formations, some gains were, perhaps, made somewhere which only made the plight of the common people, the bulk of whom live in the rural areas, stand out more sharply than ever.

One wonders now, what did we aim at? We wanted to follow the very same path that the West had taken, without taking into consideration their peculiarities and experience, and expected to reach the same goal. We thought that economic growth was the same as improvement in the overall quality of human life and we did not take into consideration the question of the distribution of wealth at home. Now that it has dawned on us that such assumptions were unfounded, we are trying to re-examine the conventional wisdom.

One thing that suggests itself is that the solution of the developmental problems in the Third World does not depend on technical skill alone. We have got to understand clearly the causal relationship among the social, cultural, economic and political factors that determine the very nature of the problems. We have got to understand ourselves and we have to have a closer look at our own experience, evaluate the successes and failures of the past and comprehend not only the structure of each of our given national formations but also the characteristics of their superstructure. This is where one could recognize the interface of development and culture.

Does it mean that we should be thinking in terms of development in isolation in a world which is increasingly getting interdependent? Does it mean that we must separate ourselves from the achievements of human endeavours of thousands of years? Do we have to remake the wheel? Does being conscious of the indigenous creativity necessarily leads to the rejection of all things exogenous? Does it mean that we will take retrograde steps and return to where our forefathers started from? Does it mean that while the world marches forward we close our eyes and cling to obsolete ideas, technologies or ideologies?

Certainly not. This sort of apprehension, however, springs out from our own experiences. In the 1960s, when Pakistan was reeling under military dictatorship, her rulers used to tell very often that the democracy of the Westminster type did not suit the genius of our people. They came out with the perfect solution to suit the genius of our people — an elixir called the Basic Democracy. Such endogenous products as Basic Democracy, Guided Democracy and Controlled Democracy, which did not have any quantum of democracy at all, succeeded only in shaking our belief in innovating any system of government for ourselves and finally led to the school or thought that we are not suited for democracy.

In Bangladesh we had lost all faith in the general elections in the 1980s because of malpractice and massive rigging, but this faith was restored by the administration of the interim government in 1990-91 which conducted a fair and free general election which could have been a model anywhere anytime.

But I have digressed, I was trying to say that when we talk of taking into consideration our historical development, cultural distinctiveness and traditional values, we are aware that such assertions may be misconstrued as an attempt to take us backward while, in fact, we are trying to post these questions so that we do not blindly replicate. We do not say this from any spirit of chauvinism but it has now become apparent that uncritical invitation, devoid of indigenous creativity, cannot deliver the goods.

Whatever the West had produced in the last five hundred years has been seen as universal, and later as modern, as the thing to emulate. When the West succeeded in colonizing to the extent of boasting that the sun does not set in the British empire, it also succeeded in convincing all and sundry that their world-view was not only the dominant one but also the only universal one. Other world-views were seen through the Western eyes as traditional as opposed to the modern and thus obsolete. This dichotomy between the modern and the traditional had a direct impact on considerations of development strategies. We could not see through that the West used to divide the world into 'I' and 'you' and this was reflected in their formulation of the typified West-East, oriental-occidental, modern-traditional dichotomy, where the West always emerges as the superior, as the holder of all knowledge. Now, in the last three decades, this aggreeable division has been challenged. We can see, for instance, that what is termed as modern is an ethnocentric view developed in the West at a given period of time. If we try to find out what modern is, we will first be told that it is a matter of, or it pertains to, the present and recent time — in particular the historical period following the Middle Ages. Not only is this explanation dependent on the precise definition of the Middle Ages and determination of the time of their close, but also it tends to put all tendencies — often contradictory ones — appearing in the last five years in the same basket. One of the characteristics of modernity has been identified as the development of a secular and rational outlook, but such outlook is known to have existed before the advent of the 'modern' period. Symptoms of modernity have been seen in the emergence of certain political systems, whereas it has been generally acknowledged that many historically 'traditional' political systems, in fact, had typologically modern structure, attributes and orientations. Modernity has been equated with economic growth without any reference to the question of distribution of wealth, and with the application of scientific and technological knowledge without any consideration for the utility of the products of such knowledge for the collective good.

Modernization, again, has been defined as 'the current term for an old process — the process of social change whereby less developed societies acquire characteristics common to more developed societies'. This is a definition heavily loaded in favour of the cultural dimension of the Western world and this is where modernization and development become synonymous with Westernization.

On the other hand one should not only see traditional values in the rejection of things modern or in their divisive forces, but also appreciate that these carry within themselves a spirit of liberal humanism and religious toleration as also a spirit, a revolt against unjust social systems.

Similarly, universalism has mostly been seen as a monopoly of the West. One often ignores the fact that universalism does not have a particular locus and that a number of universal thoughts had developed outside the Western world. To take a comparatively recent example, Rabindranath Tagore, the poet, had time and again in the present century appealed to the Western world and also to Japan to refrain from inculcating nationalism which was causing wars and human misery. His message of universalism fell flat because the powers of the day found it convenient to pursue the course they were following rather than pay heed to a poet's message.

If universalism has a particular locus, it ceases to be universal. If it does not have one, if it be a product of the human mind, then we should look for and find it in all nook and corners. As in the name of development and modernity, what we often do in the name of universality is to see that all cultural or national entities give up their specific characters and become uniform. For instance, we are asked to adopt the Western technocentric path of development. One often forgets that one-third of the countries of the world, having less than a third of world population, possess practically 97 per cent of the world science. The multi-national corporations' monopoly prevents small nations from reaping the benefit of the scientific knowledge which should be considered not only universal but also a common inheritance of man anywhere. On the other hand, the capability of underdeveloped nations of making use of the scientific knowledge is limited, as also seems to be their will to do so. But that is another aspect of the problem.

The fact remains that, in the name of universality, we tend to apply uniform norms, categories, institutions or ideology to the reality of the South, without taking into account its objective conditions and historical specificity. Unless we allow specificity to develop, endogenous creativity to flower, we shall never achieve anything substantial by replication. That will only perpetuate not only our economic dependence, but also our intellectual dependence on our former colonizers.

We do not want to get back into the past nor do we want development in isolation. We fully appreciate the need for cooperation and interdependence; we believe that knowledge should not have any borders or barriers. But, we also want to be ourselves, and not somebody else. Civilization, cultures and nations are like woven circles. We belong to one circle, then a larger circle and then the largest circle of humanity. Ours is not only one identity but many, the foremost being that we are human beings. We must fulfil our destiny as man — drawing from and contributing to the pool of human achievements. But we must do so from our own area. We would like to be universal, but not uniform; we would like to develop our specificity without restricting ourselves to narrow fields or ideas. We believe that our specificity will carry within itself what will be seen as universal. As it takes all sorts of people to make the humankind, the sum total of the specifics will be the results of human achievements. Diversity and specificity will make unity and universality meaningful. Diversity does not mean contradictions but a source for streams to follow from and converge. Many years ago this was expressed simply in three words: unity in diversity.

Note

The paper is based on an earlier publication, Anisuzzaman and Anouar Abdel-Malek (eds.), *Culture and Thought*, Vol. 3 of the United Nations University Series, "The Transformation of the World" (London: Macmillan Press Ltd., 1983).

5

Identity, Tribesman and Development[1]

Mrinal Miri

A. The question, "Who am I?", or "What am I?" has been treated differently in different styles of philosophical thought. It may seem, for instance, to be a question not about the mundane or the earthly, but about the metaphysical or the transcendent. As a question about the mundane, it can — so it has been thought — never have an adequate answer, for every possible answer leaves a crucial residue which is beyond the pale of the answer. Thus, "I am this body", "I am this mind", "I am the same as this set of properties, or memories" cannot — none of them — be an adequate answer, because the 'I', as it were, is detachable always from any particular body, or mind or any set of properties. One might, then, say that the answer to the question is not something that can be articulated in the ordinary way; it is something that is ultimately a matter of mystical realization.

The non-mystical mode, of course, rejects the idea of the detachability or irreducibility of the 'I' as merely apparent and insists that the question in principle, can be answered in a mundanely adequate fashion. There are several such mundane approaches to the question. I shall mention just two: (1) the approach where the autological version of the question is suspended in favour of what is considered its equivalent non-autological — neutral, so to speak — version, viz., "What is a person?" "What constitutes personal identity?" The answer to the question, then, is sought in terms of the correct **analysis** of the concept of a person and of specifying the criteria of personal identity. The debate here proceeds from the initial idea that the concept of a person, of personal identity, may be significantly different from any other concept, and that, therefore, our search for criteria might have to follow a correspondingly different track. However, every such search seems to have got bogged down in logical puzzles of an intractable nature, thus giving rise to the suspicion that perhaps the question ought to have been framed differently, and that the search for an answer ought to have been along a different route, or that mysticism was perhaps unavoidable. (2) The second way is to retain the autological version of the question, and to treat it as demanding an answer, which, while being indeed mundane, will require an ever deeper cognitive-moral luminosity about oneself. It is different from the first way in that it does not regard the problem of identity as an issue about the correct **analysis** of a concept and of specifying the criteria of its application, but as an issue about embarking on a moral intellectual journey into oneself.

In this paper, I shall not be overtly interested in the mystical — not because I think the mystical is erroneous or illusory — but simply because I feel more at home with the non-mystical mode of thinking. However, it should not be surprising if the mystical is found to be lurking behind some of the things that I have to say. Of the two mundane approaches that I have mentioned, I shall ignore the first and partially explore the second. This is both because I find the second more interesting in itself, and because it is more relevant to the theme.

B. Who, then, am I? The question is asked against the background of certain kinds of knowledge about myself that I already possess, e.g., that I am a human being, that I am a self-reflective as well as a self-evaluative creature, that my capacity to wield language is a condition of my being such a creature. Given that I know all this about myself, what further illumination does this questions seek?

A very useful line of thinking in relation to this last question is suggested by a distinction that Charles Taylor makes in a recent paper[2] between two orders of evaluation. He calls them 'weak' (or 'simple') evaluation and 'strong' evaluation. Weak evaluation — to put it rather starkly — does not make any **qualitative** distinction between one desire and another. It is not based on considerations which yield judgements of the kind: desire **x** is intrinsically superior to desire **y**; there is something unworthy, reprehensible about having desires of a certain kind, persons motivated by desires of a certain kind have moral or spiritual depth. A weak evaluator desists from the pursuit of a certain desire not because of the kind of desire it is, but because of considerations of the following sort: its time and place is not quite convenient; the pursuit of another desire will lead to greater overall satisfaction, the object of some other desire is more attractive. To take examples:

should I eat now that I am hungry, or wait for another hour when I know that my favourite dish will be there? Should I do my daily shopping on my way back from work so that I shall not have to come out again, and therefore, shall have time to listen to music and do a bit of gardening, or should I do it later when I know that there will be a greater variety of fresh vegetables and my favourite fish? Should I watch the recording of last year's Wimbledon men's singles final or should I rather watch the recording of the world cup football final, when it is the case that if each were available separately, I wouldn't resist either? In each of these cases my choice is not between desires which are, in any strong sense, qualitatively different from one another. Also when making a choice considerations of convenience, consequences, attractions etc., are exhausted, the weak evaluator has nothing to fall back upon, by way of reflection, but perhaps just a shrug of the shoulders.

By contrast, in making a strong evaluation, the agent is guided primarily by considerations of the **quality** of one desire as opposed to that of another. A desire is considered qualitatively superior to an alternative and this superiority is expressed in the language of "higher and lower, noble and base, courageous and cowardly, integrated and fragmented and so on" (Charles Taylor, p. 23).

But because of this language of qualitative contrast available to the strong evaluator, his evaluation is also 'deeper'. "To characterize one desire or inclination as worthier or nobler or more integrated etc. than others is to speak of it in terms of the kind of quality of life which it expresses and sustains. . . For the strong evaluator reflection examines different possible modes of being of the agent. Motivations and desires do not only count in virtue of the attraction of the consummations, but also in virtue of the kind of life and the kind of subject that these desires properly belong to" (*Ibid.*, p. 25). This additional dimension adds depth, "because now we are reflecting about our desires in terms of the kind of being we are in having them and carrying them out. Whereas a reflection about what we feel like more, which is all a simple weigher can do in assessing motivations, keeps us, as it were at the periphery; a reflection about the kind of being we are takes us into the centre of our existence as agents" (*Ibid.*, p. 26).

"Reflection about the kind of being we are" is precisely also reflection about our identity. Our identity is thus bound up with the strong evaluations we make. The answer to the question "What is my identity?" cannot consist in a simple enumeration of properties that I happen to possess. These may indeed figure in the answer, but they figure only insofar as they are important in my assessment of what I fundamentally am or ought to be. Thus, suppose I answer the question, "Who am I?" with "I am an Indian above all else", this means that my being an Indian defines me in a way which no other description of me can — descriptions such as, "I am a teacher, a tennis player, an occasional writer of philosophical articles, an admirer of Western classical music, a bird-watcher and so on. To be deprived of this identity is for my being — my human being — to be eroded in a way profoundly different from the way in which the non-availability of any of the other descriptions might possibly erode my human identity.

While my identity is thus bound up with my strong evaluations, my self-identifications are frequently clouded with uncertainties, and are, therefore, subject to clearer, finer articulations. They are, for the same reason, also liable to be distorted by self-deceptions, and, therefore, corrections which will have powerful evaluative overtones. Although greater articulacy is a necessary correlate of strong evaluations, it is similarly not necessary that at any particular point of time, I articulate, or even am capable of articulating a strong evaluation of mine or a self-identification with any degree of clarity and assurance. Sometimes there is assurance, but not clarity. In fact my most fundamental evaluations — those that constitute my identity — touch me in the centre of my being — are also evaluations which are the least articulated; I am the least clear about them. "It is these evaluations which are closest to what I am as a subject, in the sense that shorn of them, I would break down as a person, which are the hardest for me to be clear about. Thus the question can always be posed: ought I to re-evaluate my most basic evaluations? Have I really understood what is essential to my identity? Have I truly determined what I sense to be the highest mode of life?" (*Ibid.*, p. 29) Yet, paradoxically perhaps, it is these identity determining evaluations which constitute the framework in terms of which as an agent I generally make my other evaluations.

Before moving on to the question of tribal identity, let me separate out a few points — in relation to the discussion above — which, I think, are important.

First, there are some powerful theories about man, according to which the distinction between strong evaluation and weak evaluation is a spurious one. Such, for example, are some theories of psychoanalysis, e.g., Freudianism and the ethical theory of utilitarianism. For Freudianism strong evaluations are spurious, because they are never genuinely operative; they are devises used by the self to camouflage the workings of desires among which only weak evaluations can be made — and it is such desires and (weak) evaluations among them that are truly operative in human behaviour. Strong evaluations are, therefore, reducible to weak evaluations. As to utilitarianism it is well-known that it does not believe in any distinction of quality between desires: all desires are of one and the same kind, and they differ only in degree. Strong evaluations thus are an impossibility. (Mill's famous statement — it is better to be a Socrates dissatisfied than a pig satisfied — is, therefore, a repudiation of his own utilitarianism. The father of utilitarianism was not himself a utilitarian!) Here, I shall merely dogmatically assert in relation to such theories that while it is certainly possible to imagine a life totally devoid of strong evaluations, any attempt to eliminate the latter is also an attempt to denude human life of its human significance.

Secondly, one's convictions about one's strong evaluations may be mistaken. (Freudianism is correct at least to the extent to which it has shown such mistakes to be a common phenomenon.) Take a philanthropist who, towards the end of his life, is disillusioned by the glamour and power of wealth, and contemplates giving away all his wealth to help feed the hunger of the world. He wishes, from now on, to live simply, to commit himself to an ever deep realization of the mindlessness of a life of ceaseless pursuit of wealth. May be he would return to his village, (which he had abandoned decades ago), in search of the solidity, integrity and wisdom which — as he now realizes — informed the life of many a village elder. But this man also has children all of whom have grown to dislike him intensely which dislike he reciprocates, without ever consciously acknowledging it, with equal intensity; and these children have never outgrown their parasitic dependence on him. Now does he wish to give away his wealth out of a genuine sympathy for the suffering of the poor and the starved, or does he really do so out of a desire cripplingly to hurt his children? It is more than likely that the philanthropist is self-deceived; also his self-deception may be of a deeper order than the above bald narration suggests; it may be the stuff of which tragedy is made.

Thirdly, and relatedly, our most fundamental evaluations — and therefore our identity — are frequently steeped in darkness which is what makes self-deceptions and distortions about identity such common phenomena. To search for one's identity is to attempt to achieve an articulation that is free from self-deception and distortion; and to realize that one may be self-deceived, and yet not able to see one's way through distortions, is to be confronted with a crisis of identity.

C. In the light of the discussion above, what can we say about tribal identity? It is clear that if the discussion is to be any guide, our interest cannot be that of the census official, however scientific his particular enquiry might be. We are interested in tribal identity in the sense of its being determined by strong evaluation — evaluation in terms of a value such as "allegiance to the tribe" — in a way such that this value overrides other values in a fundamental way. That tribal identity, in this sense, can become a powerful reality we all know. It is something for the sake of which one may be prepared to give one's life, and frequently, as we know too well, to take another's life. What greater proof, one might ask, can there be of the reality and power of tribal identity.

The question, rhetorical as it is, must make us pause, because violence, to oneself as well as to another, is the result of darkness and fragmentation rather than motivated by the illumination and integration of successful strong evaluation. Terrorism in the cause of tribal identity may quite likely be an expression of a profound sense of emptiness and impending moral fragmentation — rather than a genuine part of the articulation of tribal identity. Yet the logic of such forms of terrorism is such that this emptiness and fragmentation cannot be allowed to be acknowledged. For, if they are, then violence loses its mask of respectability without which terrorism — in such forms, at any rate — cannot be sustained. But what would it be like for "allegiance to the tribe" to be a genuinely integrating, 'deep' value? A tribe gets its particular specificity from:

- (i) its history;
- (ii) its ecology in which the natural, the cosmic, the moral and the aesthetic and the spiritual are integrally united in a living relationship of meanings;
- (iii) its own peculiar way of dealing with questions about itself. An adequate articulation of my "allegiance to my tribe" would naturally involve my gaining clarity about all these three.

But think of the difficulties for me as a tribesman

- (i) of making clear to myself my relationship to my history;
- (ii) of gaining an authentic insight into the ordered world of meanings and values into which I am born; and
- (iii) of asking questions of my own tradition — questions to which the tradition itself might provide creative answers. (Every living tradition must have room for a *yugadharma* without

which the tradition will stagnate and collapse)

Many of these difficulties are, of course, general in nature, that is, they are involved in any attempt to articulate one's allegiance to a community as such, and not just a **tribal** community. I shall not here talk about these general difficulties. I wish instead to talk briefly about the specific difficulties of clarifying my allegiance to my tribe in the particular historico-civilizational context in which I am willy-nilly situated. This is the context of modernity. The special features of this context that are important for my purpose are: its unitary vision of knowledge; its 'whiggish', linear conception of the progress of knowledge as embodied in the movement of modern science; its moral awareness dominated by the idea of humanism and circumscribed by utilitarianism with its consequent rejection of traditional moral-spiritual visions.

At earlier times my history came down to me orally in a chain of living memories; and it was the history of a community of beings ordered morally and ontologically into a matrix of meaning-laden relationships in which the tree, the animal, the river, the mountain, the human being as well as the sky, the bird, the stars and the sun and the moon were equally significant elements. (see Appendix) The telling of this history had naturally to be in terms of what we call 'myths'; for, otherwise, how would the tree, the animal, the sun and the moon figure in it? But the mythical is not a notion that is part of the tribesman's self-awareness. (This is not to say that the tribesman has no use for the distinction between the true and the false, the real and the illusory and the actual and the imaginary. Without distinctions such as these, no communication and no language would be possible. But for the tribesman the lines are differently drawn and are a function of his **perspective** just as much as the distinctions that the modern man makes are a function of his perspective. This is again not to say that perspectives are necessarily mutually exclusive and cannot meet.) This notion of history has to fight a lost battle with a conception of history which would reduce tribal history into a soulless narration of abstract events: soulless because the narrative must ignore those very elements which constitute the moving force of the **world** of the tribesman, and, therefore of his past; and abstract because the 'truth' here can be achieved only in a general way. For a tribesman to turn to what we might call scientific history such as this in the search for his identity is already for him seriously to doubt the authenticity of this search. It may be said that this kind of history does not necessarily oust the older kind and that the important thing is that the older kind may still be available to the tribesman. But the fact remains that this availability, if it is at all there, is being rapidly eroded.

The unitary vision of knowledge of modern man with its own variety of aggressive cognitivism has pulvarized the traditional epistemic and moral-spiritual space of the tribesman. The main features of the modern vision are: (i) a 'granular',[3] atomistic conception of reality, a reality, therefore, which is devoid of meanings — a reality that is not saturated with concepts; (ii) an insistence on a singular mode of explanation and understanding, and, therefore, on the exclusion of the extraordinary; and (iii) a rejection of the idea of a profound interrelatedness of things (an interrelatedness without which, say, in the tribal vision, there is no world at all; a causal order, understood more or less in the Human way, is the only order that reality allows).

The strident exclusiveness of this vision is strengthened by the extraordinary growth of scientific knowledge in the last three centuries and its even more extraordinary technological spin-off. Within this exclusiveness there also emerged a newer concern for man embodied in the idea of humanism. This is a concern where the central significance of man's life is seen to lie in the fact that man is a consuming, producing, procreating being with an emotional life[4] — a life which is modulated by the fact that man is also a 'free' being — this freedom consisting in his capacity to choose between courses of action. The humanistic concern manifests itself in the pursuit of the ideal of serving life in precisely this sense — in the pursuit of the goal of man's welfare in all these aspects; and the means to such welfare is to be made available by science. The tribal — or indeed the traditional — conception of the good life is centred not around the welfare of man in this sense but around a deeper vision — if you like — of the cosmic order. And in this conception freedom is not seen as man's capacity to choose between different courses of action, but as the natural flowing of action from this vision. But such has been the power of science, technology and the attendant liberal-humanist discourse, that, under its exclusivist domination, the tribal vision has been exiled to a life of continuous, rapid dissipation. And it has become willy-nilly impossible for the tribesman to try and reclaim it in any deep and illuminating way.

Given this state of dissipation, there does not seem to be any possibility for the tribesman to have a genuine creative argument with his tradition — an argument that is also within the tradition. And hence the question of a *yugadharma* within the tribesman's tradition does not seem to arise.

The search for tribal identity seems thus an endeavour that is doomed, and the tribesman's desperation accompanying this realization is immense. While allegiance to the tribe is still a powerfully motivating force (perceived strongly in our sense), instead of the earlier density of material in terms of which this allegiance could be clarified, there seems now to be a void. There are frantic efforts, on the part of the tribesman, to fill this void by borrowing someone else's past (e.g., the Christian past), and by adopting a moral-spiritual stance the connection between which and the old vision is painfully unclear.

Is, then, everything lost for tribal identity? Not quite perhaps. Things that could happen which might create a situation that is better than the one prevailing are: (i) an open-eyed awareness on the part of the tribesman of his real predicament; (ii) a turn in human thought which will, as it were, put the coercive, uniformity imposing regime of modernity in its place. (Signs of this happening are, of course, already there); and (iii) the development of a genuine self-assurance on the part of the tribesman — a self-assurance which will enable him to face the world outside without being completely overwhelmed by it.

D. What, then, about development? It is, of course, widely acknowledged that development in the sense in which the West is developed and much of Asia, Africa and Latin America is underdeveloped or only semi-developed is incompatible with what is called the tribal way of life. The central motivating force of this development is humanism, and its agencies are modern science and technology. It is also not unusual to doubt whether development in this sense constitutes genuine progress at all — progress understood in the minimal sense of greater clarity — clairvoyance — about life and greater freedom that should naturally accompany such clarity of vision. This doubt finds its most acute expression in the belief that different systems of knowledge are but different forms of bondage and that mankind has moved only from one such system of bondage to another in its long history (Foucault). I do not wish here to enter into this debate — a debate in which positions ranging from unfettered celebration of diversity of truth and the good life to extreme pessimism about the very possibility of knowledge and freedom are held with equal passion. I shall content myself with merely pointing out that the 'whiggish' notion of progress as an inevitably linear process is widely acknowledged to be a highly questionable idea. I shall end this essay by saying a word about the notion of appropriate technology.

The important question to ask is: appropriate to what? The short answer to this might seem to be: appropriate to the form of life of the tribesman. But this means that the devising of appropriate technology would depend upon: (i) there being such a form of life as a going concern; and (ii) our having achieved an adequate understanding of such a form of life. But I have already argued that the tribal world is no longer available in its living palpable form to the tribesman himself; it is, therefore, even less available to the would-be technocrat from outside. I have also argued that the material in terms of which this world could present itself to the tribesman with clarity and immediacy seems to have lost its former potency and coherence. There is, therefore, the initial difficulty of defining appropriateness. It may, however, be suggested that this difficulty is only marginal. For in spite of all the obstacles to exploring the moral and spiritual depth of "allegiance to a tribe" that we talked about above, it is certainly possible imaginatively to reconstruct the tribal form of life in an abstract, general, if entirely functional way. Such a reconstruction might represent a tribe as a group of people which is strongly community-oriented: its social structure simple (unlike the highly bureaucratized modern society), its hierarchy broken by naturalness and spontaneity of all interpersonal relationships — a community which believes in an abiding continuity between nature, earth, and what we call the supernatural, instead of in the divisive distinctions between these that modern man makes, a community which is also free from numerous stress and anxiety-producing distortions of natural biological life that modern man is subject to. Given that this is an authentic, if abstract and general, representation of a tribe or *Adivasi* in its originality, then the task of appropriate technology might be thought to be to initiate changes which will be such that they will help, as best as possible, the tribe move from his present state of disintegration and dissipation to something like its original integrity and coherence. Such appropriate technology must, of course, include appropriate political strategy. It is extremely doubtful, however, if people who advocate appropriate technology take the notion of appropriateness in this sense. For appropriateness in this sense does not seem to have much to do with 'humanism'-inspired development and progress, and advocacy of appropriate technology really arises in the context of the discourse of development and progress. One suspects that what is really meant by appropriate technology in this context is the following: a technology which will ensure a slower, less traumatic pace of change towards "development and progress" for the tribe — which is really to say that the tribesman will take a longer time to get there with appropriate technology, but this is the only way to ensure his arrival as modern man in one piece. This may be a noble end, but is modern man in one piece? and, most importantly, the epistemological and moral assumptions implicit in this discourse of appropriate technology is far from being self-luminously valid.

If, on the other hand, we take 'appropriate' in the first sense of being appropriate to the tribal form of life — something that will not only help preserve such a form of life but enhance and enrich it — then we must take content as seriously as form, because it is the content that breathes life into the form. And it is here that the difficulties, I mentioned earlier of articulating tribal identity come to the fore again. Perhaps one thing that could possibly help more than most is to bring tribal self-awareness even in its present fragmented state in living contact with great traditional modes of awareness, of being and acting whose heart is, as it were, in the same place as that of the tribal mode. Examples of such traditional modes might be the Buddhist and the Jaina. Here, of course, one must distinguish the doctrinaire and the institutionalized from the pure and the living. And the contact here must not be motivated by an intent of aggressive exclusion, but inspired by a spirit of what Gandhi used to call fellowship — and mutual enrichment. It is possible — just possible — that such a contact might result in the quickening of the tribal soul once again.[5] But the odds against this are, of course, enormous.

Appendix

In 1855, President Franklin Pierce of the United States made a request to Chief Sealth of the Suwanish tribe of Indians, who live in what is now the State of Washington, to 'sell' his land to the government. In reply Chief Sealth sent the following letter to the President:

> The great Chief in Washington sends word that he wishes to buy our land. The great Chief sends us words of friendship and good will. This is kind of him, since we know that he has little need of our friendship in return. But we will consider your offer, for we know that if we do not do so, the white men come with guns and take our land.
>
> How can we buy or sell the sky, the warmth of the land? The idea is strange to us. Yet we do not own the freshness of the air or the sparkle of the water. How can you buy them from us? Every part of this earth is sacred to my people. Every shining pine needle, every sandy shore, every mist in the dark woods, every clearing and humming insect is holy in the memory and experience of my people.
>
> We know that the white man does not understand our ways. One portion of the land is the same as the next to him, for he is a stranger

who comes in the night and takes from the land whatever he needs. The earth is not his brother but his enemy, and when he has conquered it, he moves on. His appetite will devour the earth and leave behind only a desert. The sight of your cities pains the eyes of the red man. But perhaps it is because the red man is a savage and does not understand. If I decide to accept I will make one condition. The white man must treat the beasts of the land as his brothers. What is man without beasts? If all the beasts were gone, man would die from great loneliness of spirit, for whatever happens to the beasts also happens to man.

. . . When the buffaloes are all slaughtered, the wild horses all tamed, the sacred corner of the forest heavy with the scent of men, and the view of the ripe hills, volted by talking wires, where is the thicket? Where is the eagle? And what is it to say goodbye to the shift and the hunt? The end of living and the beginning of dying.

There is no quiet place in the whiteman's cities. No place to hear the leaves of spring or the rustle of insect wings. But perhaps because I am a savage and do not understand. The clatter only seems to insult the ears. And what is there to life if a man cannot hear the lovely cry of the whippoorwill or the argument of the frogs around a pond at night? The red Indian prefers the soft sound of the wind itself cleaned by the midnight rain, or scented with a pine. The air is precious to the red man, for all things share the same breath, the beast, the trees, the man. The white man does not seem to notice the air he breathes. Like a man dying for many years he is numbed to the smell.

We might understand if we know what the white man dreams, what hopes he describes to his children on long winter nights; what visions he bores into their minds, so that they wish for tomorrow. But we are savages. The white man's dreams are hidden from us. And because they are hidden we will go our own way. If we agree it will be to secure our reservation that you promised. There perhaps we may live out the brief days as we wish. When the last red man has vanished from the earth, and the memory is only the shadow of a cloud moving across the Prairies,[6] these shores and forests will still hold the spirits of my people.

Notes

1. This is an extremely tentative essay as, perhaps, is to be expected. Much of the material for the paper is borrowed from an earlier paper of mine which is

yet to be published, but which was presented at a seminar not long ago. I do hope I have been able to add some new things too.

2. "What is Human Agency?", In *Human Agency and Language*, Cambridge, 1985. Taylor's distinction, as he acknowledges, is based on a distinction, between first and second order desires, made by H. Frankfurt in his article "Freedom of the Will and the Concept of a Person", In *Journal of Philosophy*, 1971. In presenting the distinction I follow Taylor both in spirit and letter.
3. See Ernest Gellner, *Relativism and the Social Sciences*, Cambridge, 1985.
4. See Clarles Taylor, "Foucault on Freedom and Truth", In *Foucault: A Critical Reader*, ed. by David Couzens Hoy, Oxford 1989, pp 72-73.
5. A copy of this moving document was given to me by Professor K. J. Shah several years ago.
6. Very significant in this connection are the works of Sujata Miri and of Ramchandra Gandhi, particularly, his latest book, *Sita's Kitchen*, Penguin, India, 1992.

6

Cultural Identity and Development in the Torres Strait Islands

Leah Lui

Since the time of the white invasion of the continent now known as Australia, the treatment of the indigenous people has ranged from attempted genocide to segregation, assimilation, integration and since the 1970s self-management and self-determination.

The underlying assumption has always been that we — the indigenous people of Australia would want to be like them — the white usurpers of our lands. No recognition was given to our cultures and our traditions. We were seen as pagans, heathens, uneducated — in short 'savages'. No recognition was given to the fact that there are other ways of living and that there may be people who wish to maintain a way of life quite unlike Westerners. It is these other ways of living which are in danger of being lost as we travel down the road of Western development. The role traditional knowledge can play in development continues to be overlooked, yet development has the potential to empower people and reinforce the cultural traditions which have allowed native people to survive (CSQ, Fall 1991: 46).

If development is to achieve anything for the people of Third World countries or for the indigenous people who live in Third World conditions in relatively wealthy nations like Australia, we, the people must have the power to decide which avenues of development we wish to pursue.

We are the ones who should build the bridge between our past and our future.

Australia has two indigenous people — the Aboriginal people of mainland Australia and the Torres Strait Islanders. I am here to talk about my people, the Torres Strait Islanders.

There are four major areas I wish to talk about today, firstly where we are from and who we are culturally; secondly, about how Islanders took action against the so-called development in the Maritime Strike of 1936; thirdly, I want to talk about the Mabo Land Case, the judgement on which secured among other things, legal recognition of Murray Island customary law, and finally I want to look at what the future holds for my people.

The Islands of the Torres Strait are situated between the tip of Queensland, Australia and Papua New Guinea. The Straits cover an area of approximately 40,000 sq km. Of this area 2.6 per cent is land; 6.2 per cent is inundated reef flats and 91.2 per cent is open ocean.

Traditionally Islanders formed three major groups. These groupings were based on similarities and differences in way of obtaining food, ritual practices and the geophysical features of the islands. The basic division however, was between East and West on the basis of language. Western Islanders spoke Kalaw Kawaw Ya, a language related to an Aboriginal language from the Cape York area of Australia, while Eastern Islanders spoke Miriam Mir, a language derived from a Papua New Guinean language spoken around the Fly River.

An extensive trade network operating between PNG, the island and the Australian mainland ensured against total isolation and allowed for the movement of necessary items.

At the time of contact the population of Islanders has been estimated at 4000-5000. Today there are an estimated 6200 Islanders living on 16 islands within the Straits as well as two additional communities on the northern tip of Cape York. Approximately 15000 now live away from the Torres Strait region on the Australian mainland.

Central to our sense of identity are our extended families, within which respect for elders is preserved, it provides the framework within which obligations to kin are met, and ensures the sharing of resources and the source of emotional and spiritual support. Given that 91 per cent of our traditional area is open ocean, the sea is also central to our sense of identity having determined our way of life, subsistence practices and ceremonial life. The sea remains the source of inspiration for many of our songs and stories and is treated with great respect.

Today Torres Strait Islanders who live in the Straits continue to rely on the productivity of the natural environment for food, trade goods or cash income.

What makes us Torres Strait Islanders are our languages, our dances, our songs, our myths and legends and ceremonies. And although these have changed shape, it is a sign of how we have adapted as we came into contact with Pacific Islanders and missionaries. As the result of prolonged contact with missionaries from the London Missionary Society and since 1915, contact with the Anglican Church, we are a Christian people. Over the time, however, our Christian beliefs have been woven into our cultural practices.

One of the main ceremonies which brings us together to celebrate our culture is the tombstone unveiling ceremony. For my people, the death of a member of our society initiates the performance of certain rites. No less that 12 months after the primary rite in interring the body, a secondary mortuary rite is performed. This is known as the tombstone opening ceremony. The ceremony involves the public unveiling of the engraved tombstone which is blessed by a priest. The unveiling is followed by feasting and traditional dancing to celebrate the occasion. Its observance is symbolic of many things; the acknowledgement of a final resting place for the spirit of the deceased; the end of the period of mourning; the fulfilment of obligation and the reinforcement of Island custom through the reunion of kin. The performance of the ceremony continues today on the Islands and the mainland.

In looking at how development has impacted on our cultural identity, I want to look at one example, which examines how the Western ideology of capitalism was thrust upon the Islanders in the 1900s.

In 1879 when the Torres Straits were annexed by the Queensland Government some measures of self-government were put in place. These included elected island councils and island law courts. Islanders were encouraged to continue participating in the flourishing marine industry which relied heavily on market prices and cheap labour for the industry to remain viable.

In the early 1900s a former London Missionary Society missionary established a company, Papuan Industries Limited, to encourage further Islander participation in the marine industry. On a family or clan basis, Islanders were able to buy their own pearling boats through the company.

By the end of the 1920s almost 1/4 of the pearling fleet in the Torres Strait were owned by Islanders. But, before too long it became obvious to administrators that Islanders were not turning into replicas of their employers and 'Protectors' (who were the government appointed officers in the area).

Two related aspects of Islander social values and cultural meaning contrasted with capitalist norms.

1. The circulation, distribution and exchange theme inherent in non-capitalist societies continued. Rather than selling their produce, Islanders chose to uphold their identity and fulfil obligations of mutuality within and between communities, e.g., in 1910, despite the demand for copra 14 pounds/tonne, one group of Islanders gave 10,000 coconuts to their island neighbours and an additional 3000 to the Papuan Industries Limited for a new church rather than selling them.

2. Islander social values manifested themselves in attitudes to work and to their boats. 'Production' was determined by obligations, responsibilities and claims required by clan leaders and Island community.

   To administrators it appeared that Islanders worked their boats casually — as if time was 'no object', often using their boats for hunting purposes. For Islanders reciprocal obligations continued and subsistence needs were being met (Sharp, 1980c).

In the late 1920s and early 30s control of Papuan Industries Limited was handed over to government administrators. The government 'Protector' became responsible for recruiting crews and controlled the earnings of Islanders who worked the boats in addition, if the boats were not worked to the satisfaction of the 'protector', they were confiscated.

Through this Islanders lost the right to control their own means of production. In addition Government teachers/supervisors were appointed on all the islands. Their presence contributed to break down of the power of the Island councils and the takeover of administration of justice via the Island law courts. The local 'protector' also introduced a nightly curfew and a permit system to control Islander movement between the Islands. To leave the Island permission had to be sought from the government teacher. As the grip of the government 'protector' tightened —

inter-island feelings of opposition were reaching boiling point.

In mid January 1936 when the Protector made visits to each of the islands to recruit men to work the boats, with the exception of 2 councillors, Islanders went on strike refusing to work the boats until conditions improved.

The strike was the first organized Islander challenge to European authority (Beckett, 1987: 54). It was seen not only as a protest against increasing control over Islander lives, it was also a demand to be recognized as a distinct people and for the right of Islanders to manage their own affairs (Sharp, 1980c).

On some islands the strike lasted for nine months and embarassed the Queensland Government into making changes. The two most important were the removal of government teachers/supervisors from the Islands and the formation of the Island Advisory Council — which is the forerunner of the contemporary Islander Co-ordinating Council. Islander communities gained more autonomy and a separate legislative identity to that of the Aboriginal people (Kehoe-Forutan, 1988). The Maritime Strike heralded the turning point in Islander and Government relations.

Since the strike, we have continued in the struggle to maintain our identity and culture and to secure control of our traditional land and sea.

In recent years the most significant event in the recognition of indigenous rights in the Torres Straits and indeed Australia, is embodied in the decision by the highest court of Australia on the Mabo Land Case which ran for 10 years.

In 1982 Koiki Mabo and four other Islanders from Murray Island in the eastern Torres Strait issued a writ in the High Court of Australia claiming distinct rights to traditional lands continuously occupied by the Meriam people since time immemorial. After six years, the case survived an attempt by the Queensland Government to retroactively extinguish any rights Islanders may or may not have.

In June 1992 the full bench of the High Court recognized Meriam rights to Murray Island ruling, ". . . the Meriam people are entitled as against the whole world to possession, occupation, use and enjoyment of the lands of the Murray Islands". (Eddie Mabo and Others *vs* State of Queensland, High Court of Australia, Order)

The Court recognized the existence of a form of title in the Murray Islands, described as 'native title', and in doing so the High Court brought Australian law into line with that of other common law countries — the United States, New Zealand and Canada — which have recognized native title for some time. Native title existed in much, possibly, all of Australia when the British claimed sovereignty over the Torres Strait in 1879. The doctrine of 'terra nullius' which says that the land was uninhabited by people with a system of law and government was overruled.

The judgement is a major victory for the Meriam people and has profound and long lasting implications for other Torres Strait Islanders and the Aboriginal people (Sharp, 1993: 235).

The decision on the Mabo Case has placed the issue of land rights squarely on the agenda. For a majority of white Australians the decision has served only to reopen an old wound, a weeping sore, they have tried to ignore for hundreds of years. But for the Aboriginal and Torres Strait Islander people it has shifted the land rights dynamic, giving Australia's indigenous people some bargaining power.

The Prime Minister of Australia hailed the decision saying it would benefit all Australians including future generations and allow the nation to address traditional land ownership. However, despite numerous opinions from lawyers and academics on the possible implications of the decision, the Federal and State governments are yet to respond publicly.

Meanwhile, mining groups have responded in outright opposition with one representative going as far as to say that legislation should be put in place to limit land claims.

Aboriginal and Torres Strait Islander people recognize that although we have won an important and very significant battle in our struggle for land rights, the war is far from over.

Today, my people live on the mainland of Australia and on small island communities scattered around the Strait. Harvesting sea species remains essential. Even though the social and political organizational context for our lives have changed with European arrival in the region, economic activity and social well-being continues to involve our traditions and traditionally use resources.

In the Torres Strait, we have a regional governing body — the Island Co-ordinating Council (ICC) — which is made up of the elected chairpersons of the individual Island Councils. The ICC was established by Queensland State Law and despite the lack of financial resources and power, it has become the primary focus for Islander political, social, economic and cultural aspirations.

The ICC is responsible for regional affairs and is currently formulating a Marine Strategy for the Torres Strait. The preservation of the marine environment is crucial for our survival and development in neighbouring countries are of enormous concern. Oil exploration and loading in the Gulf of Papua, vessel traffic in the strait, a pulp mill in Indonesia, lead loading in the Gulf of Carpentaria and oil development in the Timor Gap all cause worry for our Islands. Within the Strait itself, we must closely watch developments on our islands. Insensitive construction, even essential infrastructure can lead to unwanted but avoidable ill effects. (Lui, 1992a)

The future for my people, though uncertain, holds much hope. Islander leaders recognize the need of taking the initiative in environmental and political issues and in addressing other needs of the region, rather than merely reacting to what are often piecemeal government initiatives. We are placed to take the initiative.

In 1988 when Islanders announced a bid to secede from Australia, the move attracted sarcasm, criticism and racist comments. But our leaders hasve persevered and, at a conference on constitutional change, the Chairman of the ICC, Mr Getano Lui issued a one page statement titled "Self-Government in the Torres Strait". The key paragraph stated:

> In looking at self-government for the Torres Strait we will be looking at practical options for securing Islander land, reef and sea tenure; managing appropriate social, health and education services and facilities; protecting the marine and coastal environments; encouraging appropriate economic development; and maintaining and strengthening our unique culture and language.

The Australian Government's response to this most recent push for self-government has been reserved. In a press statement in December last year, the Federal Minister for Aboriginal and Torres Strait Islander Affairs ". . . that the Government has made no decision on this matter and any changes will have to be the subject of exhaustive consultations" (Tickner 1992). In March this year his position on self-government in the Torres Strait had not changed.

The ICC considers that the Torres Straits are well placed for self-government, particularly since we are a majority in a definable region of Australia.

Most importantly, self-government will give US the power to negotiate our future in the world context.

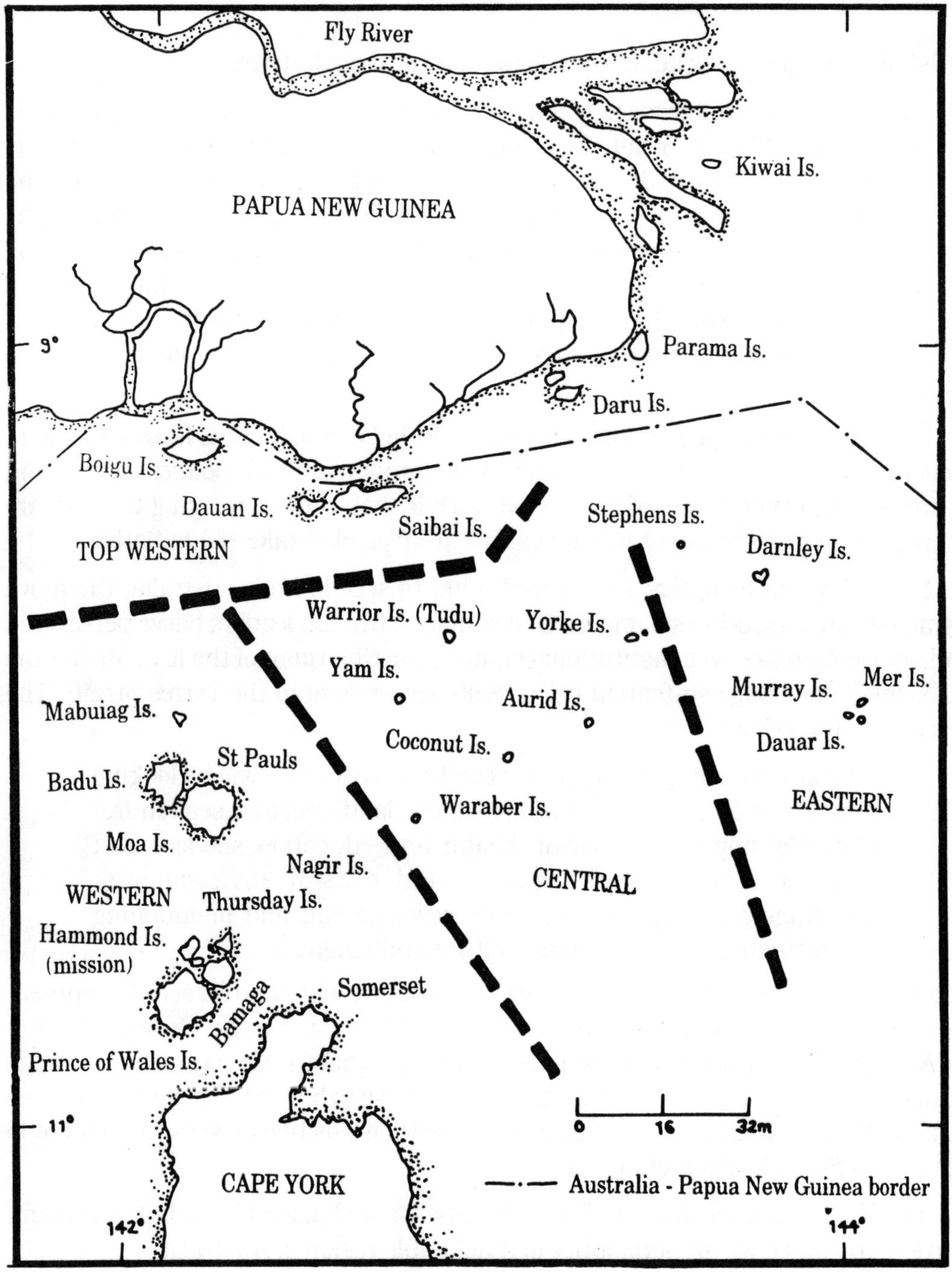

Islands of the Torres Strait

References

Beckett, J., 1987. *Torres Strait Islanders: custom and colonialism*, Cambridge, Cambridge University Press, U.K.

CSQ, 1991. "Grassroots Devèlopment", In *Cultural Survival Quarterly*, Volume 15, No. 4. Cambridge, U.K.

Kehoe-Forutan, S., 1988. *Torres Strait Independence: a Chronicle of Events*, Department of Geographical Sciences, University of Queensland, Brisbane, Australia.

Lui, G., 1992a. "The Torres Strait Islanders of Australia". Presentation to UNCED Earth Summit, Rio de Janeiro.

———, 1992b . "Self-Government for Torres Strait". Press Statement, Darwin, October 1992.

Sharp, N., 1980c. *Torres Strait Islands: A great cultural refusal. The meaning of the Maritime Strike of 1936*, Melbourne, LaTrobe University, Department of Sociology.

———, 1993. *Stars of Tagai.*

Tickner, R., 1992. Media Release, "Torres Strait Islanders on National Agenda", Canberra, 18 December 1992.

7

Identity, Ownership and Appropriation

Aspects of Aboriginal Australian Experience in Tertiary Education

Olga Gostin

This paper springs from a chance encounter with Professor B.N. Saraswati during an excursion to one of Australia's most enigmatic art sites in the Laura area of the Cape York Peninsula, in August 1992. During three days of extensive travelling and occasional intensive walking, we shared thoughts and exchanged views on our common experience as professional anthropologists engaged at some time (and in my case, currently) in teaching in an indigenous tertiary program.

Professor Saraswati thought that my background as a person of mixed Russian-Belgian descent, with first hand experience of African and New Guinea cultures, yet teaching for the past 13 years at Australia's first and foremost national tertiary program for Aboriginal people in Adelaide, South Australia, merited airing at this learned forum. I am pleased and indeed greatly honoured to be here today, though it is a matter of profound regret that my Aboriginal colleague, Mercy Glastonbury, had to cancel her visit at the last minute for family reasons. We had hoped to present complementary papers. I therefore seek your tolerance and understanding in my standing here and talking, not on behalf of Aboriginal Australians, but simply as one passionately committed to the cause of Aboriginal participation in tertiary education.

Aboriginal higher education has emerged as a significant initiative only in the past twenty years. Indeed, the first Aboriginal person to receive an undergraduate degree was Charles Perkins in 1966. The neglect of tertiary education can be directly correlated to the overall neglect of Aboriginal education from primary school onwards. This in turn is a legacy of Australia's colonial past and the policies which informed non-Aboriginal attitudes towards the first Australians from the time of contact in 1788. Without engaging in a lengthy historical review, it is possible to summarize the causes of neglect as follows:

(i) a fundamental lack of respect for, and/or appreciation of Aboriginal culture and capabilities so that the original Australians, with a few notable exceptions, were not deemed capable of systematic instruction at the same level of expectation that applied to non-Aboriginal persons;

(ii) repressive practices which saw the physical, psychological and cultural dispossession of the first Australians. These ranged from forceful physical removal and dislocation from traditional areas, removal of children from their parents, to deliberate cultural suppression where people were actively forbidden to speak their own languages, practise vital customs and/or engage in hunting/gathering activities which formerly had ensured a healthy diet and ongoing bonding with land through custom;

(iii) the imposition of an alien value system which saw Christianity and Anglo-Saxon culture as a major 'civilizing' force, while at the same time denying equal access to the benefits of that civilization;

(iv) policies of segregation, assimilation and later integration — all of which were based on the premise of asserting the dominant (Western) culture. This was extended to the point that the true history of the invasion of Australia, the resistance of Aboriginal people to it, their remarkable survival and their ensuing dispossession remained largely hidden from the Australian consciousness until the mid-1970s.

Against this background, it is not surprising that Aboriginal people on the whole performed rather poorly in what educational opportunities were offered to them. By the 1970s, however, new political forces led to the emergence of Aboriginal tertiary education. The reasons for this were as follows (Bin-Sallik, 1990:1):

(i) following the 1967 referendum giving the Federal Government the authority to act on behalf of Aboriginal interests (which had formerly been the exclusive responsibility of the States) the need to redress the educational disadvantage of Aboriginal people became a matter of priority;

(ii) the Federal policy of self-management generated a need for Aboriginal leadership;

(iii) government policy deliberately sought proportional Aboriginal representation in the private and public sectors thereby creating new avenues of employment and a demand for qualified people;

(iv) Aboriginal people themselves demanded increased access to tertiary education;

(v) this was made possible by the release of federal funds for tertiary institutions to launch new programs.

The first tertiary program for Aboriginal people launched under this initiative in 1973, was the so-called Aboriginal Task Force at the South Australian Institute of Technology, now the School of Aboriginal and Islander Administration (SAIA) at the University of South Australia. This program was supposed to be a once-off event aimed at training community workers for the Department of Community Welfare. The success of the course lead to its evaluation modification and consolidation over the next two decades during which it moved from delivering awards in welfare and community development to a fully accredited Bachelor of Arts degree in Aboriginal Affairs Administration. Since its inception in 1973, the Aboriginal Task Force as it is still informally and fondly known, has produced some five hundred graduates almost all of whom have found employment in government departments, Aboriginal organizations and private enterprises. The success of the program was largely due to its operating on a two-strand, mutually supportive basis with one sector delivering academic programs and the other offering support under the so-called Aboriginal Higher Education Unit (AHEU) or 'enclave' system.

The National Aboriginal Education Committee (NAEC) defines enclaves as follows:

> An enclave support program is where Aboriginal students enrolled in standard courses within institutions are given additional support appropriate to their culture, lifestyles and educational background (1984: 16).

The functions of the AHEUs have been enumerated by Bourke *et al.* (1991: 4) as follows:

(i) to design and administer specially targeted advertising and recruiting programs;

(ii) to conduct alternative selection procedures, and recommend on admission;

(iii) to provide ongoing academic tutorial assistance and study skills programs to enrolled students;

(iv) to provide personal counselling, as needed;

(v) to assist students in a range of non-academic areas such as housing, child-care and financial support;

(vi) to provide designated space and facilities for the specific use of Aboriginal students.

The success of the Aboriginal Task Force with its enclave program made it a model for tertiary institutions throughout Australia many of which adopted enclave support functions as a back-up for Aboriginal students studying conventional or so-called mainstream courses. The Task Force remained distinctive in that both its academic program and its support functions were tailored specifically for an Aboriginal clientele, a feature which will be discussed later in this paper.

Table 1 shows how Aboriginal and Torres Strait Islander student enrolments have increased almost sixfold in the past decade. It is interesting to note that women make up a consistent 60 per cent of Aboriginal enrolments and that an annual growth rate of some 30 per cent has been recorded for the past five years with the exception of 1990.

Table 2 shows the correlation between Aboriginal enrolments and the establishment of support programs. Thus in 1969 with no support there were only 18 enrolments; in 1982 with 10 support programs there were 854 enrolments; and in 1989 with 62 support programs there were some 3,307 enrolments. (Bourke *et al.*, 1991: 3)

Table 7.1

Aboriginal and Torres Strait Islander Students in Higher Education, 1982 and 1987-91:

	Enrolments			Annual Growth Rate	Females share of Aboriginal enrolments (%)	Aboriginals % share of total enrolments
Year	Females	Males	Total			
1982			854			0.3
1987	1,166	767	1,933		60.3	1.5
1988	1,614	951	2,565	32.7	62.9	0.6
1989	2,025	1,282	3,307	28.9	61.2	0.7
1990	2,286	1,323	3,607	9.1	63.4	0.7
1991	2,987	1,820	4,807	33.3	62.1	0.9

From: *Higher Education Series*, Update No. 2, October, 1992.

Table 7.2

Aboriginal Enrolment and Support Programs Expansion since 1972

	Year	Aboriginal enrolments	Support Programs
*	1969	18	nil
	1972	72	nil
	1979	748	5
**	1982	854	10
***	1989	3,307	62

* CDE Survey of Aboriginal Access to Tertiary Education, AGPS, undated.

** NAEC *Aborigines and Tertiary Education: A Framework for the 1985-87 Triennium*, AGPS, 1984.

***DEET *Higher Education Series* Aboriginal Torres Strait Islander Students, Report No. 3, April 1990.

From: Bourke., *et al.*, 1991. *Career development in Aboriginal Higher Education* Australian Government Publishing Service, Canberra.

Fig. 1 compares the age distributions of Aboriginal and all higher education students, showing a predominantly older Aboriginal student body.

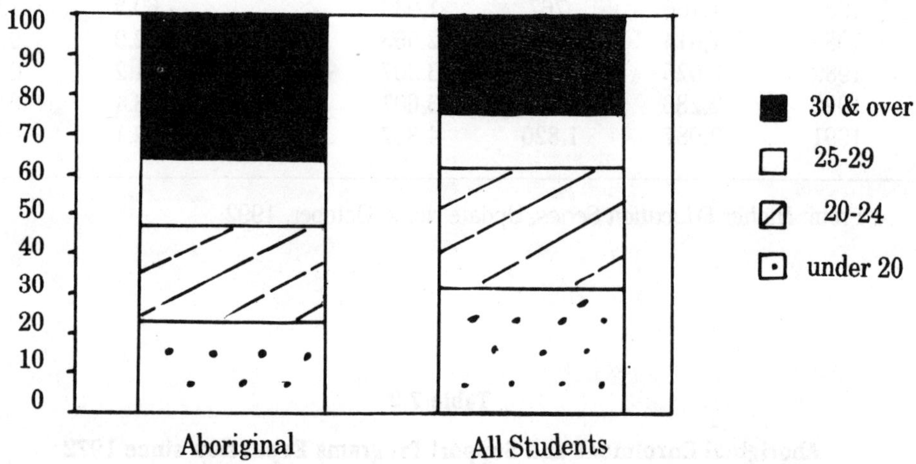

Fig. 1

Distribution of Aboriginal and All Higher Education Students by Age Group (%), 1991.
From: *Higher Education Series,* Update No. 2, October 1992.

Fig. 2 shows the distribution of Aboriginal and all higher education students by course, showing that Aboriginal students are more likely to be enrolled in diploma, associate diploma or non-award courses (*Higher Education Series* — Update No. 2, October 1992).

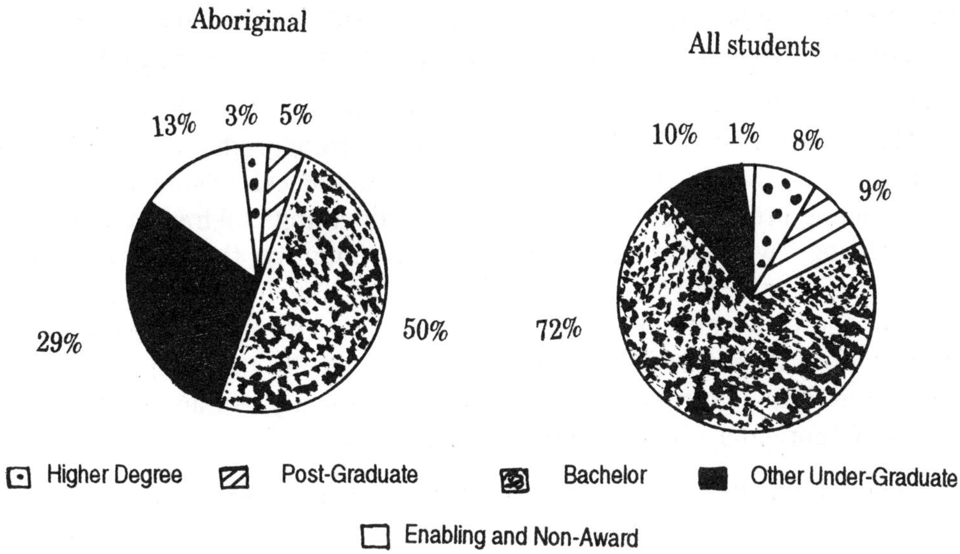

Fig. 2

Distribution of Aboriginal and All Higher Education Students by Level of Course (%), 1991.
From: *Higher Education Series*, Update No. 2, October 1992.

It can thus be seen that Aboriginal involvement in tertiary education has taken off, thanks to the role of supportive programs developed in the last 20 years. Even so, it must be noted that proportionate Aboriginal participation in the tertiary sector still remains at one-third that of all Australians (Department of Education, Employment and Training [DEET] 1988: 34).

The second half of this paper addresses the use and relevance of culture-specific material and the structuring of awards specially designed by and for Aboriginal people to meet their self-defined social and cultural needs. The realization in the 1970s that 'mainstream' education was not succeeding was clearly shown by the low retention of students at primary and secondary school levels and by the mere trickle of students entering the tertiary sector. While a variety of socio-economic reasons might appropriately be forwarded to explain the Aboriginal negative experience of formal schooling, e.g. poverty, poor health, broken families, poor role models, discrimination and racism, one could also attribute the failure of Western type education at all levels to a profound sense of cultural alienation. In a word, mainstream education was seen to be both alien and alienating, with little relevance to the real-life experience of the students. This resulted in poor attendance and performance right across the spectrum, from primary to tertiary education.

The reality of this dilemma was recognized in a *Report to the Schools Commission* by the Aboriginal Consultative Group (1975) which strongly advocated the need for an increased number of Aboriginal teachers and the establishment of special teacher-training programs to meet the need of educating children in a culturally relevant setting. Two programs resulted from this initiative: that of Batchelor (*sic*) College in the Northern Territory, and the Anangu Teacher Education Program (ANTEP) at the University of South Australia (cf. George, 1992; Stewart, 1991). Graduates from these programs are trained specifically to teach in their own culture areas. Although regional differences undoubtedly will apply, the overall approach in Aboriginal education represents a quest

> for total education which includes cultural education. Such education begins from different premises and aims at different outcomes, and as such is a study from within; an exploration, an analysis, a probing of one's own world, of one's people and their history (Bourke, 1992: 17).

On a national scale, the NAEC in 1984 set the target of training 1000 Aboriginal teachers by 1990, an initiative which has until recently soaked up much of the resources designated for Aboriginal higher education (Bourke *et al.*, 1991:5).

For the most part, however, Aboriginal tertiary programs have focused on delivering enclave-type support to Aboriginal students enrolled in mainstream higher education courses. Until recently there has been a heavy bias of enrolment in the fields of teacher training, social science and the humanities, with only negligible enrolments in agriculture, architecture, computing and engineering. Business courses, health, science and law are gaining greater popularity.

The most distinctive initiative, however, relates to the development of courses and awards which are specifically designed for Aboriginal students in consultation with Aboriginal advisory groups. This approach was pioneered by the Aboriginal Task Force in 1973 and has since been imitated in several other universities. The characteristic of these courses is that they are vocationally oriented in areas of demonstrated professional need. Thus SAIA has developed special courses in Aboriginal administration aimed at training graduates for the public service, community organizations and statutory authorities. The University of Newcastle has developed a special medical course while the Charles Sturt University has launched a special Aboriginal Community Ranger course. Other initiatives are in the pipeline as tertiary institutions increasingly recognise that they must meet the needs of Aboriginal people in a socio-political climate which acknowledges the rights of indigenous people to formulate their own socio-cultural agendas and priorities. More relevantly, Aboriginal academics are increasingly calling the tune themselves and are defining what to them is considered to be appropriate tertiary education. This was the theme of the second annual National Aboriginal and Torres Strait Islander Higher Education Conference held in Hervey Bay, Queensland in December 1992.

The current trends were in fact anticipated in 1988 when the Aboriginal Education Policy Task Force recommended that certain conditions apply to funding Aboriginal education. These required institutions to consult with Aboriginal communities, define and implement access outcomes, establish long-term planning, develop culture-inclusive and sensitive curricula and practices, and undertake reviews consistent with national goals and priorities in Aboriginal higher education (Bourke *et al.*, 1991: 9-10).

The evolution of such culturally determined programs can perhaps best be demonstrated by taking the case of the original Aboriginal Task Force. Bin-Sallik identifies several stages in its development (1990: 22-23):

(i) the creation of a two-year training program for welfare workers leading to a non-accredited certificate (1973-75);

(ii) the entry of Aboriginal students into an accredited mainstream social science course facilitated by the Task Force's special entry program (1976-82);

(iii) the establishment of nationally recognized, accredited courses specifically designed for Aboriginal vocational needs through a consultative process with, and input from, the Aboriginal community, and where the bulk of the curriculum reflects Aboriginal needs (1983 cont.);

(iv) the South Australian Institute of Technology (now the University of South Australia) accepts full responsibility for the program by incorporating it administratively and financially into its formal structure by proclaiming it the School of Aboriginal and Islander Administration (1987);

(v) the University of South Australia launches the Faculty of Aboriginal and Islander Studies, the first of its kind in Australia, which includes the School of Aboriginal and Islander Administration and other Aboriginal-related teaching and research programs within the University (1992).

A major ongoing feature of all these initiatives was the continuation of the enclave support program funded by the Federal Government through its Aboriginal Participation Initiative (API), which in 1990 allocated A$18m on a nationwide basis. Subsidiary funding is also available through the Aboriginal Education Strategic Initiatives Program (AESIP) which in 1990 committed A$7m nationwide (Bourke *et al.*, 1991: 12).

The success or otherwise of programs and their enclave support systems specifically designed to meet Aboriginal needs has not yet been properly evaluated on a national scale. Bin-Sallik, however, conducted a survey of past student evaluation of the Aboriginal Task Force/SAIA (1990: 24). The salient points which emerge are that the program:

(i) reinforced/developed identity and pride in Aboriginality;

(ii) increased self-esteem and confidence;

(iii) developed an awareness of problems confronting Aboriginal people;

(iv) improved employment opportunities.

Most importantly, because the program was allowed to evolve over two decades, it has been able to incorporate and respond to the socio-political changes which have affected Aboriginal affairs. It would be true to say that the original Task Force has been a main contributor to the development of a national Aboriginal intellectual community (Bin-Sallik, 1990:33).

The future, however, is not plain sailing. For a variety of reasons, above all economic, there has arisen a strong drive to rationalize university courses and to trim budgets. The time of preferential API and AESIP monies is fast passing and Aboriginal supportive programs as well as vocational awards are under direct threat. The tendency is to streamline courses with the foreseeable outcome that mainstream awards will dominate. This trend may well set back the progressive initiatives of the past two decades which saw such a positive response of Aboriginal people to tertiary education. As Bin-Sallik points out: "tertiary studies are fundamentally acculturative by intent and rationale; [they] therefore constitute a potentially destructive experience for Aborigines" (1990: 141).

The threat of homogenization, uniformization and Westernization of hitherto distinctive Aboriginal programs is very real in Australia today. It is to be hoped that Aboriginal academics will take their cause on board and challenge the trend towards mainstreaming, if that is indeed, perceived as an undesirable direction. Much is at stake. In the words of Eleanor Bourke, Director of the Aboriginal Research Institute at the University of South Australia:

> Appropriate education is critical in the survival of Aboriginal Australia but only if it is in harmony with Aboriginal aspirations and cultural contexts. The alternative is to loose Aboriginal values and lifestyles and to become Europeanised. Aboriginal people have to find the balance between gaining the necessary degree of expertise from western education and the enhancement of Aboriginality at the same time (1992: 17).

References

Aboriginal Consultative Group, 1975. *Education for Aborigines: Report to the Schools' Commission.* Australian Government Publishing Service, Canberra.

Bin-Sallik, Mary Ann, 1990. *Aboriginal Tertiary Education in Australia: How well is it serving the needs of Aborigines?*, Aboriginal Studies Key Centre, South Australian College of Advanced Education, Adelaide.

———, 1992. "Aboriginal Studies and Academic Reconciliation", In *Kaurna Higher Education Journal* Issue 2: 1-7.

Bourke, Eleanor, 1992. "Aboriginal Australia", In *Kaurna Higher Education Journal* Issue 2: 12-17.

Bourke, Eleanor; Farrow, Rosie; McConnochie, Keith and Tucker, Adrian, 1991. *Career Development in Aboriginal Higher Education*, Australian Government Publishing Service, Canberra.

DEET, 1988. *Report of the Aboriginal Education Policy Task Force*, Australian Government Publishing Service, Canberra.

George, Rigmor, 1992. "Emerging Models of Educational Delivery in Remote Aboriginal Contexts". Paper delivered at the National Aboriginal and Torres Strait Islander Higher Education Conference, Hervey Bay, Queensland. *Towards 2000: Maintaining the Momentum.* 6-11 December 1992.

Higher Education Series, Update No. 2, 1992.

NAEC, 1984. *Aborigines and Tertiary Education: a Framework for the 1985-1987 Triennium*, Australian Government Publishing Service, Canberra.

Stewart, Ian, 1991. "Focus on Learning Styles: Aboriginal Teacher Education in the Northern Territory", In *Access* 5 (1): 19-22.

8

Crisis of Cultural Identity in Mongolian Nomadic Civilization

Otgonbayar

It is the matter of honour for me to attend such a gathering of distinguished scholars, who are discussing one of the important issues facing the contemporary world crisis of cultural identity and to share my own ideas in this regard.

Today, at the turn of the twenty-first century all human societies have become increasingly interlinked with one other through global markets and the spread of a universal consumer culture. The need of development, which probably every country faces, gives a need in modern technology from the available source, i.e., from the West. This, on the one hand makes possible the development of the backward societies and accumulation of material wealth, on the other hand, this process results in an increasing homogenization of all human societies, regardless of their origin or cultural inheritances. This process dictates unescapable unification of education pattern, replacement of traditional institutions like tribe clan or family by new economic units, in some cases resulting in progressive modernization or Westernization of many societies.

I am not against modernization, but against the modernization with the increasing effect of Westernization, eroding the traditional values in many eastern societies. The effect of Westernization or, I would rather say, Europeanization one can clearly see in the example of the Mongolian nomadic civilization.

Before deliberating on the crisis of cultural identity of the Mongolian nomadic society I would like to dwell on the formation and description of this type of society.

Around the third millenium BC the vast region from today's Central Asia till the Korean peninsula in the east, from the forests of Siberia to the valleys of Yellow River, was inhabited by number of cattle breeder tribes. The type of economic activity, characteristic to these tribes, was dictated by the natural conditions, in which they had to exist as a major part of the region is steppe or low altitude hills. At present when we speak about the nomadism in central Asia, we will have to make one major distinction for the muslim nomadic societies in the Central Asian Republic of the former Soviet Union and Chinese Turkestan and Buddhist nomadic culture, comprising Mongolia, some regions in Russia and China.

The vast area of Buddhist nomadic civilization with dominance of Mongol-speaking people had its own cultural identity, born of the speciality and peculiarity of their existence and due to many historic, social circumstances. This civilization, mostly misunderstood by the Western audience, or I would say by the settled societies, claimed to be barbarians without any cultural heritage or tradition, had its own highly developed culture and quite sophisticated technology suited to their own living conditions. Their cultural and technological inheritance was denied publicity mostly because the scholars from the settled societies could not understand that these are simply different societies, living in different circumstances with completely different measures.

The formation of Mongolian nomadic culture can be divided into three different steps of development. These are:

1. Early period of nomadism (struggle for dominance in the region by the Turkic and Mongol tribes)
2. The period of unified Mongolian State
3. Adoption of Buddhism.

Early Period of Nomadism

The period starts from the third millenium BC and lasts till the twelfth century AD. During this period the Great Steppe was inhabited by the tribes of Mongol and Turk origin, who were co-existing and struggling for the dominance over the region. In the third century BC the Huns established their hegemony over the region thus laying the foundation of Mongolian nomadic culture. Besides having enough achievements in the field technology (they had quite sophisticated scientific observations on nomadic cattle breeding) they were successful in creating a unique culture (they had the script called Orkhon Enisei Script, similar to Runic scripts). The Huns were defeated in the first century AD by another tribe of Mongol origin, Xianbis. From the first century AD till the twelfth century a number of tribes established their dominance over the great steppe region: Xianbis (Mongol origin) from first to third century, Niruns (Mongol origin) or Jou Jians fourth-sixth century, Turks sixth-eighth century, Uighurs eighth-ninth century, Kirgizs ninth-tenth century, and Kidans (Mongol origin) from tenth to twelfth century.

This was a period of intermixing of Mongol and Turkic speaking culture, both sides acquiring many customs, traditions and cultural achievements of each other. The Empire of Kidans has a special place in this period. The Kidans, a tribe of Mongol origin who established the hegemony over the Great Steppe in the tenth century, later retreated to the Chinese territory, losing their control over the nomadic Mongolian tribes. In China they established the Empire of Lyao but were assimilated in the settled Chinese culture and underwent physical sinification. But during the dominance of Kidans in the steppe region they established two Academies of Sciences and adopted two scripts as their State scripts: one based on Chinese script, Ikh, and the other based on the Uighur script, designed for the nomads. Later the Uighur script was adopted by Mongols and some other tribes of Turkic and Tungus origin.

This period gave to the Mongolian culture not only sophisticated military science, which later was successfully elaborated by Genghis Khan, but also the veterinary and quite sophisticated agriculture science. There is evidence that the Mongols started to conduct selection among their horses in order to get the best breed and many other examples could be cited here.

The Period of Unified Mongol State

The great Statesman and leader Genghis Khan, born Temujin, united all Mongol tribes in the valley of Tuul, Orkhon and Onon (known as Mongols of three rivers) and conducted a series of conquests, bringing the tribes of Great Steppe under his leadership.

Besides the great conquests, the name of Genghis Khan is connected for Mongols with the acquisition of their own national and cultural identity. He gave to the Mongols their State script based on the Uighur script and first Constitution Ikh Yassa, and the most important, starting from that time Mongol tribes found their identity in single national unit.

The Great Empire, comprising vast territories with both settled and nomadic population, was created during the rule of Genghis Khan and his immediate Successors. China, Central Asia, Persia, Middle East and Russia were brought under the control of the Mongols. To rule such a great empire, populated mostly with hostile defeated nations which limited and outnumbered the Mongols heavily (Historians believe that the population of Mongolia was around 400 thousands while China had estimatedly 65 mln and Russia 20 mln population), was not possible without well-thought and thoroughly designed system of governance. The basis of such governance was the preservation of its own identity over the conquered nations. In fact the nomadic identity of the tribes, inhabiting the vast territory of the Steppe region with its stronger identification against the national, as the nomadic culture provided such varying degrees of identity, proposing settled population as alien to the nomadic one, which was promoted by the Mongol rulers, has played a greater role not only in governing but also in conquering other settled nations. The Mongol conquest had been successful, among other things, for the military discipline of the Mongol armies or the policy of fear and repression so much exaggerated in historiography, as the majority of the Mongol cavalry consisted of the tribesmen, who were only yesterday conquered by Genghis Khan, not only of the Mongol origin but also Manchu, Turk and Tungus origin. But why they showed so a high degree of obedience to their commanders and won battles after battles in alien territory far from their motherland in hostile environment, conquering numerically superior nations? After the death of Genghis Khan his grandson Batu was given only 4000 cavalrymen and Batu raised an army of hundred thousand soldiers from the conquered territories to fight and defeat the Russian kingdoms and European countries. Only the death of Great Khan Ogodei was the reason for his return to Mongolia. According to the common logic his army must have revolted against him and killed the negligible amount of Mongol cavalrymen, half of which were left behind to guard the headquarters. But they did not revolt, rather they fought with dedication to put their conqueror in control of Russia and Europe. The only possible explanation is that the tribesmen identified themselves with the nomad Mongols and the settled population of Russia and Europe were alien to them more than their suzerain Mongols.

The tribal community, divided by the language and origin, had one unified identification in the way of living, cultural heritage and technology. During the great Empire many scholars from the conquered nations were working the academies of sciences founded by the Mongol rulers, thus enriching the knowledge of the Mongols by the achievement of other civilizations. It was the Mongols, who introduced paper currency to the world, it was the Mongols, who brought canon to Europe, it was the Mongols, who laid down the principles of the modern postal system. The cultural achievements of the Mongols were enriched by the achievement of the other settled civilizations.

Already from the third generation of the Mongol rulers the Mongols lost their single cultural identity, some of them adopting Islam, some Christianity, some Buddhism etc. The feeling of national unity and identity was still high, as when the soldiers of Khubilai Khan refused to fight against provincial ruler Khaidu on the ground that they did not wish the slaughter of their fellow countrymen, but the religious and cultural alienation was stronger. So Muslim rulers of Central Asia were fighting against the Christian Mongols settled in Russia and the discipline which united the Mongols fell down and the Mongols started to fight against each other. The Mongol Empire as a single unit came to its end and the Mongols settled abroad were absorbed by the local population in the absence of their own identity and from the past glory of the Empire only nostalgia of belonging to the Great Genghis Khan continued merely as a slogan. By the fourteenth century the last Mongol Empire in China Yuan Dynasty had fallen and the outnumbered and alienated Mongol tribes had to confine themselves again to the Steppe region of Mongolia.

Adoption of Buddhism

By the fourteenth century military power of the Mongols faded and they lost the feeling of cohesive cultural identity among themselves. The virus of communalization by religious criteria has spread all over the Steppe and the same tribes living on the same steppe ceased to consider each other as the same, because one was Muslim and the other was Buddhist. The Golden Order ruling over the Siberia, Russia and part of Central Asia stopped to consider themselves to be part of the Empire and its Muslim rulers started to look more to west and southward. The Chagatais and the Nogais faced the same situation. Even the Mongols in Mongolia had been divided into three parts by the tribal criteria and were engaged in bloody war.

Neither military power nor nomadic identity feeling played a role anymore and the Mongol Khans felt that there should be something, which would keep the Mongol tribes feeling homogeneity between each other.

Buddhism was chosen to be a State religion. The choice of Indo-Tibetan version of Buddhism was not incidental. Buddhism had succeeded to unite Mongol tribes spiritually and assisted the great degree to the Mongol rulers to counter the threat posed by the Christian, Russia and China.

Introduction of Buddhism to Mongolian society had positive impact at that time. Buddhism has become one of the most important criteria of Mongolian nomadic identity and also Buddhist monasteries have turned into the unique cultural centres of the society. Monasteries kept quite big libraries where not only Buddhist texts, but also many books related to the traditional science and history were preserved. A lot of traditions and customs of the Mongols were enriched by Buddhist meanings and already by seventeenth century the Mongol speaking Buddhist nomads were quite different from the Muslim nomads both by religion and language.

Buddhism was the final touch in the formation of the nomadic Mongol society and a society with distinct characteristics of nomadism appeared in the country.

The distinct characteristics of the nomadic Mongolian society were:

1. A special, peculiar way of life, customs and tradition were formed due to the nomadic way of life, providing clear distinction from the settled population of both Russia and China The Mongols elaborated not only agricultural science, fitted to the nomadic civilization, but also bred a special type of cattle suited for the nomadic way of life. The Mongolian livestock does not give plenty of milk or meat as in the settled civilizations, but all milk, meat and other outcomings were available in equal proportions. The livestock was fully prepared to live in the extreme natural conditions of the country. Only by the 30s of this century with the introduction of settled civilizations' achievements, like cattle fences and preparation of fodder, the original Mongolian type of cattle started to lose their characteristics.
2. Special customs were developed connected with the nomadic way of life: gatherings in connection with the felt making, hair cutting of a baby, songs to make cattle to accept the rejected baby etc. With the introduction of Western or European science of cattle breeding these customs started to fade away.

3. A special type of dwellings called *ger*, was developed by the Mongols: wooden structure dismembered in one hour, brought to other place and fitted in two hours.
4. The calendar designed to fit the nomadic way was designed with a number of holidays fully suited to the need of their way of life. The main events of this calendar were Tsagaan sar, or the Mongolian new year (usually after the new year the cold of the winter comes down), Hansh Day (the day, on which all animals start to wake up after winter sleep and all plants start to blossom etc.).
5. The Mongols developed their script, originally acquired from Uighurs, but developed to the extent that suited all the dialects of the Mongolian language (In fact the Mongols used a dozen scripts out of which only the Uighur script has survived due to its highly developed structure).
6. The Mongols kept a tradition of written history, tradition of respecting the books. The best silk was used to wrap the books, no Mongol would allow himself to step or sit on a book. World famous books like *Secret History of Mongols, Golden History* and *Crystal Mirror* were written by the Mongols.
7. Buddhist religion gave to the Mongols not only the clear distinction from the neighbours, preserving the nation from Christian Russia, Confucian China and Muslim Central Asia, but also Buddhist monasteries were turned to the cultural centres of the Mongols. Most of the educated people lived in the monasteries, creating cultural valuables. Between the nomadic herdsmen and the settled monasteries a special type of symbiosis developed, which at the first instance looked like a religious relationship, but had deeper roots for the meaning of the way of life of society. The Nomads were supplying food, money and other items and supporting the monasteries financially, while the monasteries were acting in their turn as preservators of the tradition and keepers of the intellectual well-being of the nomads.

By the beginning of the twentieth century and after the establishment of the communist regime in Mongolia, the nomadic way of life had undergone serious changes. First of all, systematic campaign to eliminate monasteries were brought on by the authorities, subsequently resulting in a near total elimination of the monasteries (out of 700 monasteries in 1921 only one remained in 1989). With the decline of the monasteries many customs and tradition, which had provided the cultural distinction of the Mongols, faded. The Uighur script was changed to the Cyrillic, cutting off the new generation from the cultural heritage of the previous generations and transforming the logic of language. Many historical manuscripts were ignored under the name of the campaign against religion. The new gregorian calendar was enforced and many holidays which earlier were celebrated by the Mongols were banned. Even the Mongolian new year was declared a holiday only for the herdsmen. With the introduction of European agricultural science the traditional structure of the livestock was deformed. Whether these transformations were made intentionally or unintentionally is a different question to be considered, but definitely these transformations severely affected the traditional Mongolian society.

City culture was actively propagated, resulting in the spread of consumer attitude among the nomads. Today the city population and countryside nomad population look like arrivals from two completely different civilization. In the cities the Europeanization was carried out systematically and successfully.

Only by the end of the eighties and beginning of the nineties, as a result of democratic changes in the country, the Mongols were able to address these questions freely. Nowadays many things are attempted to discover and revive the old cultural and traditional heritage. The religion is on the way to revival: only during the last three years the number of monasteries has reached 100.

The Government is taking steps to reintroduce the Uighur script. In fact the English language and Uighur script are now facts for everybody. Also many efforts are being made to revive the customs and traditions lost by our generation.

One thing is clear. Despite all these efforts it is now impossible to revive fully the old traditional society. Nowadays the most important question is how to find a proper combination of modernity and traditionality in Mongolian society. The Mongols should revive the nomadic technology, fitted to their own way of life, old traditions and customs and cultural heritage, which provided distinction from other civilizations, but on the other hand, they should adapt themselves to the challenges of the twenty-first century and realities of the modern world in order to find their own place in the fast modernizing world community. How well it is done only the time will show.

9

Quest for Cultural Identity in Turkey

National Unity of Historical Diversities and Continuities

Bozkurt Güvenç

Because of our traditions
everybody knows who he is.
Fiddler on the Roof

Deep in sleep, I ask myself:
who am I tonight?
In which age, where?
My task is to give life to words
to spin the yarn of the mind
to weave the human spirit
in all its passions, yearnings, jealousies and loves
into this narrow yet boundless frame.
Epilogue, the play, I, Anatolia,
Dilmen and Halman (1991: 64-65)

I, against my brother,
I and my brother against our cousin,
I, my brother and our cousins against the stranger.
Arab Saying (Gellner 1981: 64)

In memoriam of
Mr Srinivas, who had
urged fellow anthropologists
to study their own societies.
Victor Turner
(Myerhoff 1978: Foreword)

Questions of cultural identity in Turkish development is hereby presented, by introducing conceptual frame of human identities, reviewing historical antecedents of the case, touching upon premises and purposes of the Turkish (Kemalist) Revolution, reflecting identity problems presently encountered, and concluding with an overview of mediations and prospects.

Conceptual Frame: Identities and Identification Processes

Identity may nowadays be taken as answers to the specific question "Who are you?" ID or bank cards, driver's licences and passports constitute one sub-type of individual identity. They certify, the names, birth place and date, a recent photo, an address of the individual, name or logo of the institution or authority issuing the document, the duration of validity, etc. Such a document or two of them is sufficient to identify or, at least, locate the person. ID cards, serving the purpose of distinguishing one person from others, may be classified and referred to as the **individual identity**.

Real persons would hardly consent or be satisfied, however, to identify their beings with their ID cards alone. One's sense of own identity or perception of self-existence would, by and large, include complementary information found in one's *curriculum vitae,* such as, sex, martial status, kinship, parenthood, schools attended, vocational, religious or political affiliations, hobbies, clubs, ranks or positions held in voluntary associations, beliefs, aspirations and the cosmologies, etc. Preferential or self-proclaimed identities as above may be called **Personal Identities**, in contra-distinction of **individual** ID's given or taken away by public institutions. Personal identity is at once subjective and objective, individual and social. Unlike the individual identities, however, personal identities or identifications relate or tie the individuals to others and institutions, private or public. In its subjective sense, personal identity is a **homeostatic** feeling of sameness or oneness, a comfort giving **continuity** through the **changing** times and spaces, including circumstantial roles that one has to play throughout life. It is an internalized image of the I-ego, in a micro-cosmos. Identity in this sense implies a self similarity between the cognizant being and the goals, values and purposes that a person defends or pursues in life.

Social contexts, value symbols and institutions associated with social and/or cultural aspects of identity are bound to change, independent of the individual's adherence to or identification with them. Hence identification with communities, societies and states constitutes a historical problem which requires readjustment, redefinition and even reconfirmation of perceived identities. For viability, modern societies and their states demand to have, at their disposal — if not command — , energies and loyalties of all their members that emerge from developmental growth. When new identities are confirmed, societal bonds are renewed and **supposedly** strengthened.

Towards the "fivefold consideration of the paradigm shift in development ideology" delineated by the organizer of the present seminar, I propose this last category as the **national identity**. When this type of identification fails, however, for many individuals and their societies, **political crises and/or cultural crises** may become inevitable. At this point, identity and ideology become complementary aspects of the relationship between the individual and the group. Ideological crises often search and strive for some higher forms or levels of historical, cultural or national synthesis. This leads to the painstaking, new phase in which old identities are joined, fused, renewed, and even transcended. (Erickson 1968: 64) Whether evolutionary or revolutionary, all kinds of social change due to techno-economic development induce some crisis of identity in functions and structures of society and man. There is no smooth or ideal way (Wilson 1945). A viable ideology by definition is a formal set of values, which guides and unifies individuals' strivings towards a new identity in the next generation. In eliminating the generational gap, the ideology may become a popular way of life or turn into a militant (patrimonial) oppression or radical restoration — often both at the same time, one inducing the other (Lichtenstein 1963).

It is in this conceptual frame of the genesis of "national identity and identification" (Güvenç 1993) that the Turkish case is hereby reviewed.

Antecedents of the Turkish Scene

Who are the Turks? What is their historical allegiance and geographical orientation? Are they an East European or West Asiatic people? Asiatic or European? Is their's a Muslim secular (*laique*) state? Are they natives of Asia Minor or 'nomadic hordes' from Turanian steppes of Asia? Are they despotic rulers or innocent bystanders despotically ruled? Are they descendents of ancient people from Hittites to Romans or the last surviving mercenaries of Genghis Khan, trying to conquer the world on a divine mission.

Are the Turks wandering orphans of the Ottoman Dynasty, defending the Muslim faith against the neo-Crusaders? Or else, as reflected, in the eyes of Western World, fearsome inmates of a prison — turned madhouse, as portrayed by the infamous movie film *The Midnight Express* (made in the late 1970s but being shown to this day, somewhere)? Or simply the trigger-happy invaders of peaceful islanders? Or still, slave-drivers of oppressed minorities, such as the Armenians and the Kurds? And so on.

Are they, in retrospect, conquerers or the conquered? Or both perhaps as in the saying, *Victi victimus*! What is the historical truth if there be such a thing as **the** historical truth? What are the historical (i.e., cultural) roots of such **images and realities**? Are the Turks themselves, solely responsible for the biased judgements or anti-Turkish feelings? (Jogschies 1987: 110)

Turks' answers to some of these relevant questions may be found in Table 9.1 A cursory evaluation of the scenario presented in Table 1, would be that Turks are all that but, of course, a little more. If, for example, other groups of the society were polled, a more diversified pattern of responses would certainly emerge. Modal answers vary by regions (Eastern, Western, Black Sea, Southern etc.); by ethnicity and mother tongue (Abhazian, Albanian, Aegean, Arabic, Armenian, Azeri, Bosnian, Bulgarian, Circassian, Georgian, Greek, Kurdish, Laz, Persian); by religious denomination of Muslims (Sunnites, Shi'ites, Alawis, Bektashis, Mawlavis, Nakshibendis, Tahtajis, etc.) and by non-Muslims (Christians, Jews etc.). Such a complex mosaic of diverse identities that Turkish citizens do remember their being Turk at cross-national circumstances and international contests. Turks have an existential philosophy for distinguishing individuals from the society, rather than integrating them with unifying symbols beyond the home community. As observed by Gellner (1983: 13), "In a traditional milieu, an ideal of a single, overriding and cultural identity makes little sense."

Before the First World War, the agrarian Turkey had become a semi-colony of imperialism. (Novicev 1937) The 'semi-colony' diagnosis, which is generally verified by Turkish economists and scholars (Cavdar 1970) and was accepted by the leader Atatürk himself (Okcun 1968).

Table 9.1

Turks' Answers to the Question : 'Who are You?'

Sub-Cultural Groups	Answers*
Eternal Peasants	"We are **villagers**, living here peacefully at the centre of the world, ever since the **creation** !"
Conservative Townsmen	"Grace be to Allah, we are true **Muslims**, defending our faith against the **infidels** !"
Nomadic Tribesmen	"Hailing from Turanian Steppes, we are **pioneers** of a noble tradition. We are not going to settle down like **peasants**. We shall endure."
Business Community (Urbanites)	"We are kin cousins of the Western Civilization. We are the first and genuine **Westerners** !"
Guardians of the State (Patrimonial Republicans)	"We are **guardians** of the Turkish Republic, entrusted to us by the late, great Atatürk.

* Modal answers of 'ideal types' as observed in the field (by Güvenç, 1993).

In the *long-duree* perspective of historical continuities (Paz 1985), the agrarians of Asia Minor have always sustained and survived the central powers succeeding one another: Say, from Hittites down to Ottomans, whether they were stable, indigenous states or transcient invaders like Darius, Alexander the Great, Crusaders, Timurlane or Mongols etc. (Muller 1958) Natives made history either by soldiering and feeding the armies of the ruling states or else, by resisting against them. Like traditional (oral) societies elsewhere, they did not write their own histories. Nor, official scribes hardly ever saw them as worthy of history. In the *Cradle of Civilization* and *Loom of History* 'eternal peasants' remained historiless. When they made history, however, the state often seemed in trouble (Inalcik 1973: 50-52). Agrarians had their time-tested cultures, in which "Mores made everything right" (Sumner 1960). There has always been a steady but one-way migration from the countryside to towns and cities (i.e., from rural to the urban). Those who went out hardly came back and the two worlds, making up the 'great tradition' (Wolf 1966), never closed the gulf yawning wide between them. By sheer irony of semantics, the most ambitious or comprehensive regional development project ever undertaken in Turkey is now known by the acronym GAP, standing for "South Anatolian Project". So observed Halman (1979: 579):

> Popular culture in the Ottoman State, keeping alive the Turkic rather than the Islamic patterns of thought and values, also constituted a sub-rosa system of deviation from the Ottoman norms.

In Asia Minor, their distinct yet distant co-existence has continued through modern times. Until 1950, the rural/urban breakdown of the settlements remained nearly six to one (85% rural to 15% urban, taking all municipalities above 2000 as 'urban'). This ratio was not much different from the Neolithic Era of Mesopotamia (Cole 1961). That is, peasants were living in their universal solitude (Cf Paz's *Mexico* 1961; with Stirling's *Turkish Villages* 1966). Historical continuity of peasant cultures is not readily affected by technological development or modernization projects drawn in far away capital cities. How could a modern nation be built out of these isolated and insulated villages based on self-subsistence? When, for example, Atatürk declared that "Peasant is our master", the age-old peasant wisely declined the honorific. He was much too sophisticated for sweet talks (see Cartoon 1). Revolutionary slogans of development did not bridge the gap.

In the 1930s Republican People's Party founded for, and entrusted with, overseeing the welfare of Turkish Revolution, held that the country had been sufficiently developed. What remained to be done was the universal education of those 'eternal peasants' over there — somewhere. Hence the "Village Institute Movement" was conceived and engineered as an "Educational mobilization for social change" (Kirby 1962 and Kazamias 1966). The editor-in-chief of the semi-official daily *Ulus* (i.e., nation), was commissioned to prepare an *ad hoc* compilation (titled "Our Villages") to convince President Inönü, who wished to be better informed about villages before giving his consent. Thereby was started the Village Education Movement. For reasons of their own, majority of villagers never approved nor supported the idea, even less its implementation. In 1950, on the eve of the first democratic election ever held in Turkey, the whole Institute Movement fell down like a dream house built of playing cards. Democrats took over the government. Despite several military interventions since for causes of national unity (1960), peace and order (1971) and the 'restoration' of "Kemalist Reforms" (1980), democratic parties and their coalitions managed to remain in power. To better appreciate social dynamics of, and reaction to, the development and change, one has to turn to premises and purposes of the Turkish Revolution, generally referred to as 'Kemalism' after Mustafa KEMAL Atatürk founder and the first President of Turkish Republic (Turkish National Commission for UESCO 1960).

Premises and Purposes of the Turkish Revolution — Kemalism

Atatürk saw the problem of his nation simply as the "Creation of a new Turk". "The foundation of the Republic will be culture" he declared. Adding however, "Not the obsolete, anachronical and foreign cultures left over from/imposed by the imperial era, but a **national culture** suitable to our character and history, which will earn a rightful place for the secular Republic among the family of modern (i.e., developed) nations of the World."

That, Atatürk was after or up to a total **culture change** may be read in the following dictum:

> The purpose of our revolution is to render the people of Turkish Republic a modern and civilized society, in every and true sense of the words, in substance and in appearance.

According to Atatürk, the only way for having national independence and safeguarding "peace at home and abroad" is to follow the path of **culture or civilization**. He described his vista-vision in a Tylorian (1871) fashion:

> Separating culture from civilization is difficult and unnecessary. So, let me tell you what I mean by 'culture'. *Culture is the sum total of all things* that a nation can achieve (a) in public administration, (b) in arts and sciences, and (c) in the field of economy; namely, agriculture, commerce and industry — including land, sea and air transportation and communication. Civilization of a nation then is none other than the end product of the three components mentioned above [Emphasis supplied]

This new concept of culture or civilization that was to create the new Turk and Turkey may perhaps be ascribed as

(1) Nominally universalistic,
(2) Positively rationalistic and scientific
(3) Conceptually holistic — rather than reductionist

CARTOONS
in humor veritas

1 Masters of the Land

—"Oh, Great Atatürk, here we'are
—"*Masters of the Country*!"
by Sadi Dinçcag (*Akbaba* 1962)

2 Secular Politics
(implied without caption)

by Turhan Selçuk
(*Milliyet*, December 11, 1957)

(4) Politically revolutionary — rather than reformist
(5) Basically Western oriented
(6) Substantially secular and/or laic(ist).

A word or two may be in order about this program. Atatürk's concept of world history is quite in line with the evolutionary thinking of the nineteenth-century Europeans. He saw civilization as the common pool of all mankind. The Ottomans have failed, mainly because they fell out of the mainstream of development. Since civilization was not under the monopoly of the Westerners Turks, like all other nations, could be a member, rather than victim of it. Towards this end he founded museums, historical research institutes, supported archaeological excavations and encouraged their publications through the History Foundation of Turkey. He boldly declared:

Science is the most reliable guide in life!

This positivistic epigraph, which has remained engraved on the main façade of Ankara University, was contrary to the popular belief that "Faith (in Islam) is the *one and only guide* in life." To counter-balance the Islamic predominance in public ethos, he spoke about the pre-Islamic existence, and speculated about bright (post-Islamic) future of the Turkish nation. Unlike the Turkish and Muslim scholars of his generation advocating in unison to adopt Western technology and preserve Eastern culture (i.e., Islam), he did not distinguish between culture and technology but saw the modern technology as an inseparable component of industrial culture. "In modernization, we shall catch with, and rise above the contemporary civilization", he willed. In this *holistic* attitude and radical program, he anticipated 'technolithic' taxonomy of cultures, later proposed by archaeologist Childe (1943 and 1951).

Atatürk was convinced that all "man-made institutions" of culture could be changed and developed by Man himself. He tried all he could and entrusted the remaining work to the future youth of the Nation. In changing the Quranic script, he was a unique revolutionary of his times. He believed that for progress change was necessary and inevitable — though admittedly all changes may not necessarily be progressive. In order to further accelerate the creation of the new man and society, informal re-education of the parents was to be realized in the Folk Houses and Chambers of culture innovated for this purpose (see Box).

School Physics or Cultural Enlightenment?

As students in six grade, in 1937, we did not have a qualified physics teacher to handle the Leybold instrument sets, just imported from Germany. I saw the first sound-movies, stage-plays, orchestra concerts, public library, Western style balls and dances, table-tennis, etc. in the Folk House of our rural town, illuminated at nights by the small and noisy power generator of the House. I missed Newtonian physics but caught a glimpse of the enlightenment — that was coming.

To improve the yield of national education the Turkish language was "cleansed and purified" from loan-words (mostly Arabic and Persian) and expressions. It was this reform which tied **culture, language and education** together and enabled the Turks to think in their mother tongue. Kemalist Revolution was committed to building a contemporary society and modern nation along the Western lines. The emphasis, however, was on **modernity and development, not imitation but creation**. Western sources and resources were examined, adapted but not adopted. The motto was *Turk, be proud, work hard and trust.*

Another maxim of the time, "We resemble ourselves" implied that we Turks are and going to be Turks. The goal was not, **Westernization but modernization**, that is, development and progress in time-space.

Last but foremost, the Kemalist Revolution tried to build a *laic* nation out of parochial communities, over 90 per cent of which professed to adhere to Islam. Alawis were more liberal than the orthodox Sunnis, but Muslims nevertheless. This program, which seemed to be well trenched in urban centres, had no visible effects in "forty thousand" or so many villages and was hopelessly grounded in conservative or provincial townships.

Identity Problems Related to Development

Democrats, who replaced the Republican People's Party in 1950, had clearly seen that the Kemalist Revolution had reached and taken over about one-third of the population. Two-thirds of the (rural) majority were either unaffected, undecided or non-committal. In the 'democratic' decade of 1950s, Governments followed a four-point development program: **Road, Water, Land and Mosque**, all for the village. In the 1960s **schools and health centres** were added; in the 70s **energy and irrigation projects started**, in the 80s **telephone networks** were nearly completed. Improvements in Public health (TB, malaria, pox etc.) and school services have rapidly reduced the infant and crude death rates and raised the national life expectancy from about 35 to about 65 years of age in less than two generations. This mild case of population explosion has so far been doubling the population in less than a generation. As a result of internal migration (attributed to rural push and urban pull), more than half of all Turkish citizens (including the unemployed) now make their living in urban centres. Moreover, nearly two-thirds of all urban dwellers are of rural (village) background. Squatter communities of the town are known as *Gecekondu* meaning 'built overnight'. As the urban centres keep on growing at this rate, quality of municipal life steadily fall. No system of management could cope with the acceleration of growing demands. Estimated unemployment rates vary between 10 to 20 per cent of the active population. Annual inflation rates have stabilized at about 65 per cent. Social dynamics have taken over the five-year development plans, and yearly programs are no longer debated by the daily press; while draft projects for **land, tax, education, health and income distribution reforms** are endlessly processed in bureaucratic or parliamentary committees. According to official statistics, the economy is growing at the rate of 5 per cent and the population 2.5 per cent. Development processes have reached a **homeostatic** phase. Hey-days are over. Consolidation (i.e., overhaul) has become a magic word. State-planned transition to liberal capitalism is well underway, the economy is struggling to privatise her state enterprises. This is where the nation stands today. What else could be done shall remain a speculation. People are presumably better off than ever before as the average per capita income (expressed in US $) is said to be rising but the parity of Turkish Pound keeps falling, irrespective of the dollar. Entrepreneurs enjoy gains, underprivileged ones sustain losses, others in between try to keep their own. Turkish nation is probably coming of age in a hurry. In the rush of daily chores there is not much time for reflecting about identity.

While well educated, well-to-do citizens with status may lean towards Turkish national identity and see themselves as Turks, private citizens of various ethnic origins may prefer their Muslim heritage. This basic dichotomy brews two intermediary identities like **Muslim Turks** and **Turkish Muslims**. While most Turks are gracefully well disposed to all religious identities, radical and orthodox Muslims do not share or reciprocate this tolerance. Muslim ideology does not allow for, or legitimize, intermediary identities between Islam and Muslims. Since the 1970s and 80s, the "Club of (Muslim) Intellectuals" (Aydinlar Ocagi 1973) has been actively trying to reconcile this ideological polarity. Their formal proposal known as the "Turk-Islam Synthesis" was adopted by the Armed Forces in 1983 as the "National Culture Plan". Güvenç *et al.* (1991) showed that it was simply a deception. The essence of the master plan was 'Islam' disguised and presented as 'National Culture'. After a decade of trial and many errors, the plan appears to be a wreck but not abandoned. Although the Muslim camp do refer to 98 per cent popular adherence, it is an assigned identity rather than volutional one. Political conflicts of interest amongst Muslim factions may be as fundamental as those between Muslims and non-Muslims. Islam is State politics *par excellence.* In Turkey, orthodox (Sunnite) and radical (Shi'ite) Muslim images are further handicapped by their rumoured affiliations with, and sources of, finance from followers of *Sharia.* Radical Muslims for their part openly claim that laics (i.e., Turkists) are heathen. Some political leaders try to mediate by announcing that *laicité* is not paganism, without clarifying, however, what it actually is. Head on conflict between laics and Muslims may thus be reduced to alternatives of **culture or religion**. If cultural identity may in fact be equated with language (as suggested by Braudel 1980) and if "Turk is he who speaks the Turkish Language" (as proposed by Roux 1979), then, the actual dichotomy is simply between language and religion (Geertz 1963). In a parallel vein, since Arabic is the language of Quran, the identity question lends itself to the dichotomy of Turkish *vs* Arabic ! Here, I believe, lies the essence of the problem. Turks find the integrity and the independence of their cultural being in Turkish language; radical Muslims violently oppose any resurrection or renaissance of the modern Turkish. Subconsciously, Turks internalize their mother tongue as a symbol of their cultural identity, **against** all likely intruders. (Fishman 1973: 79-80) [cf. the Arabic epigraph of this paper, quoted from Gellner]

Caught in this multi-faccted flux, where "everybody is against everybody else", is a distinctly Turkish phenomenon, which has come to be known as 'Arabesque' According to anthropologist Stokes (1979), the **Arabesque** (as observed in films and heard as distinct music), reflects the drama **(alienation)** of Turkish peasants who cannot adopt, or integrate with, the urban way of life. Scenarios and librettos are all in Turkish with Arabic decoration, dramatic stories sound Turkish but monophonic and monochromatic melodies favour Arabian flavours. It is, at best, a naive caricature of the Turkish-Arabic synthesis. Melodies and stories leave an *Avare mu* (melancholic, bitter) taste, similar to the famous film made in India by the same title, which was very popular in Turkey for many years. **Arabesque** heroes — not so much the heroines — seem to enjoy their depression, solitude and sufferings. They yearn, try their best but get nowhere and resolve, at the end, to accepting their fates. Japanese culture's traditional *mono no avare*, too, interpreted by Tazawa (1973: 1), as the "saddening beauty of autumn", rather sounds like the Turkish **Arabesque**.

Both Western and Islam oriented Turks have displayed anti-**Arabesque** attitudes. Born in collective taxicabs, driven by migrant country boys, **Arabesque** had once grown into several hundred million dollar media industry and was doing until recently rather well in the R-TV networks. According to the video and audio sales and ticket-box returns of popular **Arabesque** stars, 20 to 25 per cent of the Turks appeared addicted to this melancholic mood. Today, however, with an unprecedented media explosion of private TV and Radio stations managed by urban youth, a healthful variety of aesthetic moods have dethroned the **Arabesque**. The episode seems practically over.

Overview of Mediations and Prospects

While revolutionary ideology had aimed to create a modern (laic) republic, the Democratic Movement collaborating with the die-hard Muslims has successfully staged an anti-laic restoration of the revolution (cf Cartoon 2). *Laïcité* equated with modernity (i.e., development and change) and Islam identified with sacred morality (conservatism and continuity) are opposing one another. The Muslim roots are certainly stronger than they appear. The Laic Front, however, is not as fragmented and disorganized as it once suspected. Mysterious killing of columnist Mumcu of the daily *Cumhuriyet*, the champion spokesman for the laic ideology of Kemalism, has brought unprecedented reactions from the left and right alike. Eventual victory is anybody's guess. A reconciliation without a show-down or a civil war seems more likely. The final round will probably be decided upon by the sweeping, **new aesthetic** mood breathing and enjoying the freedom of expression. The outcome of liberal economic development will be another factor to contend with. People still have their trust in development and democracy. They prefer to believe that, in the long run — though "in the long run we will all be dead" according to Keynes — it will soon be possible to overcome structural handicaps and join the family of developed nations. If the liberal economic policies fail, however, radical Islamic and/or neo-corporatist praties may become strong alternatives for power. Since the revolutions must and do export their ideology, Turks already had a first hand chance to observe what they will be like. Unofficially there are nearly one million political refugees in the country. Though, the Radical Islam cannot certainly be ruled out; it seems possible but highly improbable. Historical conflict between Sunnites and Shi'ites is another obstacle. Turkish society, by and large, seems to have cut the theocratic *Rubicon*. Despite the propaganda that Islam is advancing for an eventual take-over, the national popularity of Radical Islam at the polls varies between 10 and 15 per cent. Hence, young Muslim ideologues seek and find conciliatory platforms. They even appear receptive to recent prepositions for re-interpreting Quran — in Turkish, of course — which may be the first revolution in the Orthodox Islam.

The question of identity *vis-à-vis* development or otherwise boils down to philosophical riddles like one or many, monism or pluralism, unity or diversity, solidarity or uniformity etc. Islam, founded on Oneness (One God, One Prophet, One State, One Belief, One People) has already diversified for survival. Western World, coming from polytheism, two prophets, several states, scores of churches and multiplicity of faiths try to be united. Blue prints of the New Architecture of Europe calls for **several culture, many languages and a variety of religions**. The motto: *Unity is diversity/Diversity in unity*, has been one of the guidelines of Western Democracies. It was a happy occasion to learn from the Preamble of Seminar invitation that unity-diversity paradigm is also one of the landmarks of Eastern Wisdom (*Ex oriente lux* !). Contrary to Kippling's false prediction, twins meet as we do.

What are the prospects of Turkish society for seeing this light, reach her horizon? Though, as a student of Mankind, I am neither ready nor willing to make hasty projections of things to come I wish to conclude with two hopeful — if not wistful — afterthoughts:

- Findings of a recent public opinion survey (conducted in Istanbul by a professional public poll agency (Konda 1993) about the self or cultural identity of people living in the city) are given in Table 2. They suggest that **We, Turks are perhaps acquiring a national identity !**
- Socio-cultural histories of mankind, rather than "official histories" of nationalistic states, may help the human ethos in appreciating "who are we?", and in anticipating or preparing for enigmatic

problems of new identities waiting ahead. **Man can and do learn from History!**

Table 9.2

Who are the Istanbulians?

Answers	%
Turk	69
Muslim Turk	21
Muslim	4
Kurd	4
Others (than above)	+ 2
Total	100

Source: Konda 1993.

Notes : (1) More than two-thirds majority of the metropolitans identify I-self as "TURK".

(2) Nearly one-fifth feels "Muslim TURK" — not Turkish MUSLIM, however.

(3) Muslims and Kurds who overtly decline the TURKISH identity are less than 5%.

(4) Sample and methodology are not yet disclosed, hence they wait to be verified.

(5) Findings should be taken as tentative.

References

Aydinlar Ocagi, 1973. *Turkiye'nin Meseleleri* (Problems of Turkey). Istanbul: Aydinlar Ocagi.

Braudel, Fernand, 1980. *On History*. Chicago: UCP.

Cavdar, Tevfik, 1970. *Osmanlilarin Yari-sömürge Olusu* (Ottomans' semi-colonization). Istanbul.

Childe, V. Gordon, 1946. *What happened in History?* New York: Pelican.

———, 1951. *Man Makes Himself.* New York: American Library-Mentor.

Cole, S., 1961. *The Neolithic Revolution.* London: British Museum.

Dilmen, G. and T. Halman, 1991. *I-Anatolia* (a stage play in verse). Ankara: Ministry of Culture.

Erickson, Erick, 1968. "Psychosocial Identity", In *IESS*, VIII: 61-65.

Fishman, Yoshua, 1973. *Language and Nationalism.* Rowley: Newbury House.

Gellner, Ernest, 1881. *Muslim Society.* Cambridge University Press.

———, 1883. *Nations and Nationalism.* Cambridge University Press.

Geertz, Clifford (Ed.), 1963, "Civic Politics", In *Old Societies and New States*, pp. 105-57.

Güvenç, Bozkurt, *et al.*, 1991. *Türk-Islam Sentezi Dosyasi* (File of Turkish-Islam Synthesis). Istanbul: Sarmal Yayinevi.

———, 1993. *Türk Kimligi* (Turkish Identity in print). Ankara: Ministry of Culture.

Halman, Talat, 1973. *Turkey from Empire to Nation: Review of National Literature.* New York: St. John University IV, 1.

Inalcik, Halil, 1973. *The Ottoman Empire Classical Age: 1300-1600.* London: Weidenfeld and Nicholson.

Jogschies, Rainer, 1987. *Das neu Lexikon der Vorurteile.* Frankfurt am Main: Eichborn.

Kazamias, A.M., 1966. *Education and Quest for Modernity in Turkey.* London: Allen.

Kirby, Fay, 1960. "The Village Institute Movement in Turkey: An Educational Mobilization for Social Change." (Unpublished Ph.D. Thesis.) Teachers College, Columbia University.

Lichtenstein, H., 1963. "The Dilemma of Human Identity", In *JAPA.* II: 173-223.

Muller, H.J., 1958. *The Loom of History.* New York: Harper and Row.

Myerhoff, Barbara, 1978. *Number our Days.* New York: Simon and Schuster.

Novicev, 1979 (1937). *Osmanli Imparatorlugunun Yari-sömürgelesmesi* (Semi-colonization of the Ottoman Empire). Ankara: Onur.

Ökçün. Gündüz, 1968. *Türkiye Iktisat Kongresi* (Economy Congress of Turkey, 1924). Ankara: Sevinç Matbaasi.

Paz, Octavio, 1961. *The Labyrinth of Solitude* (translated by Lysander Kemp). New York: Grove Press, Inc.

———, 1985. *One Earth, Four or Five Worlds: Reflections on History.* New York: Harcourt Brace-Jovanowich.

Roux, Jean-Paul, 1979. *Turquie.* Paris: Librairie Arthaud.

Stirling, Paul, 1966. *Turkish Village.* New York: John Wiley.

Stokes, Martin, 1979. "Music, Fate and State: Turkey's *Arabesque* Debate", In *Middle East*

Report. Sept-Oct.: 27-30.

Sumner, W.G., 1960. *Folkways.* New York: Mentor.

Tazawa Yutaka, *et al.*, 1973. *Japan's Cultural History: A Perspective.* Tokyo: Teikoku-Shoin.

Turkish National Commission for UNESCO - 1960s *Atatürk* (in German, French and English). Ankara:UNESCO.

Tylor, E.B., 1871. *Primitive Culture I.* London: J. Murray.

Wilson, G., 1945. *The Analysis of Social Change.* Cambridge University.

10

Popular Culture and Arabesque Music in Turkey

Meral Özbek

The so-called 'arabesque' music in Turkey has been the most popular musical genre since late 1960s. Although the founder and still the 'king' of this genre is a middle-class, self-taught musician Orhan Gencebay, its first consumers were the people of the 'gecekondu' (literally, built-up over night), that is the rural migrants of the squatter settlements around the big cities who worked mostly in the informal sector. The consuming public has thereafter expanded to include the rural and middle class people, and also a fraction of the new economic and ruling classes of the 1980s. The musical genre has diffused so much that arabesque began to be considered a trans-class taste and people have also come to accept the arabesque with its "neither Eastern nor Western" quality has become a way of life.

Arabesque music is very melodic and emotional. The main theme of the lyrics has always been 'love'. Every other theme, especially in the early lyrics, melts into and speaks through the authority of love. The early lyrics are usually made up of 'traditional' concepts but the articulation of the words and the sound of the music reveals an overall meaning as an invention of tradition, with connotations able to be articulated to a popular discontent referring to a mode of living at the corners of an urban environment. Still, the abstractness of the language and the fact that no directly concrete daily problems related to the life around the big cities are mentioned in the lyrics need be explained. The musical structure of arabesque is hybrid, blending both Turkish Classical and Folklore music's rhythms, modes, forms and instruments and popular Western rhythms, instruments and scoring system for individual instruments. Although the music is homophonic, attempts are made to render it polyphonic. And since the end of the 1960s the genre has undergone change, given birth to many versions, differentiated as it got more popular and thus reproduced itself with different audiences, as the music industry developed and social relations and people changed. In time, especially in the 1980s, it became more of a medium of entertainment, football game's musical slogans and political campaign songs, while it also produced its so-called 'revolutionary arabesque' and 'Islamic arabesque' versions. Arabesque music influenced other popular musical genres too, that is classical Turkish music, folkloric music, pop music which are also officially permitted on the state TV, especially with its melodic patterns, rhythmic emphasis and performance of the instruments and the singer.

The diffusion of arabesque music has for almost 20 years been primarily by the cassette-industry, music halls, taxi's (through cassette-recorder and the police-radio) and street peddlers, since its transmission from the state-controlled TV and radio was prohibited. Arabesque music's some leading singers had shown on a couple of New Year nights entertainment programmes and films of some of the leading names had been shown on the TV since the end of the 1970s and the viability of its prohibition began to be discussed at the state level at the end of 1980s. There was no solution to the discussion except for an attempt to ameliorate arabesque officially beginning by a production of a 'nongrieved/griefless' arabesque songs which did not succeed. So it was the 'illegally legal' private TV Star-1 which first opened its screens widely to arabesque in 1992 with the motto "people want it".

The bureaucrats and intellectuals of diverse political inclinations in Turkey have shared the opinion that arabesque is tasteless and grieved and reflect the alienation of the new urban migrant citizens who brought the village with them to the big cities degrading the city (esp. Istanbul). "A music of alienation" is the major concept coined to arabesque in the Encyclopaedia of Music. The left in general emphasized that arabesque is traditional (backward), preaches fatalism, suffering, suitable for manipulation and does not embody any protest; it is at most 'the opium of the masses'. The Turkish Classical and Folklore musicians condemned it for corrupting classical forms due to the both Arabic and Western influences. As a matter of fact, the word 'arabesque' has carried a negative connotation from the beginning and its meaning grew like a snowball with each new connotation. The word was first coined in the 1960s to mean that the new music was an imitation of arabic music due to the infusion of the Egyptian melodic nuances and the style of the string performance. Then the word came to be used as an adjective to name almost everything and every aspect of social life considered to be degraded, which really meant matching neither with 'traditional' nor 'modern' forms (arabesque democracy, economy, people, situation, taste, feelings, way of thinking and living). But after the 1983s it also gained a negative political connotation. This is because although the majority of 'gecekondu' people had voted for (a populist) social democracy between the years 1969 and 1977 (and the 'gecekondu's had built up in some areas left militancy in the late 1970s), in the first elections after the 1980 military coup majority of them voted for the neo-liberal ANAP. And though the prohibition of arabesk on the state TV continued till the competition created by the private TVs forced it to change itself, the new ruling elite (most notably the then prime minister of the ruling ANAP) liked versions of arabesque music and used it in their election campaigns.

I have serious objections to the mainstream conceptualization of arabesque and argue against its basic assumptions by trying to explain the complexity of arabesque formation and its historical transformation from a critical perspective. The arguments raised are against what the mainstream assumes: the social significance of popular songs can be understood only by analyzing its lyrics and only with reference to the alleged 'alienated' characteristics of its consumers; 'degradation' is a suitable 'scientific' concept to explain and understand the rich complexity of the concrete processes or forms; and only the educated and the elite can create Culture. It assumes cultural forms must be pure in national-ethnic sense and that there is a natural correspondence between tastes, political choices and social positions, that cultural forms and forms of practical consciousness are unified totalities with no contradiction and complexity, that popular culture is a product of total manipulation and arabesque culture is fatal preaching only suffering. The mainstream states that the articulation of arabesque into the 1980s dominant ideology can be explained by its already segregation and openness to manipulation, and that arabesque culture or any other aspect of social life in Turkey can be analyzed by a framework based on a traditional-modern duality derived from the Modernization Theory — although modernization as a Westernization process in Turkey with its mono-cultural politics has a lot to do with the formation of arabesque music as a resistance. The implication of all these assumptions is the pessimistic implication that arabesque-loving people are already lost for any emancipatory ideological/political struggle or the commanding implication of the necessity of 'manipulative' education or the too optimistic/ simple implication that economic development will eventually restore everything.

11

Cultural Pluralism and National Cultural Identity

The Case of Nepal

Dilli R. Dahal

'Culture' and 'Cultural Identity' are sensitive topics. Often, they are hard to define. While explaining the diversity of human cultures or developing a concept of nation state, these topics are discussed either narrowly or broadly by philosophers, political scientists, cultural historians and anthropologists. It is easy to define an indigenous culture or a culture of a particular group, as most anthropologists do. However, it becomes an immensely difficult task to define a national culture or cultural identity of a nation, especially when a nation is composed of diverse ethnic/caste groups with different race, language, religion and culture. History has already shown that when there is an 'artificial' conglomeration of cultures, a nation gradually falls apart in the name of language, religion, race or culture. The tragic conflict between the Tamil and the Sinhala, the breakdown of the Soviet Union and Yugoslavia and the frequent Hindu-Muslim riots in India are recent examples. The problems in each case are the cultural identities of the people as expressed through language, race, religion, caste and culture.

In this article, I provide a case study of Nepal, which has been facing a serious cultural identity crisis in recent years, despite its long unified cultural history. I argue that this has happened because of the regular attempt by rulers, who wanted to develop a homogeneous Nepali culture within the frame of Hindu political ideals and without seriously considering the diversity and complexity of the Nepali culture. Here, I put together facets of history, sociology and politics to argue my case.

Historical Perspective of Nepali Culture

Nepal, a small Himalayan Kingdom sandwiched between India and China, is a cultural mosaic forming a unique kind of multi-ethnic and caste society, throughout its history. There are about 140 distinct ethnic/caste groups, who have lived side by side for the past 2,000 years, maintaining separate yet related cultural traditions of their own. This has come to be collectively known as 'Nepali Culture'.

Today, the Nepali culture in essence, is the combination of the following three distinct elements:

(i) A culture representing the four distinct categories of people: (The caste-origin Hindu groups; the ethnic/tribal groups; the Muslims and others, Sikh, Bengali, and Marwari and Christians). Of them, the caste-origin Hindu groups represent approximately 70 per cent of the total population of Nepal.[1]

(ii) Racially, two distinct groups of people: the Indo-Aryan (Caucasoid) and the Mongoloids, and

(iii) A culture heavily influenced from the Indian Hindu civilization from the south and the Tibetan Buddhist civilization from the north. In terms of cultural tradition or civilization, Nepal as a whole can be distinctly placed as an interface between the Hindu and the Buddhist civilization (Fisher, 1978).

As Nepal was divided into small kingdoms and principalities before 1768, it is difficult to give an overview of the totality of the Nepali culture. However, it can be said that the Nepali social structure was traditional in nature. There was little ethnic tensions or conflict between ethnic groups or cultures. The family, kinship caste and village were the main forces of social institutions. The people were highly orthodox in their religious attitudes and divided in geographical, linguistic and cultural units. Nobody was seriously concerned about a common language or culture. So, the 'Nepalese' social structure comprised localized and thriving 'local' or 'small traditions' or of 'indigenous village civilization', hardly crossing the caste, creed and ethnic boundaries.

After the unification of Nepal by the Gurkhali King Prithvi Narayan Shah in 1768, the Nepali social structure was gradually enticed with the Hindu model of Great Tradition, albeit without intensively disturbing the local cultures. This peaceful transition was affected through the implementation of the Legal Code of 1854. This Code categorized all the people of Nepal into four distinct orders, without seriously considering the diversity and complexity of the Nepali culture. The orders were:

1. Tagadhari (castes wearing sacred thread),
2. Matwali (liquor consuming castes),
3. *Pani na calne choi chito halnu naparna* (castes from whom water is not accepted, but whose touch does not require aspergation of water), and
4. *Pani na calne, choi chito halnu parne* (untouchable caste).

This Code embodied certain distinct features: commensality, supremacy of Hindu values and religious orthodoxy, and caste as the basis of social mobility. A member, irrespective of his cultural background, breaching these features of Code, was either severely punished, excommunicated or had to accept demotion within the caste hierarchy (Sharma, 1977: 96).

In brief, the regime before 1950 was authoritarian in political structure, without any opposition from any ethnic or cultural group or political parties. Social harmony as well as national cultural identity was maintained by strictly enforcing Hindu laws. In other words, the rulers consolidated their powers by arranging all groups of Nepal in a hierarchial framework of the Hindu caste structure. The Hindu values of morals and merits were enforced to provide the support base for the despotic regime.

Along with the overthrow of the Rana regime in 1950, Nepal opened her door to the outside world encouraging the process of democratization and modernization. But Nepal could not develop a new model of ethnic pluralism. With the introduction of the Panchayat government in Nepal in 1962, the political and social structures of Nepal became more rigid and orthodox. One of the significant aspects of the Panchayat system was its ban on political parties; there was no place for organized political activity and opposition within the system. But even within this given structure, one of the most dramatic changes that took place was the introduction of New Legal Code (Naya Mulki Ain) in 1964. According to this Code, nobody could claim inferiority or superiority on the basis of race, caste and creed; everybody was equal before the law.

No doubt, many of the strictures of the caste system such as the 'defiling' of food and water by the low castes and religious sanctions against anti-caste behaviour have weakened after the introduction of the New Legal Code. But the caste system is alive and, in some cases, has become more distinct and prominent over the years. Caste forms the basis of social interaction among the majority of Nepal's diverse ethnic population and there is a fairly uniform order of caste ranking even today. This is because those ethnic/caste groups whose social position is higher in the traditional hierarchy have usurped much of the power, influence, wealth and prestige available within the system. Thus Brahmanical values have become a model to raise one's socio-economic status and even to identify oneself in the existing structure. This has invariably led towards the process of Sanskritization or Hinduization, providing for more orthodox, stratified, caste-hierarchial values even for those who were originally outside the framework of the caste frame. The process of Sanskritization and Hinduization of a group (whether an ethnic Limbu or an ethnic Thakali) is, therefore, an affirmation and not a negation of the caste system and their values (Jones 1976; Ijima 1977; Sharma 1977; Bista 1971). That is why an untouchable still finds difficulty in locating one's own position within the framework of the *New Legal Code.* Untouchability is not enforceable in courts. The system inadvertently provides a new basis for caste exclusiveness and this has given rise to the creation of ethnic/caste associations such as *Manka Khala* (an association of the Newar community), *Thakali Samaj Sudhar Samitee* (Thakali association), *Magurali* (a joint association of the Magar, Gurung, Rai and Limbu), *Kamatapuri* (a joint association of the Koche, Meche and Tajpuria), *Sadbhawana Parishad* (an association of the people of Terai) and many more. The objectives of these associations, at least theoretically, are to protect one's own language and culture from outside forces, but they see themselves as part of a historical cultural unit which is both exclusive and in opposition to the 'outside'. Cultural identity has already taken the shape of political identity in the context of confrontation over issues such as language, religion, economy and culture.

In brief, though the introduction of the New Legal Code was a bold attempt in the traditional Nepali society, it was already too late to maintain ethnic harmony and integrity as Nepal could not move a step further towards economic modernization. Over the years the people became poorer and economic disparity widened more than before. In other words, the economy could not be transformed to service the projected caste-neutral social structure. This problem has been compounded further by the liberal political structure in the recent years.

Democracy and Forms of Ethnic Tension

After a long struggle, Nepal was able to forms a democratic government in April 1990. This political structure provided avenues for public debates. This has, among others, helped to bring out ethnic tensions in the streets. Three main forms of ethnic divides deserve attention. The first is between the *Pahade* (hillmen) and the *Madhesiya* (plainsmen) based on the regionalism and ethnicity. The second is the split between the high caste Hindu groups (particularly the Hill Brahmin, Thakuri, Chhetri and Newar) and the so-called 'indigenous groups' or *Janjati* of Nepal. The third is the split between the Brahmin and Newar groups and the high caste Hindu groups and the low caste Hindu groups.

Three main groups of people reside in the Terai: the original inhabitants (e.g. Tharu, Dhimal), the people of 'Indian origin' and the hill Nepali people. The influx of hill people suddenly increased in the Nepal Terai after the malaria eradication programme of the late 1950s. Historically, neglect of the Terai people by the hill-dominated government created an outburst of ethnic tension in the Terai. Some Terai leaders, particularly those representing the Hindu caste groups in the 'Sadbhavana Party' have started a *Pahadiya Hatao* campaign to physically remove the hill people from the plains — which might be considered a disturbing trend in national politics These leaders also advocate the use of Hindi as a link language in the Terai, challenging Nepali, the national language of Nepal.

The division between hill people and plains people also seem linked to the uncontrolled flow of Indian migrants crossing the border to settle in the Nepal Terai. Because so many of the groups on either side of the border are culturally identical, it is difficult to differentiate between the Nepali Terai residents from the Indian settlers. Daily familial, cultural and commercial interactions which take place between these groups further complicate matters. In recent years, more and more Indian workers have been coming into Nepal, who settle with their wives and children. That a problem of national identity should arise among the Terai people, as also the fact that hill Nepalese thus question the allegiance of the Terai residents seems natural (Dahal, 1992).

The divide between the high caste Hindu groups and the *Janajati* are also on the forefront these days. The *Janajatis* also feel that they have always been neglected by the Hindu high caste dominated governments of Nepal. They claim that they are the indigenous population of Nepal and demand a share of power in national politics and insist on the recognition of their cultural and linguistic rights. They consider themselves as non-Hindu groups, although the Hindu dominated government of Nepal has always tried to incorporate them within the Hindu caste hierarchical model. The Hindu caste culture is considered as an 'alien culture' by the *Janajatis*. Furthermore, the Brahmin's predominance in every field of life—political, economic and social— is labelled as 'Brahmanbad' and thus the Brahmins have been the subject of attack in recent years in Nepal (Bista 1991; Sharma, 1992).

Likewise, social and political competition between the Newars and the Brahmins is creating serious problems for the nascent democratic structure of Nepal. The Newars of Kathmandu Valley feel that they have been gradually displaced in their home, and by the 'outsiders', particularly the *Parbatiyas* (the hill people), the *Madhesiyas* (the plains people) and the *Bhotiyas* (the Mountain people). (Malla, 1992) Newars actually claim that as they are the original inhabitants of the Valley, they should have access to all fields of Nepalese life-social, economic and political. In fact, considering the present population size of Newars in Nepal (5.5% of the total population), Newars are one of the most benefited groups in the social and economic developments of Nepal.

Finally, conflicts between the high castes and the low castes are emerging rapidly. About 12 per cent of the total population of Nepal consists of untouchables.[2] The New Legal Code, after its three decades of implementation, has not been effective in changing the socio-economic status of the untouchables, and they have the lowest social and the economic status compared to other groups in Nepal. As a consequence, they are raising voices against the dominant Hindu castes.

Finally, the language issue has come on the forefront in recent years. About 60 different languages and dialects are spoken in Nepal. No doubt, all of the languages must be preserved as the cultural heritage, whereas a national language is also most essential for Nepal. The Nepali language has been functioning as the national language of Nepal for over the last two centuries. It is spoken as the mother tongue by more than 50 per cent of the total population. Over the last three decades or so, the Nepali language is being widely adopted throughout the kingdom and spoken by almost all people. But the government is adopting an ambivalent language policy. The Sanskrit language has been made compulsory up to the high school level without considering the diverse language groups whereas the Nepali language is withdrawn as one of the compulsory papers in the examination of Public service Commission in Nepal. How can one be a good official if one cannot write the Nepali language well?

Likewise, the Hindi language is merely a tool for playing politics in the Nepali Terai today for those who feel themselves outside of the Hill Nepali mainstream. Most of the Terai people (excluding the tribal ethnic groups and the hill people) in fact speak not Hindi but the Maithili, Bhojpuri, Bajika (mixture of Bhojpuri and Maithili) and Awadhi languages.

Conclusion

In brief, cultural similarity is not necessarily a diagnostic of common origins (Barth 1969: 9-11). My discussions have demonstrated that social, economic and political conditions of Nepal over the years motivated people to show serious concern over their own ethnicity, race, caste, language, religion and region. This concern is being demonstrated more intensely and publicly after the restoration of democracy thus contradicting the assumption that democracy is the ultimate solution to all ethnic problems of Nepal. The elites as well as the political leaders use the community identification as a tool for their own ends even today. The people who are better educated are becoming more and more culturally self-centred and religiously orthodox. The process of urbanization, transportation, communication and mass-media and new occupations are not helping much to change people's traditional cultural values. This is leading towards a process of cultural disintegration rather than cultural cohesiveness and assimilation. In considering the present changing socio-political contexts, I feel that the government must adopt some cultural policies to develop this country as a multi-cultural nation.

(i) In lieu of the current emphasis on Hindu values-based national culture, a redefinition of Nepali culture is desirable which can incorporate various threads of cultures scattered from the east to the west of Nepal. This task is not easy. We have to develop certain common denominators from every culture of Nepal which can be harmonized as elements of a distinct national cultural identities of people. In other words, these traditional cultural elements must develop themselves into a national culture of Nepal.

(ii) It is an irony to note that Nepal attempted to develop social and political superstructures without an adequate economic base. This has not helped to push democratic institutions forward within the multi-ethnic society of Nepal. Most of the Nepali people feel that they do not share adequately in the economy, polity and social life of Nepal. Hegemony of certain ethnic identities over other identities is seen in many aspects of Nepali society. This is one of the root causes of ethnic and political discontents of various groups in Nepal.

The crucial problem today remains how to cross these socio-cultural barriers of status, language and culture in order to establish relationships of parity and reciprocity. The only solution lies in the promotion of performance based democratic institutions, which requires a stable government with strong commitment in action.

Notes

1. According to the 1991 Census, 89 per cent of the total population of Nepal are Hindus. In fact, only the caste-origin groups can be considered strictly Hindus and others not.
2. According to the 1991 Census, the untouchable hill populations only such as the Kami, Sarki, Damai and Badi make up 8.4 per cent of the total population. There are significant numbers of untouchables among the Newars and within the Terai Hindu communities of Nepal.

References

Barth, F., 1969. *Ethnic Groups and Boundaries* (ed. F. Barth), Boston: Little Brown.

Bista, D.B., 1971. "The Political Innovators of the Upper Kali Gandaki", In *Man*

———, 1991. *Fatalism and Development*, Orient Longman.

CBS, 1991. "The Census of Nepal, 1991", In Central Bureau of Statistics, Kathmandu.

Dahal, Dilli R., 1992. "Grasping the Terai Identity", In *Himal* (May/June).

Fisher, Jim, 1978. *Himalaya Anthropology*, Hague: Mounton.

Iijima, Shijeru, 1977. "Ecology, Economy and Cultural Change among the Thakalis in the Himalayan Kingdom of Central Nepal", In *Changing Aspects of Modern Nepal* (ed. S. Iijima), Institute for the Study of Languages and Cultures of Asia and Africa, Tokyo.

Jones, Rex L., 1976. "Sanskritization in Eastern Nepal", In *Ethnology* Vol. XV, no. 1.

Malla, K.P., 1992. "Bahunvada: Myth or Reality", *Himal* (May/June).

Sharma, P.R., 1977. Caste, Social Mobility and Sanskritization in a Tribal Hindu Society: A Study of Nepal's Old Legal Code", In *Changing Aspects of Modern Nepal* (ed. S. Iijima), Institute for the Study of Languages and Cultures of Asia and Africa, Tokyo.

———, 1992. "How to Tend This Garden", In *Himal* (May/June).

12

National Identity and Development in the Plural Society of Indonesia

S. Budhisantoso

Most developing countries are generally engaged with national development activities with the aim to strengthen national unity and to improve the welfare of the population. In the field of politics national development efforts reflect in the build-up and the strengthening of ideology or other symbols which can accelerate their national unity by throwing away any mark of the old politics and replace them with new ideas.

Several problems usually begin to appear at a time when the nation concerned succeeds to chase away the old regime and starts to constitute a new one. The most outstanding problem they usually have to face is how to unite a nation which consists of a certain number of communities, formerly independent and with diverse social, economic and cultural backgrounds. It is the diversity of a new born society which demands a symbol, acceptable for the whole population and really able to play the function as a basis for the development of the national identity.

Developing countries like Indonesia therefore are ever trying seriously to develop their cultural identity not merely as a specific mark to differ from other nations, but also to create a firm identity for all the citizens. In countries, which are coincidently socially very diverse like Indonesia the building up of a national unity has been often ignored. Lack of attention to the diverse character of the society might result into an asymmetry of development, which could hamper the realization of the unity of the nation (M.G. Smith 1960: 763-77).

This phenomenon is not difficult to understand as the community often has to make a choice of priorities in the implementation of the building of the new borne nation.

Generally a newly independent society tends to put the development of the political sector as the first priority to foster the national unity and at the same time to wipe out all leftovers of the 'foreign' power. In this context people tend to stress their attention to matters to improve the role of the society in political life and to develop public functions and services.

To interpret and channel political aspirations of the people several forms and organizations are developed and maintained in order to create an adequate political condition for the sake of national stability and security. Several laws and regulations for political parties are issued to grant equality of rights and to establish a suitable political condition for the realization of the national desire. Also administrative structures and mechanism are developed and performed by referring to several laws and regulations, which undergo improvement processes from time to time in line with the trend of the social development.

Meanwhile there are also countries which prefer to develop the economical sector as a means to strengthen the national unity of their developing societies. In this case national development are more directed to the development of national systems of currency, banking, trade, transportation and communication as infrastructures to achieve the national development's objectives. The establishment of an integrated economic system often arouses social reactions, not because the society rejects the efforts to improve the national welfare, but they are caused by differences of preceptions and methods to adjust the existing social traditions with the regulations, which are indeed sometimes really strange and invite wider participation of the society. It is also worth considering the reactions of the society against the ever growing intensity of contacts between groups and tribes as motivated by the higher social mobility and information flow, due to the achievements of communication and transportation.

Although social tensions and frictions are usually of temporary character, preceding the readjustment process of the living structure of the community concerned, they should be taken into consideration and properly mended as to achieve the objectives in line with the goals of the national development. Lack of clearly determined objectives and adequate management in the development process of an economic system often arouses social jealousy and frictions, caused by the ever widening of the dividing line between the more fortunate and the less, and the success of the less able in taking the advantages of, and in adjusting themselves to, the new opportunities and challenges.

National Cultural Development

Many of the developing countries ignore the socio-cultural challenges in developing their countries. They take for granted that the culture will develop as their people try to adapt to the new condition. The national leaders think that their people will react to the new challenges in the same way as they do, regardless of the different socio-cultural background and experiences.

In a plural society like Indonesia, development of a national culture as a common frame of reference for the whole nation is inevitable. It is a fact that since the proclamation of the independence, the development of national culture as the many manifestations of the active disposition of the Indonesian to the new challenges has been proceeding very fast.

An American anthropologist has described the national cultural development in Indonesia as an integrative revolution due to its nature. It is an integrative revolution because it succeeds in breaking up the primordial ties based on the family, tribe, local original, belief and language which undergo a widening process of diffusion into a larger integrated group. It means that the success of the building of a nation of national integration of plural societies is actually a readjustment of local traditional primordial ties towards the forming of a new national identity (Deutsch 1961: 449). However, the need for a national cultural identity to unite the plural and previously independent societies is generally ignored by political leaders. The need of a national culture as a common frame of reference for the whole nation is generally defeated by political issues which stimulate a political action instead of cultural response.

Development

Fortunately the Founding Fathers of the R.I. were fully aware of the need of a national culture as a uniting force in the plural society of Indonesia. The awareness is reflected, especially, in paragraph 32 of the National Constitution which orders: "The Government promotes National Culture." In its explanation paragraph, it is mentioned that the National Culture should be based on the "old and genuine" cultures as they are manifested in the paramount cultures of the 'regions'

It was not so difficult for the government to establish the cultural foundation of the national culture, because the paramount cultures of the regions have been discovered and formulated by the Founding Fathers of the Nation in the form of *Pancasila* or the Five Principles. And the *Pancasila* as a set of core-values has been accepted by Indonesia as the National Cultural Identity and it was formally confirmed in 1988.

However the acceptance of *Pancasila* as the national cultural identity is not the end of the national cultural promotion as it is ordered by the National Constitution. The cultural identity of *Pancasila* should be implemented and institutionalized in the daily life and socio-political and economic activities of the nation. It means that the social acceptance of the national cultural identity must be followed up with the inculcation of the core values of the national culture as the national frame of reference to facilitate an even intensive inter-ethnic and regional social interactions.

In its implementation the government has to face the internal as well as external forces which sometimes do not support the endeavour. The internal force which is less favourable in the promotion of the national culture is the plurality of the society with the heterogeneous cultural background. Although the plurality of the society and the heterogeneous cultures of Indonesia is formally considered great national assets, sometimes it caused problems in the promotion of national culture. In fact the ethnic as well as the regional community generally interpret and express the national cultural identity according to the ethnic and regional cultures. The multiple interpretations and expressions of the commonly accepted symbols may invite social tension even if they do not stimulate social conflicts. However the multi-interpretation and expression may be accepted as a great contribution in colouring and enriching national culture in the future. As a matter of fact, the selection of cultural elements which will be contributed to the development of national culture is in the hands of the people in general. The intensive involvement of the government may raise the suspicion of the people as it is reflected in the fading issues on Javanization and Islamization of national culture. What can be done and in fact it has been carried out by the government is providing public facilities and guidance to prevent the deviation growth from the nationally accepted principles of Bhineka Tunggal Ika in promoting the national culture.

It is worth to mention that the National Constitution recognizes three categories of Indonesian cultures. Apart from the ethnic cultures, some regions or provinces have their own local or 'pasar' culture, while the third category is the National Culture which has been developed since the independence. The three categories of culture each has their own function and social arenas. Therefore the Indonesian may interpret and make his strategic choices referring to three different cultures. The choice depends on the most beneficial to response with and the social arena they are involved in. On the other hand the government may also make its own interpretation and develop action to facilitate and direct the development of national culture. However the government interpretation and direction has recently invited a strong reaction from the public, especially from those who identify themselves as the Democratic Forum. The Forum believes that culture will develop freely, as it reflects the active responses of its bearers in the course of history. On the other hand the government group accuses the Forum as traitors and opposes to the Constitution which orders the government to promote national culture with definitive directions.

The heterogeneous cultural interpretation and action of the plural society of Indonesia are also reflected in their response to national development programmes. To improve the social welfare the government has emphasized the endeavour in the economic sector. Application of the modern technology with large scale capital investment and intensive organization in the process of mass production is inevitable. The industrialization trends has obviously stimulated the development of industrial culture which facilitates those who can afford to control the national resources. Consequently it raised public reaction, especially in deciding the development approach.

Heated polemic on the development approaches is reflected in mass-media. Those who can afford the cost of development argues that the development cake should be enlarged before it can be distributed evenly. While the starving commoners prefer to share the cake initially to enable them to participate in the development programmes.

Indeed most of the commoners have nothing to contribute to the national development except their labour. The economic poverty has strongly influenced their interpretation and action in the development programme. On the other hand, the rich has different ways in interpreting and taking part in the development programmes though they are sharing a common principle of the national identity of *Pancasila*, both the poor and the rich referring to one of the five principles of *Pancasila*, i.e., "Social justice for all the Indonesian citizens."

Diverse interpretations and actions based on *Pancasila* as the National Identity have touched almost every industrial sector, such as the capital raising, management of production and the nature of labour. The *Pancasila* working arrangement is always multi-interpretable. It depends on who, in what capacity, under what situation and why it happens. Generally the factory owner will never let any Trade Union carrying out their campaign in the factory. Those who join the Trade Union will be facing difficulties in getting promotion and salary improvement. Striking is considered a 'tabu' and it may cause the production failure and therefore the workers have to share the risk. On the other hand, the Trade Union has different interpretations in defending their right to strike and join any organization. In many disputes both sides firmly hold a common principle of *Pancasila*, i.e., "Just and civilized Humanity"

The heterogeneous interpretation and implementation of *Pancasila* as the National Culture Identity is also effective in people's responses to the increasing intensity of international cultural encounters. Most people react to the ever-increasing foreign cultural influences and try to legitimize their actions by referring to the *Pancasila*. People react to the youth and woman's way of dressing, using *Pancasila* principles as their reference. Likewise people are trying to hold the control of artistic life and preventing the government involvement by referring to *Pancasila* as their source of justification. Not to mention that *Pancasila* has been exploited to legitimize socio-political interpretation and action either conducted by the people or the government agencies.

In conclusion cultural identity is highly needed by every nation, especially for the nation with a plural society and heterogeneous cultural background. The cultural identity is functional not only as an integrative symbol but it may help the society ultimately to reach a common interpretation and action. It may also help the fighting parties to reach a compromise without losing face to each other.

However to promote a strong cultural identity in a nation with a plural society it needs a responsive freedom to facilitate the people to interpret and implement the values into daily life activities. The responsive freedom is also necessary to enable people to respond to the new challenges with appropriate actions in line with the respective social developments, advancement of modern science and technology and the changing environment. Such a responsive freedom will, accordingly, help the National Cultural Identity retain its function as a source of cultural wisdom for the respective nation.

13

Cultural Pluralism, National Identity and Development

The Indian Case

A. R. Momin

Every civilization evolves certain unique features of its own which, in their entirety and inter-relatedness, constitute its dominant configuration and differentiate it from other civilizations. Indian civilization is distinguished from other civilizations of the world in respect of its continuity and heterogeneity, its accommodating ethos and its composite character.

Since the middle of the second millennium BC, Indian civilization has played host to several streams of migrant groups and communities from different parts of the world. The advent of the Aryans, the Tibeto-Burman speaking Mongoloid groups, the Kushans, the Sakas, the Greeks, the Huns, the Arabs, the Persians, the Turks and the Mongols at different points of time testifies to the pervasiveness of the migration process during the successive periods of Indian history. The migrant groups and communities brought their respective traditions and behaviour patterns from their native lands. In the course of time they lost contact with their places of origin and underwent an extensive process of indigenization. The process of adaptation and interaction among the various groups brought about, on the one hand, India's characteristic diversity and, on the other, a composite cultural tradition. This fact is borne out by historical sources and contemporary surveys as well as researches in folklore.

The composite fabric of Indian civilization has been woven with strands and shades of varying textures and colours. It is no exaggeration to say that since ancient times India has represented a melting-pot of races and cultures. Indian civilization may be likened to an expansive river and the various cultural traditions within its confines to streams or tributaries which join the river at different points and thereby give it a distinctive character.

I

Archaeological evidence points to the existence of commercial and cultural relations between the borderlands of north-western India and Iran and Central Asia even before the dawn of the Harappan Culture.[1] The Harappan civilization had extensive trade and cultural contacts with Mesopotamia, Persia, Afghanistan and the Mediterranean world. The process of acculturation which was set into motion as far back as the third millennium BC continued unabated during the successive periods of Indian history and led to the intermingling of a variety of cultural traits and features. Among other things, the Indian astronomical lore was influenced by the Babylonian arithmetical system as well as the Greek geometrical system.[2]

Successive waves of Aryan-speaking people from Central Asia began entering India from the middle of the second millennium BC. It is interesting to note the close parallel, testified by philological evidence, between Vedic deities and ancient Iranian as well as Hittite deities.[3] There are frequent references in Vedic literature to the migration of foreign people, who are described as *Mleccha*.[4] The *Atharva Veda* refers to the Vratyas who were outside the fold of Hinduism. The Brahmans made considerable efforts to draw them to the mainstream of Vedic society.[5] The *Mahabharata* refers to the Yavanas (Ionians or Greeks) who are later mentioned by Panini in the fourth century BC. The Sakas (Scythians) who entered India around the first century BC established their kingdom in India and were accorded a Kshatriya status.[6]

Four important and interrelated dimensions of the process of acculturation in ancient India deserve mention. One of them is the diffusion of cultural traits and technology; the second relates to miscegenation; the third comprises the process of Aryanization or Sanskritization; and the fourth refers to the incorporation and assimilation of regional, as well as foreign, beliefs, rituals and customs.

The Aryan-speaking people introduced the horse-drawn chariot and iron in India. They had probably learnt the use of iron from the Hittites towards the end of the second millennium BC.[7] On the other hand, advanced plough-agriculture, which was known to the Indus people, was borrowed by the Aryans.[8]

The classical literature provides ample evidence of the extent of inter-marriages between the Aryans and other groups, both indigenous and foreign. The Vedic texts refer to Aryans of Dasa descent, the *dasiputra* Brahmans, who were a progeny of Brahmans and slaves.[9] The non-Sanskritic names of several prominent Brahmans in Vedic literature and the Puranic tradition indicate racial admixture. Later Indian sources mention the Abhira Brahmans, who were contemptuously described as *Mleccha* because they were a product of inter-marriages between Brahmans and the Ambasastha caste.[10] Similarly, a seventh century inscription from South India mentions the Boya Brahmans, the Boyas otherwise being described as a Shudra tribe.[11]

There were inter-marriages between the Brahmans and the forest-dwelling Naga tribe. It is significant that Naga genealogies and myths are accorded a prominent place in the opening canto of the *Mahabharata.*[12] It is also interesting to note that in the folk tradition some of Krishna's sixteen thousand wives seem to be of foreign extraction.[13] One can discern a reflection of social reality in the mythological tradition.

The *Sama Veda* refers to a ritual whereby non-Aryans were admitted into the mainstream of Vedic society. There are frequent references in the early sources to non-Aryan Brahmans. *Manu* mentions that several foreign tribes who had entered India at different points of time and came into contact with the Aryan-speaking people were accorded a place within the fold of Hindu society.[14] The process of Aryanization or Sanskritization often entailed the adoption of Sanskrit names, rituals, customs and habits. However, it did not always bring about uniformity and homogenization. Often, the adoption of Brahmanical customs and features was a selective process. Furthermore, it was often blended with regional customs. For example, the Brahmanical institution of *gotra* was adopted by non-Brahman, including tribal communities in different ways. In some cases, Brahmanic and regional *gotras* were blended. In some communities the *gotra* exists only nominally and does not entail exogamy.

From early times, tribal and folk cults and ritual practices were incorporated and assimilated into the corpus of Brahmanism. Totemic deities such as fish, tortoise and boar were made into incarnations of Vishnu.[16] Shiva was formed by a fusion of the Vedic Rudra with some non-Aryan deity, including the Indus deity which has been described as proto-Shiva.[17] Similarly, Narayani and Durga, manifestations of Shiva's consort, which were associated with non-Aryan tribes, later came to be absorbed into classical Hinduism.[18]

The cult of sun-worship was brought to India by the Magas who came to India around the first century BC from Sakadvip or Persia. Initially, they were not admitted to all the rituals and ceremonies but subsequently they came to be absorbed into the mainstream of Vedic society and known as Sakadvip or Maga Brahmans.[19] The Krishna cult was substantially expanded and enriched by the Abhiras, who were a foreign pastoral tribe.[20] The deities of tribals and low-caste groups were absorbed by Brahmanism. This is testified by the popularity of the Jagannath cult in Orissa and that of Viththala in Maharashtra.[21] Similarly, serpent worship and phallus worship which later found their way into classical Hinduism were taken over from forest-dwelling tribal communities.[22] Heterodox sects and cults, such as Shakta and the Tantric tradition, incorporated several esoteric features from indigenous, particularly tribal cultures.[23]

The incorporation and assimilation of regional features into the mainstream of Vedic culture is attested by linguistic and philological evidence as well. Certain kinds of echo formations which are characteristic of the Austric family of languages found their way into the Indo-Aryan speeches. The presence of non-Aryan elements, especially Proto-Dravidian, in vocabulary, syntax and phoenetics, in Vedic Sanskrit is now fairly well established. The later Vedic texts indicate an even greater admixture of non-Aryan words.[24]

The foregoing discussion makes it fairly clear that from very early times Vedic society was internally differentiated and pluralistic, rather than monolithic and homogeneous. It was an amalgam or synthesis of Aryan and non-Aryan, including tribal elements. In other words, since its very inception Hinduism appears to be a "mosaic of distinct cults, deities, sects and ideas", as Romila Thapar puts it.[25] The point which I have tried to establish is that since ancient times Indian civilization has had a pluralistic and composite character, the pluralistic and composite ethos of Indian civilization, which began germinating during the Vedic period, was supplemented by the rise of Buddhism and Jainism, and was further reinforced during the early medieval period which witnessed the early flowering of the Bhakti Movement. This composite tradition attained efflorescence during the late medieval period.

II

A certain dialectic or complementary between pluralism and syncretism seems to pervade the fabric of Indian civilization. Three interrelated themes or dimensions of this dialectic may be delineated: (a) pan-Indian, (b) within the fold of Hinduism, and (c) the regional context. The pan-Indian, civilizational dimension of cultural pluralism and syncretism encompasses racial diversity and admixture, linguistic heterogeneity as well as fusion, and variations as well as synthesis in customs, behaviour patterns, beliefs and rituals.

Pluralism has been one of the quintessential features of Hinduism both at the metaphysical as well as socio-cultural level. At the metaphysical level, truth was considered pluralistic. For example, it is believed that if two *Sruti* traditions are in conflict, both of them are to be held as law. The inherently pluralistic ethos of Hinduism is reflected, on the one hand, in the wide and divergent range of beliefs and ideas and, on the other, in stratification, customs, traditions and behaviour patterns.[26] Syncretism is conspicuously evidenced in the survival of non-Aryan deities, rituals and ceremonies in villages which have been the heartland of Aryan expansion.[27] The epic tradition, in both textual as well as folk forms, bears the imprint of pluralism. For instance, the *Ramayana* has several variants or versions.[28]

The process of acculturation and integration has been extensively at work at the regional level. Though each group or community has a distinctive identity and ethos of its own, it does not exist in a social vacuum. Rather, it forms part of an extended and dynamic network. Often, interaction, exchange and integration characterize inter-community relations. The sharing of space, regional ethos and cultural traits cuts across religions and sectarian differences and binds the local people together.[29]

The distribution of material traits at the regional level indicates a certain complementarity in that it is marked by both local differentiation and inter-penetration. Often, a cluster or complex of material traits at the regional level unites different sections and communities.[30]

The unity of India is often assumed and taken for granted; it is seldom subjected to a critical examination in a diachronic framework. This is so because the sense of unity which pervades the fabric of Indian society is rather elusive, nebulous and enigmatic. Nevertheless, at the pan-Indian level, five interrelated sources of integration and unity may be delineated:

(a) Sanskritic Hinduism at the ideational and institutional levels and through a network of centres of pilgrimage,[31]

(b) a composite cultural tradition born out of the protracted interaction and exchange between Hindus and Muslims through the length and breadth of the country, which is best exemplified in the Sufi and Bhakti Movements,[32]

(c) patriotism and nascent nationalism, which emerged during the War of 1857 and culminated in the freedom struggle,[33]

(d) the secular-democratic ethos of modern India which is enshrined in the Constitution of the country, and

(e) the country-wide process of modernization which was set into motion during the British period and which got accelerated in the post-Independence period.

The above-mentioned themes or currents have a wide geographical and cultural distribution and are manifested both at the macro as well as micro levels.

Since the late medieval period witnessed a creative synthesis of Hindu and Islamic civilizations and thus represents the zenith of India's composite tradition, it merits some elaboration. The protracted interaction between Hindus and Muslims gave rise to what may be termed the Indo-Islamic tradition. There are two interrelated dimensions of the Indo-Islamic tradition. On the one hand, it manifested itself in syncretistic traditions of music, art, literature and architecture.[34] On the other, it found expression in folklore, dress patterns, food habits, names and surnames.[35]

The Sufis played a crucial role in the development of this syncretic tradition. Their broad human sympathies, their message of love and brotherhood and their identification with the poor and the dispossessed attracted thousands of people, Hindus, Muslims and Sikhs to their fold. Even now their shrines, which are located through the length and breadth of the country, are thronged by millions of people and thereby serve as focal points of integration.[36] The Bhakti Movement, which had a far-reaching impact on Indian society during the medieval period, was significantly influenced by the ideals and precepts of sufism.

III

The question of nationalism and national identity is embedded in the broad context of Indian civilization. The foregoing discussion on the structure of Indian society is based on a dynamic and creative vision of civilization. A civilization should be seen, not as a closed system or a finished product, but as a dynamic and unfolding process. As Kroeber has perceptively remarked, what is characteristic of any civilization is not its being but its becoming.[37] By virtue of its characteristic pluralism and its continuously evolving synthesis, India represents a nation in the making, a nation which is continuously unfolding its civilizational potentialities. This view is reflected in a statement of Jawaharlal Nehru to the effect that Indianness is a matter of feeling, a dream, a vision, and an emotion.

The view that nationalism and national identity are rooted in a broad civilizational framework should not make us oblivious of the role of primordial, ethnic, religious and regional identities. One of the remarkable achievements of Indian civilization lies in its tolerance and accommodation of diverse identities as well as the facilitation of a creative synthesis of these identities. This has been one of the major factors in the continued survival and resilience of Indian civilization. At the same time, one should not gloss over the fact that from time to time there have been conflicts between the over-arching national identity and sub-national identities. Similarly, sub-national identities sometimes tend to acquire rather pathological overtones and thereby threaten the unity and integrity of the country. This is true of communalism as well as other fissiparous tendencies. In recent years the distinction between the two has acquired a sharper edge. This phenomenon has global manifestations, as attested by the disintegration of the erstwhile Soviet Union and the continued ethnic strife in Bosnia-Herzegovina. In the prevailing climate of increasing democratization and collective self-consciousness, ethnic and other corporate identities cannot be suppressed for too long. What is therefore required, in the global context as well as in India, is a flexible and accommodating, rather than constructive and strait-jacketed, notion of national identity.

The issue of national identity in India is reflected in the secular-democratic framework which is enshrined in the republican Constitution of the country. The ideal of national unity is reinforced by cultural pluralism and the composite heritage of the country. It is foolhardy to suppose that there is perfect harmony between national identity as it is enshrined in the Constitution and the whole corpus of Indian tradition. Indian tradition has its blind spots as well: the scourge of caste and untouchability, degradation of women, child marriage and restrictions on widow remarriage, to mention a few. What is required is a critical re-interpretation of tradition in the light of cherished national goals. Therefore, the concept of national identity should be seen as essentially an ideal-critical concept which is embedded in a broad humanistic framework.

As an ideal-critical concept, national identity is to be safeguarded from external threats as well as internal corrosion and ossification. The latter variety of threat may arise from narrow chauvinism and cultural solipsism. In the present context, this kind of threat to India's national identity has been posed by what has come to be known as the *Hindutva* syndrome. The ideology of *Hindutva*, as propounded and popularized by the right-wing political formations in contemporary India, entails three interrelated sets of fallacies. First, it presents a grossly over-simplified and distorted picture of an otherwise amorphous and pluralistic Hindu ethos. Secondly, with its accent on homogenization and regimentation and its misplaced identification between Hinduism and nationalism it tends to be xenophobic and exclusivistic, which is at variance with the spirit of Indian civilization. Thirdly, one can discern a hegemonic, tyrannical and even fascist streak-lurking behind the pseudo-nationalist rhetoric of *Hindutva*.[35] Likewise, the political motivation of the movement is only thinly disguised.

The issue of national unity and integration is closely intertwined with cultural policy. A policy of integration, which discounts cultural pluralism and the composite character of Indian society and seeks to impose uniformity, homogenization and regimentation on the country's heterogeneous population, will ultimately prove to be self-defeating. What is required is a humane vision of integration which would take due cognizance of India's pluralistic ethos and at the same time strengthen the long-standing bonds and inter-linkages among the people, especially at the grass roots level. Indian society is to be seen, to use K.S. Singh's evocative metaphor, as a honeycomb in which communities are engaged in vibrant interaction, sharing space, ethos and cultural traits.[39]

IV

The notion of development in the Indian context should be viewed in tandem with cultural pluralism and national identity. It is worthwhile to bring out three inter-connected dimensions of development. The first of these is of a general nature. Civilizations do not emerge and develop in isolation. This has become a truism in our times, thanks to the process of globalization. In recent years, a serious rethinking of the notion of development and its linkage with human welfare has taken place. For too long development has been regarded as a fetish and modernization as the promised Messiah of mankind. The relevant question now is: development for what and for whom? The first part of the question focuses on a holistic and integrated perspective on development, and the second underscores a people-oriented approach. Development is now seen, not as an abstract ideal, but as a correlative phenomenon involving necessary reference to ecological balance as well as human resource development. The new vision of development stresses that the development process must take into active consideration people's grass roots institutions and organizations and must enlist their initiative and participation. Furthermore, development cannot be measured in quantitative, statistical terms alone.[40]

Since the development process must ensure the participation of people at the grass roots level and take cognizance of their perceptions and felt needs, the question of development has to be closely linked to cultural policy. The cultural policy in respect of development needs to be embedded in the framework of cultural pluralism and democratic decentralization. A corollary of the above is that a policy which seeks to impose unitary solutions regardless of regional variations and specificities will prove to be counter-productive. Thus, though the policy for development needs to be attuned to national interests and aspirations, it can ill afford to ignore the culture-specific dimensions of development.[41]

To conclude: the interface of development and cultural identity in the Indian context has two interrelated dimensions: the pan-Indian, civilizational, on the one hand, and regional-cultural, on the other. At both the macro and micro levels, the development process needs to be informed and guided by the pluralistic and composite ethos of Indian society.

References

1. G. Possehl (ed.). *Harappan Civilization*, New Delhi, 1982, p. 79.
2. R.A. Jairajbhoy. *Foreign Influence in Ancient India*, Bombay, 1963, pp. 69-75; P.M. Joshi (ed.). *Studies in the Foreign Relations of India*, Hyderabad, 1975, p. 46.
3. K.C. Chattopadhyaya. *Studies in Vedic and Indo-Iranian Religion and Literature*, Vol. II, Varanasi, 1978, p. 43; D.D. Kosambi. *The Culture and Civilization of Ancient India*, Delhi, 1987, pp. 72-91.
4. R.S. Sharma. *Sudras in Ancient India*, Delhi, 1958, p. 32; Romila Thapar, "The Image of the Barbarian in Early India", In *Ancient Indian Social History: Some Interpretations*, New Delhi, pp. 152-92.
5. The noted Indologist Basham considers the Vratyas as one of the prototypes of the Gypsies who migrated to Europe during the Middle Ages. A.L. Basham; *Classical Hinduism*, Delhi, 1990, pp. 58-59.
6. Romila Thapar. *Ancient Indian Social History*, pp. 176-77.
7. D.D. Kosambi. *The Culture and Civilization of Ancient India*, Delhi, 1987, p. 77.

8. Romila Thapar. *Interpreting Early India*, Delhi, 1992, p. 11.
9. Romila Thapar. *Interpreting Early India*, p. 84; R.S. Sharma. *Sudras in Ancient India*. pp. 63-64.
10. Romila Thapar. *The Past and Prejudice*, New Delhi, 1975, p. 31.
11. Romila Thapar. *Ancient Indian Social History*, pp. 178-79.
12. D.D. Kosambi. *The Culture and Civilization of Ancient India*, p. 94; Romila Thapar, "Social Mobility in Ancient India", In *Ancient Indian Social History*, pp. 122-51.
13. D.D. Kosambi, *op. cit.* p. 116.
14. N.K. Bose. *Society and Culture in India*, Bombay, 1967, pp. 207-08; Romila Thapar. "The Study of Society in Ancient India", In *Ancient Indian Social History*, pp. 211-39.
15. G.S. Ghurye. *Two Brahmanical Institutions: Gotra and Charana*, Bombay, 1992; K.S. Singh. *People of India: An Introduction*, Calcutta, 1992, p. 56.
16. D.D. Kosambi, p. 170.
17. K.C. Chattopadhyaya. *Studies in Vedic and Indo-Iranian Religion and literature*, vol.II, pp. 47, 91-92; R.G. Bhandarkar. *Vaisnavism, Saivism and Minor Religious Systems*, Straussburg, 1913, p. 104.
18. Romila Thapar. *Interpreting Early India*, pp. 178-79; J. Gonda. *Vishnuism and Saivism: A Comparison*, New Delhi 1976; S. Shivapadasundaram: *The Saiva School of Hinduism*, London, 1934.
19. R.G. Bhandarkar. *Vaisnavism, Saivism and Minor Religious Systems*, pp. 153-55; Jairajbhoy. *Foreign Influence in Ancient India*, pp. 153; P.M. Joshi. *Foreign Relations of India*, p. 179; Benjamim Walker. *Hindu World*, London, 1968, vol. II, p. 3.
20. R.G. Bhandarkar. *Vaisnavism, Saivism*, pp. 37-38.
21. Some tribal communities have been associated with Hindu temples and shrines for a long time. The Todas of the Nilgiri Hills, for example, serve as palanquin-bearers of Shiva at the Bhavaneeshwar temple in Ooty. The Chenchus are attached to the Hindu shrine of Sri Sailam in Andhra Pradesh. The Savara tribe in Orissa has been associated with the Jagannath temple at Puri. In parts of Chota Nagpur, Central and the Western Ghats, the custodians of Shiva temples and shrines are tribals. The Sri Venkateshwar temple at Tirupati has been associated with the Kurumbas and Lambadis. The Yerukulas have been associated with the Sri Subramanyam temple of Palani and Tiruttani. K.S. Singh. *Tribal Society*, Delhi, 1985, p. 98; S.G. Tulpule, "The Origin of Viththala: A New Interpretation", In *Annals of the Bhandarkar Oriental Research Institute*, 1977-78, vols. 58-59, pp. 1009-15; G.D. Sontheimer, "Some Memorial

Monuments of Western India", In *German Scholars in India*, II. New Delhi, 1976.

22. R.G. Bhandarkar. *Vaisnavism, Saivism*, pp. 114-15.

23. John Woodroffe. *Shakti and Shakta*, Madras, 1951; Agehananda Bharati. *The Tantric Tradition*, London, 1965; S. Dasgupta. *Obscure Religions Cults*, Calcutta, 1962.

24. T. Burrow. *The Sanskrit Language*, London, 1965; M.M. Deshpande and P.E. Hook (eds.). *Aryan and Non-Aryan in India*, Michigan, 1979; Romila Thapar. *Interpreting Early India*, pp. 11, 94. It is interesting to note that the most commonly used word for plough in Vedic literature, *Langala*, is derived from Munda. Similarly, the word for rice, *Vrihi*, is of Dravidian origin. Romila Thapar. *Ancient Indian Social History*, p. 217.

25. Romila Thapar. *Interpreting Early India*, p. 68; Romila Thapar. "The Study of Society in Ancient India", In *Ancient Indian Social History*, pp. 211-39.

    Interestingly, the word Hindu is of Persian origin. The Persepolis and Naqsh-i-Rustam inscriptions of Darius (died 486 BC) refer to the frontier regions of the Indus as Hindush. Later on, the term is frequently used in Arabic geographical and historical sources. D.C. Sircar. *Select Inscriptions*, vol. I, Calcutta, 1965, pp. 7; Andre Wink. *Al-Hind. The Making of the Indo-Islamic World*, Delhi, 1990, p. 5.

26. Irawati Karve. *Hindu Society: An Interpretation*. Poona, 1961, pp. 1-14.

27. McKim Marriott. *Village India*. Chicago, 1955, pp. 209-10.

28. Romila Thapar, "The Ramayana: Theme and Variations", In S.N. Mukherjee (ed.). *Indian History and Thought*, Calcutta, 1982, pp. 221-53; V. Raghavan (ed.). *The Ramayana Tradition in Asia*, Delhi, 1980; Paula Richman (ed.). *Many Ramayanas*, Delhi, 1992.

29. K.S. Singh. *The People of India: An Introduction*, pp. 96-101.

30. N.K. Bose. *Peasant Life in India: A Study in Indian Unity and Diversity*, Calcutta, 1961.

31. M.N. Srinivas. *The Cohesive Role of Sanskritization and Other Essays*, New Delhi, 1991; S.M. Bhardwaj. *Hindu Places of Pilgrimage in India*. Berkeley, 1973; B.N. Saraswati. *The Spectrum of the Sacred*, New Delhi, 1984.

32. Tara Chand. *Influence of Islam on Indian Culture*. Allahabad, 1936; H.K. Sherwani. *Cultural Trends in Medieval India*, Bombay, 1968; Yusuf Husain Khan. *Glimpses of Medieval Indian Culture*, Delhi; Aziz Ahmad. *Studies in Islamic Culture in the Indian Environment*. Oxford, 1964; Ashim Roy. *Islamic Syncretistic Tradition in Bengal*, Princeton, 1983; S.C. Misra. "Indigenization and Islamization in Indian History", In *Secular Democracy* (VII) 1974; A.R. Momin. "The Indo-Islamic Tradition", In *Sociological Bulletin*. 26 (2) 1977, pp.

242-58.

33. Bipan Chandra. *India's Struggle for Independence*, Penguin, 1989.

34. Interestingly, the *Ramayana* of Tulsidas contains scores of Arabic and Persian words. There are over thirty translations of the epic in Urdu and over a dozen in Persian. In some villages, the *Ramayana* is ritually recited before Hindu audiences by a Muslim sage. Not too long ago in imperial Delhi, a Hindu *pandit* taught the *Quran* to Muslim children. Even now in several villages of northern and western India Hindu bards and mendicants recite Muslim epics before Muslim, as well as Hindu audiences.

35. At the regional level, the penetration of the Indo-Islamic tradition is evidenced by linguistic diffusion. In Bengal and Orissa, for example, the commonly used word for *prasad* is *Shirini*, which is of Persian origin and which has the same connotation in Muslim usage. Similarly, the Persian word *Pir*, which refers to a spiritual mentor, is used in Hindu religious context as well. One comes across, for example, the name of Ramdev Pir. Likewise, the chief of a *Nathpanthi akhada* is known as *Pir* (G.S. Ghurye: *Indian Sadhus*, Bombay, 1953, p. 157). Scores of names and surnames in India, which are largely derived from occupations, are originally of Arabic or Persian origin and thus betray the blending of Hindu and Muslim traditions. Consider, for example, the following occupational names: *halwai, bafand, bawarchi, hajjam, bazaz, bazigar, daftari, madari, saraf, lashkari, noongar, rangrez, nilgar, sangtarash, munshi, khazanchi.* These names are commonly found among Hindu as well as Muslim communities.

36. S.P. Jain. *The Social Structure of Hindu-Muslim Community*, Delhi, 1975; Christian W. Troll (ed.). *Muslims Shrines in India*, Delhi, 1989; Currie, *Muinuddin Chishti of Ajmer*, Delhi, 1991.

37. Quoted in N.K. Bose. *Society and Culture in India*, p. 289; A.L. Kroeber: *An Anthropologist looks at History*, California, 1963, pp. 4-5.

38. Jan Breman, "The Hindu Right: Comparisons with Nazi Germany", In *The Times of India*, March 15, 1993.

39. K.S. Singh. *People of India: An Introduction*, p. 98.

40. Michael M. Cernea (ed.). *Putting People First*. Second Edition, New York, 1991; J.V. Ferreira and A.R. Momin (eds.). *Nemesis: Critical Perspectives on Modernization*, Bombay, 1984.

41. A.R. Momin. "Social mobility and Development among the Tribal Communities of India." Paper presented at a seminar on Social Mobility and Development, organized under the auspices of the Joint Indo-Russian Commission in Moscow on September 27-30, 1992.

14

Secular Sovereign and Artha

Parthasarathi Banerjee

Welfare is not possible without a sovereign. Welfare is the endurance or stability of the livelihood (or the disposition to livelihood) of the entire human multitude, as is under the sovereign authority, along with the implied endurance of the species of lives and the earth contained under the sovereign. Endurance of lives and livelihoods are necessarily spread over the temporal horizon, and therefore this implies the enabling of the propagation of all life-forms and earth. Both the sovereign and the welfare is defined by the acquiring of an earth possessed by the human multitudes and other life-forms and by its up-keeping (endured livelihood). This is our central argument.

Theories of development, or the actions and rhetorics of development (which we may call development-in-action) do very often either deny or disregard such a supremacy of the sovereign authority in development. To distinguish our hypothesis, we would therefore use the term welfare as defined above. Our demonstration would be to show that the secularization of development is not only misconceived but also that an autonomous development is actually in a certain sense morally purposive. The clock of scientific factuality and causality in this system cannot be maintained against the demands raised by the very construction of science and causality. This theoretical and actual system of development thereby necessarily brings in the purposive morality (which may also be termed evangelization), and by doing so this system intends to bring under its universally evangelizing fold the entire globe. The resurfacing of natural law, of human and community rights, of the rights of the communities to overcome the boundaries dictated by the sovereign, etc. are all part of this common evangelic initiative. We would demonstrate, arguing on only a few points, that such theories cannot either offer the welfare as defined above, or guarantee and envision a truly secular sovereign. Our contention is that our position, which follows Indian theoretical vantage of *arthasastra*, can offer and guarantee this both.

Therefore we have to speak on the notions and relevances of law (and law-state), and rights. We would argue, though briefly, against it, claiming that both the sovereign and the welfare need not be defined by law (or system of law). Our attempt would be to enlighten the causality inherent in the constitution of sovereignty and the welfare, for and by the multitudes (and the other species and the earth). It may be claimed then that this is superior to the utilitarian formulation by being 'scientific' and secular; and certainly our claim is not moralizing, thereby claiming its superiority to various theories of natural law, legal traditions and potentiality-fulfilment (of human individuals). The arguments offered here would therefore have to touch, partially albeit, upon the penal authority (or law) and understanding community — (or civil) societies. We would depend upon a cognitive understanding of the poena (somewhat comparable to *danda*). Interestingly in our endeavour the individual human figures very prominently, and yet we are able to put aside 'individual differences', 'liberty', or 'freedom of the will', etc. The point is that individual welfare (*abhyudaya*) is free of 'moral' considerations, and can under a proper sovereign act cognitively. This means, and if we define the cognitive as the rational, that given the sovereign and therefore the poena, and also given the fact of individual's learning through discourses, human actions-for-welfare are causal and we need not depend on the ideas of 'fall', *akrasia* or weaknesses of the will. We argue that the welfare, as defined above (i.e., *artha*), is possible through a sovereign — (who seeks to win), who therefore is *artha* wielding the penal, the *danda*. We claim that this alone is secular, and the other notion of global imperium (of development) cannot properly define a global authority that is both secular and definable for secularized individuals. The contemporary notions of, and attempts at, a global developmental imperium is liable to be both non-secular and penal.

Our arguments do not therefore allow us the constitution of a moralized, penitential and penalizing global authority. Consequently it does not threaten the commonsensical life or culture. This therefore is a secularization of the universal and the welfare, achievable through the sovereign — (who seeks to win).

It is needless to emphasize that in the short span that this present essay is allowed, it is simply not possible to examine satisfactorily the issues raised above. We would therefore limit ourselves to the discussion of only a few points.

II

Commonsense valuation implies that development is a progress aiming at bringing in more and more people, from multitudes of communities under a common principle. This principle could be considered as that of the brotherhood. Another notion in currency in the Western tradition is to create a stronger state, and thereby to achieve a supremacy over the neighbours in terms of power and prosperity. It is not necessary that these two idea-types should be considered as opposed, and in fact detailed formulations might recognize a unity. This latter, the unity of the two types, in fact constitutes a third principle. To give examples from the past, Thucydides in his *Peloponnesian War* represented the second strand. "Different states encountered different obstacles to the course of their development" and that led to the succession of wars, defeats and conquests. Aeneas, in Virgil's epic was concerned with his people alone and, lest he forgot the ordained mission at Carthage, he was led into the hell of the future of his own people. His people could thereby develop themselves and build an empire. The ordained mission was the protection of life and prosperity of its own people and a strong sovereign was indeed necessary for that. Later, this same people following the defeat of their states at the hand of the northerners were told by St. Augustine a common principle — a principle of brotherhood. Augustinian formulation was not directed against the necessity of a sovereign, neither so much against the 'necessary' wars but it had aimed at a common and unique spiritual media, one god and unique ethic for the multitudes of Roman people. This was then a synthesis of sovereignty and culture, which was to make possible an imperium over nations, races, civitas and towns, which Dante dreamt, and argued for, much later in his *Monarchy*. The Augustinian principle is then not a sovereignless principle. The latter, a sovereignless type, possibly could be traced to the Jewish tradition, which remained often without a sovereign. Its strength was in a common principle.

Against the contemporary global standard, the size of population that it involved or of the size of the geographical expanse over which these above ideas and actions took place could indeed appear small. An increase in size as such, without any corresponding change in the principles, would indicate increased information which might lead fabulously to a tower of Babel. It would appear then, and since no conquest has been made over these old principles, that these principles remain valid. Development could be considered either as an expanding extension for the space of varieties of human multitude by bringing them under a unique principle or, at least in enabling a certain people to retain their own principle. None denies the necessarily important question of prosperity of the population. Prosperity is a principle of life and, even if unsaid, it remains supreme. Moreover sovereign is of supreme importance in all the strands of action excepting one.

It may be observed that contemporary notions of development do not present a coherent, rigorous formulation of its agenda. In the absence of the same we may take up development-in-action, that is, as it is being performed. Such a documentation, over that period which we often call modern, of the performance or the acts is indeed what we cognize and what we are concerned with.

In this sense neither population nor its prosperity is the object of development. People act and prosper and development is performed. It is like an autopoeisis, a constructivist undertaking, though our position is sharply different from that. This people, however, is not an amorphous mass but as has been noted above, do have both variabilities and magnitudes. Till recently such variabilities used to be measured by the modernists in terms of lobotomical differences and similar other 'racial' markers. Race has been replaced largely by other artifacts recently. Culture, traditional communities or epistemic communities are contemporary artifacts. Race was defined earlier in terms of a cognate structure (i.e., of blood or of lineage), defined materially. The contemporary (racial) culture or the (racial) epistemic communities are symbolic, semiotic — either as defined in the field or defined in a territory (which is either geographic or abstract-communicational).

Before we embark upon these racial constructs in a little more detail, it would not be pointless to consider the issue of the size of the population. While even the Roman state was based upon the notion of citizen and used to conduct census, it was only with the post reformation modern states, which often are called nation states, that quantitative issues turned out to be important. In England, with the Elizabethan reform of poor law by which the state took upon itself the charity-endowment, the controlling interest of state in population became significant. The size of the population as such, albeit owing to many other reasons, became a matter of active state interest. In the beginning, for much of mercantilism, nation was a near equivalent of population and rise in quantity was favoured often by that nation which did not have the same desired quantity. But possibly owing to changes in methods and organizations of production, the later *laissez-faire* lost interest in the rise in population and the state was to remain detached as it were, not from the issues of population but from its rise. Shortly thereafter it was argued, to begin with Malthus or Wicksell later, that the state's active containment of population quantity would possibly be desirable. It would be worthwhile to note Heckscher's observation that mercantilist economics, a division in economics, was made into production, exchange and distribution, where production and exchange were to be run competitively and distribution were to remain in the hands of the state. Quantities of population in the spheres of production and exchange were noted but as legitimate such factors were not only to be determined by the market, (competitively which alone, without the sovereign's interest, would turn out to be accidental), but also their gross requirements were to fall uninterruptedly. Active quantity, therefore, was to be reduced and made into the accidentally caused and allowed to survive. The state was to provide for the distributive justice, which having been dissociated from the spheres of commutative justice was a reduced minimum. This flotsam population therefore became a burden to the exchequer. It was no longer for the sovereign to look after, and actively promote, the prosperity of its population in its entirety. On the contrary what we see in the twentieth century is often an active bid by the sovereign to enhance accidentally, the risk to livelihood and promotion of such instrumentalities as reduce the quantum.

It has been noted that the Roman state was based upon citizenship which was defined as the negation of aliens. This state was, therefore, based on a variability— a differentiated group of population. Moreover it was a law-state, where citizenry (the various cives) was legally defined and the state defined accordingly, i.e., on both the quantity and differential of a population. It is also worth noticing, while the early state was exclusively based on a select group, defined on blood relation and descent, a social group, the last stages of the empire saw the inclusion into citizenry various other groups, drawn from both other racial and mixed groups. This latter were in general put into various hierarchies, with corresponding rights and privileges. One primary reason for the expansion of the hierarchy of citizens was the enhancement of the collection of taxes. In terms of the legal scope the differentiation in the hierarchy was drawn in the civil sphere — either by denying it such rights altogether, partly or by providing the scope completely. Slaves, drawn from various races, were one large group which, either through manumission (a kind of relief from slavery) or through the offsprings, provided indeed by way of a default scopes of racial intermixing. There were others, such as the original Latinis or the Peregrines in distant occupied parts who had but little scope of overcoming racial differences and, indeed, were often allowed to continue with their own customs, especially in select matters (though, for example, often denying inheritance). The civil law provided for various checks and scopes on acceptable marriages and inheritance, but as explained above, this was primarily meant for a small group or race. State's actions, primarily legal, were therefore either limited to containing or, at the most, accepting partly a current state of affairs in the differentiated population. In the long history thereafter of various states, or the empires in Europe and adjoining areas, we see either endemic racial wars and conflicts, 'racial' or customary civil law or very violent migrations, wars and settlements. Migrated settlement virtually never did lead to what Hobbes defined as 'conquests', but it usually attempted to exterminate or displace the original inhabitants — such as had happened with Charlemagne or the Angles and Saxons displacing Celts. Small communities, such as the Jews, had to suffer throughout history. The very feeble attempts at popularizing pilgrimage or the various crusades could not either achieve any result or only led to even bitter and violent racial skirmishes.

Inter-racial or inter-national mixing, therefore, being limited by its spare occurrences, even the law-states or kings and such other states did not have much to do with corresponding legal artifices. The Roman state used to apply ius gentium (natural law, in a certain sense), often in dealings with those who were outside the bounds of civil law, i.e., the others, the Latinis, etc. The ius natural, though mentioned in a few cases, was otherwise indistinguishable from the ius gentium. Possibly, the most important distinction that this system has is its separation of law civil from natural. It appears that this distinction was the result of a law-state as defined on its citizenry. The ius gentium was not for a universal philosophic demand, as to some extent it was with the stoics, or Cicero or as it was to be later with Grotius or even later with Pollock; but the same was for both the maintenance and prosperity of commercial transactions, that too primarily of trade. Moreover, natural law could not have been in existence without sovereigns; and natural right had to have two parties, i.e., no claim to natural right could be made without accepting the reciprocal duties. To an insignificant extent the slaves and otherwise the Latinis, the Peregrines of the empire or others were in the range of this artifact.

Its purpose, that is, of natural law, is therefore not to be confounded with some hypothetical purpose of universalization, a common principle, say, of brotherhood which, as it seems, the state was not directed to. Similarly later with the canon law, though it was to be common (or universal) in matters ecclesiastical, it had its wings clipped by the various civil or common laws, as evidenced, for example, in the murder of Thomas Beckett much later in the cathedral and described by Maitland. As a result, natural law disappeared virtually till its rearrival in the early modern times.

III

Apparently natural law has the twin bases of universalism. The first basis is provided by the *ius gentium* and the second basis is provided by an individual. In fact, the two are complementary. Stoic and Augustinian explanation on natural law was that which was beyond the bounds of necessity, and that what could have a free will was to be the individual. Augustine, however, provided a divine prescience on this free will and, therefore, for him the natural was part of an 'order' to which the stoics could not make any claim. In this 'natural order' then there is no cleavage between the free will and universal order, and it is necessary too. Therefore those who would act for this temporal peace and desert, would also receive the supreme desert. This schema remains even today, for the establishment of a truly universal empire.

A brief discussion on this order of causes seems necessary here. Contemporary debates do in fact seem to be hovering around the twin positions of natural law, represented by the Stoics and Cicero. It is possibly to overemphasize the stoical view that Bloch does not appear to discuss Ciceronian free-will libertarians of our own time. A rather hypostatized natural law doctrines may be found in Augustine first, and then of course in Hobbes. Augustine clearly delineates the three Ciceronian free-willing senses of causality, viz., the fortuitous, the natural and a voluntary. Augustine then can show that the fortuitous is but latent, the natural as of prescience, and he says that there is no efficient cause without the voluntary causes. The point is that he draws a distinguishing line between cause that makes and causes that make and are made. Material causes, therefore according to him, is not efficient because it is virtually of the made-type. Will therefore is a power, which belongs to the stronger man, which as a cause both makes and is made. For Hobbes too in the 'motions' of deliberation, consisting of aversions, appetites etc. the last thing that adheres to the action is the will. Will, therefore for Hobbes, is part of an action — it is acting; and willing is not the part of a rational faculty. Augustine too clearly states, that, by failing to act even while willing to act by remaining under the compulsion of a stronger power, does not mean that a separation of free-willing and necessity is necessary. By this inability will's freedom is not invalidated, but the fact is that the prescience has not endowed the unable will as much power.

It is thus Hobbes' sovereign is constituted of congealed will, and not of contracts. Hobbes' contracts of one to another are artificial (and not natural) first; and second such artificials are there only to acknowledge the congealed will — that Will, which alone can act in those things which concern the common peace and safety. This Will, the 'real' unity, called as the Leviathan (Psalm. 104.26), by Augustine and by Hobbes — has that power and strength the use of which enables it to form the wills of the multitude by the terror thereof. This construction of Leviathan is both necessary and is a 'mockery' of itself thereby. It is a mockery of the evil, of the temptation, and of those wills — such that it is through evil willing (through the united Will) that the good will come forth.

Cause of volition or of voluntary actions, that is the will therefore is by free choice only insofar as it is enabled by the united Will to do so, within its respective realm. Other artificial unions, which are entered into through contracts are by names; and unless, as Hobbes asserts (which later was developed by Mill, in his theory of names) these names are properly defined, the artificial unions, similar to the syllogistic failure, would fail. The Leviathan, the sovereign thus can legitimately suppress all such artificial unions. Natural order of cause, for Hobbes (and to a certain extent for Augustine) requires an external force, which enables it to act. Enabling the action, therefore is through the will, more particularly by the causality of terror and punishment.

The first law of nature for Hobbes is concerning peace, and the second law pertains to forsaking the claims to such rights as are inimical to peace. Justice comes third only and is characterized by the primacy of two other natural laws. Justice comes therefore only as a performance of covenants, entered into through the application of the second law of nature. It has to follow therefore the constitution of a 'commonwealth'. The performance of covenants has to follow the causality — caused by the Leviathan. Nothing is just or unjust in a state of nature. Locke was rather unable to define clearly and defend his views. Contemporary proponents of Locke (Nozick for example, with a doubtful heritage of Locke) forget easily such Hobbesian explanation of causality; and go ahead instead without a proper theory of names, of causation, of peace and towards such inherently and wilfully, risky artificials as cause, violation of laws of nature, to which ironically and incidentally they swear. Groups, communities, etc. are all artificials, and would be acceptable to the Leviathan only if the syllogism — the defining of names are correct. Such groups cannot be defined by covenants alone, as regards their actions or performances are concerned. Union of will would be necessary. Hobbes' scheme alone does not give rise to multiplicities of sovereign.

As though, as a result Hobbes gives special importance to bodies, those who can have a definite name, extension, and inertia, etc. Spirit, or the means or the middle term in a syllogism are reduced to bodies. This territorial expression is then combined by Hobbes, especially in his arguments relating to Christian Commonwealth, to a territorial nation — which is based on civil laws and held together by a sovereign. Hence, he can argue that though all the nations of the world are of the prescient omnipotent, yet some are especially His, i.e., some are sacerdotal. Significantly, Hobbes draws upon St. Peter and, St. Paul, for arriving at the notion of a unique body, a unique nation that is Christian as the only rational interpretation and he categorically rejects the spirit, the entire globe of all the nations, which can be of a sacerdotal dominion. Moreover, in his reference to the threefold divisions, regarding the 'Blessed Saviour', which are the 'Radeemer', the 'Pastor' and the 'eternal King', he says that these are of three different times, as it were the divisions laid out serially in the history. Therefore the laws that are said to be canonical, are indeed civil, and are actually given the force of law by the civil sovereign for a specific territorial body. Excluding a very small domain of moral laws, the laws are certainly not penitential (in contrast to Kant's law, which is simply penitential) but are positive, given a force by the sovereign till, and as an intermediate guidance to, the days of judgement. In sharp contrast to this bodily, territorial expression, Augustine and most later exponents argue for a spirit as well. The temporal city and the city of God are created together to pave the way for an imperium that extends beyond territory to all the nations.

One important distinction needs to be noted that while ius gentium did not wish to conquer the gods of the gentiles and of similar other extant groups and remained limited to such international areas of legal actions — it failed in both integrating (or universalizing) the variabilities of human multitudes and in erecting a truly universal empire. Augustinian and also similar later formulations wished to conquer all local 'Gentillistic' aberrations (local gods) by the singular 'supreme' principle and wanted to erect thereupon an integration of the humanity, differentiated no longer by localities or communities. Distinctions having been effaced, this is but an amorphous mass if all the wills are active for the supreme desert. An uniformity exists but an integration, that is a government (or empire) is both a contradiction and an impossibility. Much later, Bentham while commenting upon the American independence, described this contradiction as a dry moisture or a resplendent darkness.

In order to overcome this impossibility, St. Augustine offered a few formulations,

(a) that the temporal city and the city of god were created together and a natural order (out of law) is possible in which the good alone dwells but it is impossible to have an order where evil dwells.

(b) hence no (free) will is evil beforehand, but is so only following the act of evil,

(c) provided the city of god is necessary (there is a prescience, or 'supreme' natural order or end), the evil can be made into a mockery of itself by allowing it to act on its own — which invariably, as it were with the Leviathan, would eliminate evil.

This was therefore a justification of a universal state, the Leviathan. However this Leviathan is not secular. To summarize, in order to universalize a variable population the natural law provides a moral scheme, which erases out all distinctions and provides the population with natural (good). This exercise of the natural will is possible through a Leviathan, a state. This state is a mockery of the evil by the evil itself and cannot be secular.

IV

Mediaeval Europe was concerned with the notion of wholes, and parts, their relative dependencies and hierarchy. This was almost always the expressions of communities, or states *vis-a-vis* the dilapidated empire. Birth of 'modern' states therefore, could not have come through a positive jurisprudence but had to be founded on a 'revolutionary' natural law, a revised stoicism. As it appears, the 'freeing' of individual had threats from a ecclesiastical order and from the last vestiges of the empire; this 'free' individual could not therefore give a call to build up an universal state or an order. Instead it gave rise to states of contingencies and races, of tribes and culture.

This new breed of theories and dogmas dissociated the common origin of the temporal and the city of gods. Histories, cultures and languages or at least a hypothetical state of nature had to be substituted as the 'beginning', the 'origin'. Will was dissociated into reason and morality, supreme good into utility and moral. The means or the necessity of state and society was to be either positive or reasoned. The redefined and reassertive sovereign though, to begin with, was described as a Leviathan (in a description including that of a Christian commonwealth) but soon were to become either the supreme authority on a hierarchy of lesser organic authorities (as in Bodin) or to become essentially limited governments, limited to the theories of double sovereignty, such as in Grotius. Notwithstanding the emergence of (natural) constitutional jurisprudence, as though the states were identical, contingencies or accidents were given a position in the theory of the state (or society). It is therefore only natural that the absence of evil and the necessary Leviathan, which alone virtually endowed the new state with the credit of a seeming secular identity, had to give rise to a state, as though 'outside in' (as used by Gierke), bent upon punishing the deviant citizens. The seeming secularism, the apparent dissociation from the church or from the canons had to secure a moral foundation first at the universal level and had to unsecure itself from a strictly defined sovereignty over its own citizens. A true secular credential could not secure a proper foundation of obedience, especially following Hume's criticism of Hobbes and therefore had to substitute the same with the 'habit' or 'disposition' of obedience (as in Bentham, Austin or Mill). And since there remains still a 'ring' of moral, since the separation of positive and moral laws/norms, as defined, seem unachievable and since law as a system (as in Kelsen) or as a process (as in Wittgenstein or interestingly as it is in Whitehead) assumes once again the old angelic spirit, the 'belief' 'norms', 'rules', processes etc. become the theme with our contemporaries. Quantity of population and its habitual identity were secured by defining the sovereign on a determinate, assignable stock of population (as in Austin).

Over this period many shocks and cracks were to appear and challenge this utilitarian and positivistic aspirations. The English experience was delimited all along by a sense of expediency, by retaining case-laws for example — it was an exercise in continuity. However the Bill of Rights (or Declaration) of Virgina or Pensylvania demanded and clearly demarcated an independent sphere of the sovereignty of the people. In terms of clear constitutional (and therefore universally public) imperatives the French Declaration of the Rights of Man set aside in concrete, a natural sphere of the 'imprescriptibles' — of the 'ante-law'; which otherwise was there in the natural law theories of the modernity. Grotius in fact had conceived of twin-sovereignty, where individuals or collectives could act as the subject of rights, internationally in a large measure independent of the sovereign authority and internally as holding together with the same authority the dominium. As a result the 'degree' of liberty that the subjects retain depend upon the concourses and accidents of their specific history. Changes in the forms of state for example cannot take away from the popular subject its rights. This popular subject, according to him, has an active personality which exists alongside the personality of the sovereign ruler, and exercises extensive authority. This provides the state, then, with a divided sovereign, but in terms of such natural rights as are not to be found in the divided governments of Locke or Bentham and Austin. Even following a conquest a sovereign ruler cannot exercise absolute authority over the people who would still enjoy some natural rights. These rights are in the form of power as over property, and the sovereign authority cannot alienate that but can have the right of usufruct.

It is even more important to notice that for Grotius the popular subjects, of differing personalities (i.e., say of different countries) by virtue of their independent rights may join agreements or contrarily the sovereign authorities would be bound amongst themselves, while for example entering into any agreement, by the various holders of popular subjects. Apart from weakening the sovereign authority the most, this scheme assumes several possibly contradictory bases. Such schemes (provided among others by Grotius, Althusius, Bodin, *et al.*) naturally had a difficulty in defining the universal which existed in its own right, a 'whole' which depended on itself. Varieties of collectivistic or corporatist proposals that had been offered were, however, limited by the mere connections, mere reciprocal rights and duties. Collectively it is the People, co-extensive with the sum of its constituent units and yet paradoxically as a single-bearer of the rights of people — as a 'Subject' of rights, it is a single unit in itself. Even the common will was then the result of the cooperation of individual wills, rendering inevitably collective or state actions, weak and contingent. The common agreement was on a common civil society, however (theoretically) ungrounded, and necessarily on the theory of representation, such that the procuratorial powers could act based on a weak theory of majority decision. So they proposed in effect, sovereignties of people, of communities, of individuals, or represented persons, of the state, etc. In Grotius, for example the original sovereignty that the community had under the inchoate conditions of primitive society, were still retained. Individuals or collectives, he argued, retained as 'Subject' externally the international rights and internally rights pertaining to 'Subjects' of state-authority.

It would appear that these spheres of rights have in recent times been defined in terms of both natural law and positively defined as science-claiming legal artifices. Amongst the contemporary natural law proponents mention might be made of Nozick, Rawls, even Dworkin or Viley; amongst the positively defined artifices are many UN or multilateral frameworks or agreements, for example, and amongst the science-claiming legal artifices are, for example, prescriptions/agreements on education, finance, stock/investments etc. In fact much of UN or multilateral frameworks/conventions derive their strength from natural-law, such as for example those on Human rights, such as the International Covenant on Civil and Political Rights. A number of these do in fact allow, such as the covenant last mentioned, 'contacts' or rights to establish and maintain the community's 'own associations' across borders. Moreover there are 'imperations' on the 'sovereign' states to emulate certain standards or refrain from doing a few acts. This when coupled with the UN statute, which empowers it to use force on 'sovereign' states under specific circumstances, would really leave not much room for a real 'sovereign' to act.

It would now be very interesting to compare the world of St. Augustine or of those European preachers, who had cleared all the sacred oak groves from the face of Europe, with the contemporary world which is rather seriously concerned with the protection of species of minorities, ethnic, religious or linguistic on a ground, which is founded on natural law and which appear to value, at least for a moral ground, governance and development. The common-universal shall then have an irresolvable conflict with the rights of an individual, or the rights of a community. These are rights against the sovereign authority, as it was the case with Grotius. It may be noted that 'minority' can only be defined in terms of a system of government, based on the notion of citizenry which excludes aliens and on the voting principles. Tocqueville had observed this majority-minority in an America, which in its days of declarations of rights did not have a standing army, a city worthy of mention or any groups of people who were not essentially peasants. The notion of 'groups' or 'group-sovereignty' or 'group-morality' (as for example in Pufendorf) of early-modern period of Europe, though not defined in terms of franchise, were defined against an emergent dogma of individual and society, and therefore against an emergent general sociology. Such a society realigned its historiography and analytical tools in favour of a collective, defined either as classes or as divisions of labour. Grotius did not accept group personality but discussed a contractual collection. However the 'identity' of a group (i.e., what early authors defined as 'personality'), if it is not considered ante-legal, what presumably Tocqueville had understood, then only through positive acts of the sovereign alone can be undone what was created earlier through the governance. If instead, the 'identity' is ante-legal or a-temporal, only then such justifying actions on the part of the sovereign be possible which do not belong to the temporal or secular spheres.

Much of contemporary concerns, such as the 'Negro problem to Myrdal, is made into a problem of valuation. Valuation here is an attitude or disposition as Streeten or Myrdal describe it. Disposition or belief is not as fleeting as interest (burdened with ends-means dichotomy), amenable to prescriptions and revisions and, therefore, to a national scheme and yet without any attached claim to a foundation of categories of universal principles. Without going into a rather close scrutiny of this issue, it may be observed that it begins with a fact of variabilities of beliefs, attitudes and respective loci in the population groups, and by transforming valuation into a fact (graded, revisable), this schema tacitly assumes a sovereign of Benthamite-Austinian type that is secured on habits. Prescriptions, revisions and gradations in this schema are not just bloodless 'rational' sand they do not take place just as a state of affairs but as part of an active sponsorship of desirable beliefs, attitudes and dispositions by a certain holder of valuation — who by the fact of its commanding a certain valuation is a claimant to sovereignty. Such a claimant is an auctioneer of valuations who begins to act through vouchsafing. It appears also not to be limited by territory or space and valuational imperatives such as are in universal education or suffrage or limiting population growth rate, competition on free-trades — all this become a part of the campaign by the power, a schema of development.

In legal discussions therefore, as Hart has argued, an "assumed common human objective" remains abiding. A purpose, an ought, many of our Western contemporaries have argued, comes as the end in our interpretation and action. Moreover this does not come alone, but as Fullen argues it, abides by as a process, as do also the means. In fact the non-cognitivist criticism of utilitarian law and politics is that the moral, the emotional, was separated from the interpretative/ actions. The utilitarian command theory and the habit theory limited cognitive reckoning, by way of primarily curtailing down causality. Later criticisms by the non-cognitivists certainly bring legal, normative or sovereign actions; decisions or fiats much closer to moral, process reality: a process that has a purpose, an end and is shared. This evangelizing process grows out of a limited understanding of cognitivity and causality. In case command is causal, it was held, law and actions are cognitive and rational. Failing which, as it is in interpretations or in discourses or in matters civil, etc., the rational is processual or moral; and such a process or end-game view, we hold, is evangelizing first, and second, an alternative which is cognitive and rational can be offered by the *arthasastra* view. This Indian theory alone then can have a claim to represent both welfare and rational together.

Such schemes of development, it may be noted, are to be necessarily plural. In the case of a singular belief or valuation, and since it is a fact, it has no end to achieve and therefore will be static. In the case of plural belief-entities alone, sovereignty can be instituted through transforming other 'classes' or groups of dispositions, through wars on mass ignorance, poverty or ill disposition towards competitiveness, i.e., on the contemporary paganism. What this wishes to achieve is the freedom of war from space or territory and therefore undermines any territorial sovereignty. It is important to note that the above schema

(a) indeed speaks for a sovereignty, but that is global and not territorial;

(b) this global sovereign, has to define itself only by way of a war or punishment, for example on such things as are 'cognoscible' (of Bentham);

(c) cannot justify its instituting itself except by the Institution; otherwise this will have to seek recourse to moral spheres, the sphere of natural law and will have to disclaim the dispositional entities as either non-moral or immoral while claiming itself alone as moral;

(d) can be institutionalized only in bodies; and

(e) cannot define, in the absence of a sovereign, the rationality of its moves. A global schema cannot cease to be either non-secular or warring.

Secular ideals demand that the sovereign is defined unto itself. In fact most definitions in the West, such as by Grotius, Bentham, von Martens or even Hobbs do define sovereignty accordingly, but in varying degrees. It seems that the specific history of West, as for example brought out by Skinner, has given rise to this unfortunate definition of sovereignty and secularism as qualifying or defining it. As we have noted earlier that for example it was not just the crowning of the emperor by the Pope Leo III or on the reverse, the donation of Constantine (the famous forgery) with which this problem originated, but as it seems it was the order, the ecclesiastical which had to be defined this way. Maitland's observations in this regard on a later period is illuminating. Without going into further details and as remarked upon earlier, it was the attempt to separate out a sphere of the temporal that created a separate problem of morality. In order to alleviate this difficulty somewhat Coke's formulations on common laws, or the ordinary disposition towards customary laws, for example, was considered positive. It is in this sense, we may presume, that the global sovereign (that it aspires to be) gives credence today to the customs, presentiments, dispositions, rights and even identity of the loci of the same.

Use of the term loci may not be appropriate. A locus is considered sometimes as the residence of a property and sometimes as the continuity of indefinitely close, discrete existents each exhibiting the property. In fact in the latter case there cannot as such be existent distinguished from a property. A person is then a set of beliefs or dispositions as in much of Humean literature, who cannot enter into a state-of-nature hypothetical contract and for whom there cannot be a sovereign except by way of customary or positively entered government. There being no substantive causality, temporality is but successions and regularity. Governments therefore are similar and a sovereign (the abiding absolute) cannot be defined as such, neither can any abiding moral realm nor any abiding good. Governments are divided and balanced. Hobbesian nominalism is not far off from this position, though it provides some remarkable distinctions. Here individuals are name-holders, distinct bodies. Properties are either by way of accidents or by way of marking out fancies (derived through senses). There being nothing in the world as universal but names. Reasoning or reckoning is but putting names into a proper account. Therefore Hobbesian bodies cannot enter into agreement with the sovereign, but have to enter into agreement with one another. The Leviathan is but a body, distinct altogether from all the assignable bodies of the subject.

It is the body of this representer which is unity and as per Hobbes there is no unity in matter civil amongst the represented. Owing to absolute differences or non-identity between names, there cannot be any causality as such. Temporality is then the unity of the representer — which under no circumstances be divided. In short, temporality is the abiding characteristic in a body, segregated from the ecclesiastical of the body. The latter, for Hobbes, is the spirited. Sense, memory, understanding, reason and opinion — what matters in the temporal, in the form of obedience to the sovereign, are not the effects of will but the will of them. This separation of body and spirit, transforms each body into secular. Owing to absolute non-identity the secular sovereign cannot be the result of secular actions of the subject bodies. In a number of other contractual theories, however, bodies are residence of properties. General contract is based on the common properties.

Sovereignty can be temporally abiding through such properties as are also temporal. Insofar as there are bodies, characterized by the unidentical, causal actions are possible. Through action results a new body. Temporality too is therefore regenerated, or remains as the abiding. For some, e.g. for Grotius or for Collegialism, through spiritualism also contracts could have been entered into though such congregations would not have sovereignty. Thus sovereignty was abiding by way of the abiding causality, limited by the fact that for some writers there was a social contract (towards a general sociology) and such contracats would have its own temporality. Secular institutions therefore got created through such bodies as were secularized (e.g., the real-nominal, being will dichotomies, etc.) with corresponding consequences, as argued earlier, on external-internal obligations or on practical-moral spheres.

It is time now to look for some suggestive answers or principles. As we have indicated in the beginning, we would take recourse to a very brief discussion on Indian theories on *dandaniti* (theories of state). The discussion would remain limited to indications alone, not just because of lack of space but primarily because, most theories are lost and the principles do not exist in fact as being practised. Moreover even a very inappropriate knowledge of the tracts makes it hard indeed to borrow upon and use intelligently.

V

It has been mentioned that welfare, or the realization of *artha* is not possible without the penal authority, the *danda*. Reason being that persons are rarely honest by virtue of the beliefs that they are endowed with (or, in another language, rarely honest by virtue of the nature of natural law) and these persons cannot experience the desired world (*bhoga*) in the absence of the *danda* (Manu). In fact nothing in this world, including the most insignificant creature, can experience the desired world or can live properly without the *danda*. In other words, this *danda* alone enables the (true) appearance of the world (*prakasa*) possible, and this together with the temporal (the temporal rhythm, the *kala*), expresses linguistically or not (*chandas*) this world, through the enabling of experiencing the desired world (*bhoga*). It is thus, along with *chandas*, that *danda* appears. It is therefore prior to the particular appearance, viz. the sovereign, and it is certainly prior to the laws.

All the mobile and immobile earthly formations (the *sthavara* and the *jangama*), that are not only apparent but that are also experiencing the respective worlds of desires as though as per the rules or laws (i.e., causally), keep doing the same out of a fear of this *danda* alone (Manu). Laws, therefore, are as per the injunctions; and there is no need to segregate natural causal laws from the normative or from the 'ought' imperatives. However, does that connote a causal relation between the *danda*, the injunction and the fear which causes the experience of world possible? This significance may now be noted that there in *danda* does not reside the causality (*hetutva*) of fear.

According to Madhatithi, *danda* and the fear are related. It may be recalled that two entities are called related when one entity qualifies the other entity, which is thus qualified. This qualified-qualification is closer to the noun-adjective type, though different from it. A qualified is not exactly a noun. Such a relation gives rise to a qualified cognition, as for example, the cognition of *danda* relate to fear. This relation however does not express the power of a container (or locus) in containing the related, but is expressive of a qualified cognition. On the contrary, the relation between the *danda* and fear is expressive of a class (or universal, *samanya*) being related.

In fact this *samanya* (class) is signified by a particular qualified (*visesya*) in such a way that the qualified appears as a qualifier, or as adjectival. As a result on this *danda* adjective (*prakara*), as though, the fear gets related and gives rise to a cognition. This cognition in turn is the cause or the actuator of desire which in turn causes action. The cognition alone, in order to cause desire, does not require *danda*, although *danda* as a qualified-universal still qualifies this cognition, assuring as it were the unobstructed experience. Fear, as the non-appeared cognition in being related to the adjectival *danda*, gives rise to that cognition which causes action or experience.

We would like to argue that desire, owing to cognition, has similarity (measure) or action, owing to the desire, has similarity. In the first case, the cognition of the accomplished happy-person appears as the past and the desire or non-appeared happy person is the future. But in the second case both the desire and the action are in the future. We would argue that the noun happy-person remains the same over causation, that is, the object (of cognition) remains the same. The noun here is of a special type being used as though adjectivally. The point is that while a pot in front is directly perceived (therefore cognized), a pot-universal (beyond space and beyond time) is perceived indirectly (*alaukika*) through an indirect nearness (*alaukika pratyasatti*) to (or with) the form (*rupa*) whose designation is universal. It is said that 'a cognition of self-referring noun appears as an adjective, and being of such property (or attribute), is a relation between the pot-universal and the eye of the beholder. In fact it is not just a pot-universal, but a designator of such an attribute which is adjectival (or being adjective) and such that the latter is similar to the universal. This special relation or nearness (called *samanyalaksanapratyasatti*) with the pot-universal, while directly perceiving the pot in front, entails also having the same relation with the pot itself (not the universal pot) in the event of a cognition of 'pot on the floor'. Similar to the cognition of 'pot on the floor' is the cognition of 'happy-person on me (being at various states or times)'. The person therefore has this special relation (*samanyalaksanapratyasatti*) with the happy-person (which is here a happy-person universal), while having a direct cognition of his having been the accomplished happy-person, or his having the cognition of his future, non-appeared happy-person. It is feasible now to have a cognition of a future object, the non-appeared happy-person or the non-appeared ability to perform the (future) action.

We argue that fear is that state where knowledge has not yet emerged. In a certain sense then absence of knowledge is fear. It is important however to note that this absence is also a real (*bhava*). Therefore action or *bhoga* is undertaken, caused either by the desire (which in turn is caused by knowledge) or by the fear (caused by the non-appearance of knowledge). These are, being causal, under a continual metamorphosis (*pratiksanaparinama*). *Danda*, the penal, stands apart and does not participate in this causation. It is only related as a *samanya-visesya* (qualified-universal) to both the qualities of knowledge and fear, to the former as though by way of sustaining it, and to the latter as though by way of restricting it. Following the above argument, it may be observed that even when *danda* can be internally perceived, that is, directly perceived, it cannot be held to be the cause. The causal chain can be enumerated as per the cognition-desire-action, etc. rule. However when the relatedness of *danda* is not internally perceived but is inferred from observing the actions or experiences of others, even then this is not held as a causal agent. As a result, *danda* and the rules or laws are known neither intuitively nor penitentially or morally (as through the attached piety).

The domain of discourse, where a certain inference achieved already by the speaker has to be conveyed to a second person, should require the employment of *hetu* (a cause, as shown in the discourse) in the fivefold (or tenfold) discourse-structure (*mahavakya*) (*Nyaya-Sutra*, and *Vatsyayana bhasya* on the same). Employment of *hetu* is therefore necessary only in the case of communicating socially an inference (*pararthanuman*), by way of showing the similarity or the dissimilarity of the inferrible attribute to the analogy. *Hetu* (reason, the middle term) has its strength in the invariable concomitance (the *vyapti*) and in the condition of being an attribute of the subject (*paksadharmata*). With the help of these two the *hetu* establishes the *sadhya* (what is to be proved) — such that *hetu* is shown as a case of the *sadhya*. Now in a discourse, which is aimed at elucidating the truth (*vadakatha*) in establishing the right inference to another, such as in communicating the hypothetical *danda* having the property of being the *hetu* (*hetuta*), the ascertaining of the two delimiters, respectively of the property and of the relation of *hetu*, is necessary. However *danda*, shown above as cognizable through the *samanya-prattasatti*, cannot have the delimiter of property because it is the qualified-universal and therefore cannot have the property of *hetu*.

We would argue on the contrary that an injunction sentence is self-contained — have a complete meaning (*svarasya*), while a sentence in an ordinary discourse does not have the same. The sentences of the latter type depend for their meaning on another different validation (*pramananantar*) which is not required by the *vidhi* sentences. The speaker in an ordinary discourse arrives at the meaning through another different validation, and to convey the meaning, sentences are used by him. The *vidhi* sentences do not signify the meaning arrived at through a different validation but as argued above by dint of sentential-instruments (*linga*) the meaning is signified. The *laksana* used in such a sentence is not meant for overcoming an alternate validation. As per sentential (or word-sound, used here in the sense of an ordinary discourse) implication, that Devadatta receives/enjoys the fruit-laden villages is valid. However, only when we pay attention to the speaker's intent or desire we cognize that Devadatta receives these only as an itinerant and that he is to enjoy thereafter the town (to be visited). This latter cognition (illocutionary) owes to another different validation — only following which the *ekavakyata* (or here, the discourse) is accepted. This *ekavakyata* is not sentential (or do not preside over ordinary discourse), but it is out of another validation. If the meaning were sentential (i.e., according to the *sabdasvabhav* — nature of the word-sound), its meaning would have been unvarying and unrelated to the existence or not of another validation. Discourse is delimited by illocution. Similarly, sentences prescribing wealth earning for example, if considered in isolation shall have only materially implied validation (*vastuvrttyanusar*) — unless these appear as part of an injunction (while the meaning appears sententially). Therefore both discourse and material implication are delimiting, and in such cases actions pertaining to that would be delimited by the obtaining of that (visible) fruit alone. *Vidhi* sentence coalesces through one sentence, and there too a fruit is obtainable. It may be noted that none of the above have been defined as the indefinable good.

It may be mentioned very briefly that this above contention can also be shown to be true by the application of *upadhi*. The entity that is wider (*vyapaka*) than what is sought to be proved (the *sadhya*) and yet not wider than the *hetu* is called an *upadhi*. A *hetu* vitiated by *upadhi* cannot draw defensible inferences. Briefly, to take an example, *danda* allows the manifestation of things or entities and this is not known to happen (or it is not knowable) with the fear; and hence the same is vitiated by *upadhi*, rendering the *hetuta* of *danda* as indefensible. Therefore *danda* cannot be shown to be the cause of the fear. To sum up briefly, *danda* is neither known intuitively or morally, nor known to be as the judge who would render justice and penalty — in short, it is not known as that which causes fear. Moreover, *danda* cannot be inferred and made known, through discourses to the others, as the cause of fear. Any pact with *danda* is thus imaginary; and neither is it feasible to enter into pact of one with another to create or erect or infer about *danda*. It is important to note that an absence, as for example, by imagining the absence of pacts of one with another, cannot create a real, viz. the *danda*; no amount of hypostatization would be of any help in this regard.

In certain tracts of these theories, properties (*dharma*) are the loci of individuals (*dharmi* or distincts), and both the properties and individuals are taken into consideration (as true). The individual is distinguished by characteristics of times past, present and future — which in turn are characterized by the state of affairs. Property again is characterized by individuation. Distinction is known through comparison. Again to have the knowledge of the common (property) of a comparable group, the cause of the non-cognition of a comparable individual may be considered as the common property. Therefore given a comparable class or group, we can discern that property of which individuals are but distinctions. Such distinctions are owing to the extensions of other properties. As a result, neither absolute in-identity nor absolute identity are considered as the case, and on the contrary, it is argued that identity (together with) in-identity prevails. The sovereign authority is such a (resident) common property as is common to the whole population, the groups, the powerfuls, etc. and it is also such as through which alone other (extensional) properties of the individuals, groups remain operative. It is therefore subtler, extensionally larger and more powerful than any. It is important to note therefore that neither a state-of-nature nor any agreement or covenant (hypothetically) at that, is indeed needful in explaining the sovereign in this case. In other words, sovereignty inheres in each individual, group or the powerful. This brings us to another very important point, that is a *desa* (near equivalent of a body or a country) is that extension which is the action (or the same as its fruit) of the sovereignty. A sovereign country, for example, should not therefore be defined on a definite countable (or determinate and assignable) population, nor on a historically limited territory. In fact, the theory does not explain a sovereign as such, but explains the sovereign who seeks to win.

VI

The causal scheme in this theory speaks about the existence of a distinctive-cause (somewhat comparable to the efficient cause) and incidental causes (the *nimitta*), such that sovereignty is the distinctive cause of the sovereign authority while it is incidental only for the others. The space (*desa*) over which the sovereign resides, and also the temporal aspect of such residence is related to the causal relation with either the sovereign or with the others etc. It may be recalled however that, there is no causal relation with the fear that goads to action. The sovereign authority is neither identical nor in-identical with the individuals, groups, etc. but is related by identity and in-identity. Therefore in contrast to the absolute in-identity, which reigns supreme in contemporary political dogmas, this Indian theoretical vantage offers something that speaks indeed of a 'participatory' sovereign-governance. Moreover contemporary theories cannot explain the hiatus that it left unexplained as either the family, or the various forms of paterfamilias, the respective potestas or power especially as regards its explanation on property (rights), owing to such absolute in-identity. Notwithstanding Sumner Maine's generalization on laws that speaks so little about sovereignty, here is a theoretical possibility that bridges the breaches between family or groups to the sovereign, or the hiatus between power, property rights of a person and the sovereign. A fundamental cleavage that remains unaddressed in contemporary polity especially as regards its developmental imperatives, notwithstanding the demands that some cooperative movements or some 'grass roots organizations' raise, is for a politically aware 'mass' an awareness of sovereignty or its duties and imperatives. Awareness smacks of will, spirit or consciousness. The vantage presented above however offers a vigorous formulation of this much needed developmental imperative.

In fact, *Arthasastra* considers it obligatory on the part of the sovereign to bring prosperity — the *sree* and *artha* to the population and the earth contained therein. This is necessary, as explained in one theoretical vantage. It is argued that the entrapment of the self (*purusa*) is because of the creation (or world, life, the *srsti*) and it is also said simultaneously that the creation is meant for making freedom from entrapment possible. There is an apparent contradiction. The theory answers that creation alone is not the cause of entrapment but there are other entrapments such as in coma (unconscious state), deep sleep or in *pralaya* (near equivalent of anarchism, revolution, i.e., a state which cannot be apprehended through sense-organs). If the self is considered to be unentrapped in these states, then the much laboured knowledge is rendered meaningless. However these states are not the states of freedom according to any of the vantages, and therefore this creation is meant for and it alone makes it possible to achieve freedom. This creation (or world) is also the *bhoga* (the experience) — the satisfaction of *dharma* (comparable to the principles of conduct and stability), *artha* and *kama* (the nearest equivalent is possibly pleasure or desire). Therefore achieving of freedom, though entrapped by these *bhoga*, is possible through the satisfaction of this and access to a knowledge of it. It should also be noted that morality cannot be a problem here and prosperity and satisfaction of desires in its full bloom remain compatible with knowledge and freedom.

As sense-reports unassisted by mind go haywire, so would also these satisfactions and acquiring of knowledge and freedom without an abiding sovereignty. Reason as argued above, is the most common property and the most extensive and the subtler is characterized in the sovereign. It is important indeed to note that the more extended and the subtler property is not only true and resident of the distinct individual, but also that such a causal relation cannot be explained or should not be compared with a relation of hierarchy or a relation of parts-whole. Without going into any further discussion on that, it may be observed that the Indian theory offers a causal and a relational scheme. Therefore without the sovereign, which ensures the distinctive cause of satisfaction of each and every undertaking (the classes of *barga*), everything — from the very true knowledge (the word, the *anviksiki*) to the worldly (the practical) is lost. Each such undertaking has its own distinguishing distinctive-necessity. This supremacy of the *danda*, the *arthasastra* and the sovereign should not be confounded with secularism as is done, for example by Dumont. In fact to the Indian debates this notion is irrelevant owing both to the non-existence of the problem as fact or being unproblematic in the construction of theories. However if a comparison is made in terms of the sovereign's separation from the organization of religion, from the action ensuring that the populace are true to their religious or moral pursuit, from the legal/normative/rule-based actions that ensure the moral sphere or the ends to be achieved, etc. the *arthasastra* sovereign is truly secular. It is also necessary to notice that in all this artifacts of secularism, hierarchy is the result of a certain ideas and culture (as elaborations of the text) — and livelihood. Hierarchy in Tellenbach or in Dumont is part of tradition (even this term is so Biblical), as for example of the Thomistic; or the primacy as secularism as in Augustine. There is no reason why such questions or categories should be considered universal and hence much of the occidental or orientalist writing on this subject — as for example of those who attempt to give primacy to the *dharmasastra* in preference to the *arthasastra* (by quoting Mitaksara and not elaborating upon such others as Medhatithi) as was analysed by Kane, Lingat *et al.* seem to be nullifying the *prasthan* of *arthasastra*. This has been brought out excellently by Yogendranath Bagchi.

Similarly attempts are made to make a general sociology possible for India, by way of theoretically instituting naturally free in-identical individuals, division of labour, symbolic discourse or interaction and as it were a separate general contract for the society. These are evidenced in Renou, Dumont or Srinivas. In fact such studies often fall short of the spirit of revolutionary-making that nature-law and as a consequence (civil) soviety — or, a general sociology took up in Europe. Reason, as we attempted to show in earlier sections, was made into a cause of both personal enlightenment (or cognition) — the associated freedom and the sovereign's legitimacy of actions. *Arthasastra* clearly states that the logic of cognition and of *danda* are separate; *danda* is not the cause of fear (or actions out of fear). *Dharma*, while it is not at all religion, is about the cognition and worldly experience. The society of India, if that term can be used, is not part of general sociology but is constituted of *dharma* — with which *danda* is not causally related as a *samanya*. The Indian vantage adumbrated above would not substantiate this approach. In fact the state here is not instituted on citizenry. It is for the sovereign to care for the prosperity of the whole of population unlike as for example Kant's idea, where the sovereign can enable achieving the Right alone. *Arthasastra* asks the sovereign categorically on this, and it also asks the sovereign to locate amongst its population those who are angry, avaricious, insulted and afraid such that the sovereign-to-win may satisfy or pacify this lot of its own, and engender a similar lot in the lands of enemy or that of friend-of-enemy. Again, in the description of the sevenfold limbs of a state etc. neither citizen nor quantity of population are mentioned. It is necessary to observe that while for *arthasastra* the prosperity of the whole of population — the earth (i.e., the land and all other living beings) contained therein is the principal concern, at the same time for the distinctive form or the individuation, viz., the sovereign, the mode of action is free of both the quantity (the countable, assignable, determinate) and the variability of the population. Explanation is, as argued above, based on the theory of causality, property and its locus, or the reverse. As regards variability, two aspects are noteworthy. First, the notion and institution of *pindas* (or *sapinda*), *pravara* and *gotra* apart from those of *jati* and *sreni*. Briefly, *pinda* is a kin to a cognate, though broader in scope in terms of descent, and is definable in terms of that which helps prosper flesh and blood. *Gotra* and *pravara* (which is as though an expansion of *gotra*) are also another property, whose descents are *sagotra* or *sapravara*. Neither of these are definable in terms of cognate or agnate, nor in terms of potestas (power) or inheritance (though in exceptional cases inheritance is applicable). All such properties are of importance in marriage, and conduct, and only sometimes in inheritance. In terms of contemporary debate or of Western practices, the most noteworthy aspect is the superior method by which various 'natural' barrier such as blood, race, ethnicity, linguicity or of locality, etc. are overcome, by enabling the distinct individuals to be located variously in the locus of variable properties. It may be noted that the scope of *nimitta* allow the same distinct varieties of loci. Further, it is not for the sovereign to make conquest over a so-called 'natural' multitude through an effacement of the 'ante', 'natural' properties but it is necessary for the sovereign to enable and allow the same multitude to be resident in the respective *desacara*, *kulacara* (the customs and principles of conduct of the *desa*, clan, etc.) in simultaneity with variable other properties of *gotra*, etc.

In this theoretical vantage, property is the locus of certain distincts and although this property is characterized by a few such distincts, it is not extensional but on the contrary limited by the temporal order of the appearance and the state of affairs. It would allow however, a feature-wise class (or group) association which is temporally present. Feature's disappearance would indicate the absence of that feature-associated name. Features are associated with, and defined by, actions. Therefore groups etc. are not temporally abiding and it is the individual's cognition and action that defines themselves on their own, or as associated with groups. Such groups are exclusively positive and, therefore, not based on any moral, natural or similar reasons. There cannot be thus any universally recurring, temporally abiding features. This lack of extensionality cannot therefore render it a scope for universalization over a countable universe. The proponents never have claimed that. This is in sharp contrast to the tradition of the opponent where 'virtue', for example, would be a universal property extendable to all. They say that no one is evil before commiting to an evil act; or everyone is naturally good. Hence justice is not only possible, but as it were the only conceivable foundation of the sovereignty even if it is taken behind 'a veil of ignorance', or a loss of certitude or ratiocination, etc. The notion of duty, imperatives and law in the Western tradition is derivable from that. Another progressive shift that is noticeable in that tradition is from 'right' as an adjectival quality to 'right' as a noun substantive (e.g. Austin's remark). Trades in rights are then entirely feasible. A right in this case associates with a single name. Extensionality and this shift are strongly related especially, as it seems, through a nominalism. Groups, firms, associations, etc. could then be considered as organizations of rights. To be brief, in this move towards a law of things and contract (as for example in Jhering's computation), enforceability appeared essential. Law there appears as positive, as though forwarded from customs, with penal portents. Duty appears more and more Ciceronian, as moral and universal or otherwise as part of utilitarian beliefs. It is with this Western scheme in mind that Lingat for example attempts to treat Indian theories and development, such that *dharmasastra* appears as customary laws. For him law is as positive and enforceable while *dharma* is about duties, and it is through law-in-action as a transformative force that *dharma* is turned into a rule of law. This however appears to be wrong. In the classification of theoretical tracts (*sastra*), for the earlier masters *dharmasastra* was not a distinct knowledge tract though *dandaniti* was. According to Vatsyayana (as pointed out by Bagchi) each theoretical tract has a twofold necessity — of gaining knowledge (or *tattvas*) and reaching the end necessity or the ultimate. *Trayi* is a theoretical tract, whose necessity is for knowing the *dharma* (the right and wrong) and the valid cognition, while for *dandaniti* it is to know when and where and with what might to apply the four instrumentalities as the *tattva*, and to become sovereign of the world as the ultimate. Therefore for the sovereign this use of four instrumentalities, viz., — *sama* (encouragement), *dana* (reward), *bheda* (differentiation) and *danda* (threat and punishment) of the individuals characterized by time and state of affairs is of sole importance but not, as is often maintained, that its concern is the judgement or the maintenance of either justice or *dharma*. *Dharma* or its abhorrence is the individual's concern, insofar as such actions are not against the property of sovereignty. The presence of *danda* ensures both the experiences of fruits of action, viz., the visibility related (*drsta*) and the invisibly related (*adrsta*). However individual's actions and resulting experiences are free of sovereign's dictate, as well as the dictates of a hypothetical society. As argued earlier, there was never a 'society' in the general sociological sense of the term, but there were as it were feature-groups; and therefore neither names the individuals, nor were the individuals bound by either the sovereign or a society, in pursuing and experiencing its actions. This sense of freedom, which is perhaps the loftiest, is Indian. Indian theory thus provides for the true foundation of positive laws individual freedom, and the sovereign who alone can ensure this positive freedom, the welfare. For proper actions the individual is rewarded (or even as an example to others), otherwise differentiated and finally threatened or punished. *Sama* is therefore the first possible action of the sovereign.

Vrtti (broadly speaking, occupation) is related to *Vartasastra*, another theoretical tract – whose first objective is to acquire knowledge of production, agriculture, trade, etc. and whose ultimate aim is to acquire wealth-prosperity. It is imperative upon the sovereign to look after the health and stability of the *vrttis*. The sovereign is thereby not defined by the enforcement of *dharma*; neither the *dharma* through law-in-action is transformed into an enforceable law, whereby the sovereign acquires as it were its sovereignty (through enforcement). In short, Indian theory says that state-and-sovereign is not legal, or is not defined legally. For *Arthasastra* a state is not a law-state. It would in fact be the closest to a development-state. We have already seen how difficult, if not impossible, it is for a law-state to be a developmental state. It may not be improper here to point out that 'renunciation' is therefore unrelated to both the general populace and the sovereign. It is only a fact that some orientalists have made *dharma* and renunciation into something they call 'Indian'. It is wrong and unfortunate.

It has been pointed out already that there is a sharp difference between the *desa* and territory. Territory is independent of the sovereignty, and possibly explained and bequeathed by such terms as tradition (Cannan was endowed) — it is therefore the duty of the sovereign to keep to it as such. In the case of *desa*, as defined earlier, it is defined by the action of the sovereign, more so by the action of the sovereign-to-win. The ultimate for a sovereign is to win over the entirety of the desired earth. Moreover, since the state is no longer a law state as defined by, say, a citizenry or the negation of the aliens, the state remains no longer limited by traditionally endowed territory but it depends on the qualities (*gunas*) and the desires which a sovereign-to-win would strive for.

In this particular vantage, there are qualities (*guna*) — ever dynamic — and an unbalance amongst which causes the appearance of the distinct individual. The disappearance of the distinct would mean that there is now an equilibrium. Any state is constituted of six qualities, the details of which may not be elaborated here. These qualities are the variabilities of treaties or pact, such as pact, conflict, etc. The eminence of one quality causes an unbalance and a distinct appearance. These are then qualities, to one of which the actions of the sovereign need to adhere at a certain time such that the sovereign is enabled to achieve a certain constituent (*prakrti*) either in his own state (who were otherwise turning out against the sovereign) or in the state of his enemy (to the sovereign's own benefit) In order to apply a certain quality (to the sovereign's action), the knowledge of the fivefold constituents of any state is necessary These constituents are *amatya* (elites, powerfuls, lords, etc.), *rastra* (state machineries, governors, etc.), *durga* (defence mechanism, fort, etc.), *kosa* (finance, exchequer, etc.) and *danda* (penal authority, power to threat, etc.). Again a sovereign should consider itself as surrounded spatially by twelve other sovereigns (each of whom has five constituents) such as friendly, enemy, enemy's friend states etc. Sovereign's actions should therefore be the total of seventy-two *prakrtis*, (sixty of the twelve surrounding states, and the twelve of his own). Actions from any of the six qualities, of these *prakrtis*, depend on the time. Qualities cannot be destroyed but the actions cause such an unbalance that a certain *prakrti* (constituents) is either lost or gained (disappears or reappears). The sovereign is, therefore, to be either a sovereign-to-win or it is lost. *Desa* is therefore not as given, but as acted upon.

It is as though a series of ceaseless actions — actions of war, conflict, diminution of enemy's exchequer or *danda*, or pact etc. that are characteristic of the sovereign. Actions ceased would mean the disappearance of the sovereign. Therefore to achieve the *tattvas* (the knowledge, etc.), i.e., the *artha* for the multitudes and the earth contained therein, the sovereign must act on the qualities — that is relentlessly on attritions, pacts, diminutions. In short development cannot be but without war, attritions, pacts or diminutions, etc. This is also what Thucydides had said but unfortunately the reigning theories in the contemporary world — the world that is ravaged most by wars and attritions, do not provide as such, this element and speak for international morality, a free trade or peace that never was or never is. We must look at development or *artha* in the light of this theory of qualities and action.

Development without a sovereign is impossible. *Artha* (or *danda*) is employed for both enabling the achievement of *dharma*, *artha* and *kama* to each individual of the multitude and disabling the threat and varieties of evil (*vyasana*). The sovereign in such employment should strive for acquiring the unacquired, preserving or maintaining the acquired, growth of the preserved and endowment of the grown-up to the appropriate station or person.

Given this, and before this essay is concluded, it is important to notice that *danda* or sovereign being non-causally related to the resident of various properties, it gives rise to alternate or possible (*vikalpa*) formulations of conjugates. Such alternates are possible and allowed but in themselves they are just variations for state of affairs, characterized temporally by their disappearance or appearance. These are not *artha*. Therefore, the temporal provenance of the sovereign may not mean much. Some say that temporality is that which abides through the *drsta* (that which is known to bear certain fruit) to the *adrsta* (whose fruit-bearing relation is not known). However logic, maxim, etc. achieve the same. Those actions that are from the qualities are marked in time (*kala*), and over the sovereign; *kala* and *danda* presides over that. That is called *rta*, and should not be confounded with justice. True sovereign ensures *rta*. Such actions ensure the employment of *artha* (in the above sense) for the multitude and enables the sovereign to acquire the world — the twofold distinct characteristic of *dandaniti*. An alternate that marked temporally does not satisfy this above is not true. A sovereign in this latter case may as well be substituted for the multitudes.

15

Technology, Man and Spirituality

Sanctifying Technology Through Sacrifice

Mohammed Reza Rikhtegaran

Is it possible to bring technology and spirituality together? Usually technology is referred to as an instrument of mass production related to profit and loss. But is technology merely an instrument? Regarding technology as mere instrument is correct but it keeps us from understanding the essence of technology and its relation with truth.

Unconcealedness and concealedness of Being are always together, and every stage of unconcealedness is related to its corresponding concealedness. The Greeks call this unconcealedness Aletheia, that is, Truth.[1] It is quite strange that contemplation about the essence of technology brings us to considering and understanding the unconcealedness and concealedness of the truth. In other words the essence of technology is nothing technical, just as the essence of a tree is not itself a tree which can be seen among other trees.

The truth or essence of technology, is the disposing and dispossession of raw material for consumption through which mastery over the universe is achieved. In other words in the realm of technology, man is confronted with a sort of unconcealedness, based on which he uses things for the mere purpose of consumption and thereafter achieving the mastery. With this dispossession the relationality of man with things goes through a transformation and things turn into fixed stock. Dispossession is the essence of technology.[2]

The question is, how is it possible that technology — the basis of which is Western, and, worldly and is rooted in the left (wrong) dimension of human existence and the preoccupation of which is the domination of, and mastery over the material universe, be brought under the domination of the right dimension of the human existence? How to make it spiritually oriented and Eastern, while preserving it, and thereby sanctify it? It was mentioned that technology is based on a particular unconcealedness and a special relationality with Being. In other words, technology is itself a culture and considering its etymology culture is a kind of interpretation of earth. Thus, the very issue may be put in a different way, i.e., how is it possible to bring forth a union between the culture of technology and the culture of spirituality and at the same time retain both. The crux of the problem, therefore, is as to which cultural aspect we are to transfer the culture of technology, in other words, in which culture is it to be included. It is the question of the confrontation of the two cultures. It is the confrontation between the left (wrong) dimension and the right dimension of human existence. Therefore, there emerges the well-known confrontation between the East and the West. However, the very essence of the West and its culture which is the basis of technology, is earthly, whereas the essence of the East and its culture is the renunciation of this world. If technology is to be adopted by Eastern culture and knowledge, there shall be contradiction between the two. Thus a union between the two is not possible and the desire to have technology along with Eastern spirituality is wishful thinking.

On the other hand, if we accept that Being always keeps the world balance through its unconcealedness and concealedness, and that today the onslaught of the army of the left (wrong) dimension of the human existence calls for a sort of spirituality through which the balance of the world is won, and if we believe that the Eastern spirituality cannot unite with Western culture, we have to admit that to attain this essential balance the world today requires the emergence of a different kind of spirituality which is not purely Eastern. In modern age, mastery of technology has taken such a shape that Being has unconcealed a totally different kind of spirituality. The historicity of the confrontation of technology with spirituality reveals that this confrontation could have emerged only in this period of history. This is because in every period of history only one sort of unconcealedness and objective relationality has got the chance to have mastery. "Every age is the time for emergence and dominion of a truth (unhiddenness of Being), and when (the predestinate) time of its dominion is expired, it (i.e., the truth) will be concealed under the reign of another truth that is to emerge".[3] The same thing was mentioned by the thirteenth century Sufi Nuruddin Abdur-Raman Jami: "This world is the world of form-worshipping in each cycle (stage) of which, someone plays the drum of Being. Thus, the Truth is manifested through different forms. Had the world been always the same, so many rays of light would have kept themselves hidden."

The ontological basis of history is man's time and presence which is based on the openness of Being. The manifestation of truth and its unconcealedness and concealedness in the microcosms and in other words man's relationality with the Being is the ontological basis of history in the macrocosms. History is nothing but the objectivization and externalization of this interior relationality of human beings with Being itself. History is the objectivization of man's spiritual journey in the various stages of Being. The nature of man makes this journey possible. It is only a human being who dwells in two houses, the house of God and the house of Satan. There are so many paradises in his heart and so many hells in his earthly aspect. It is only the human being which is the interface of these two dimensions. His station is where two seas meet. Now, the major point is which dimension he may be inclined towards to attain either a sacred, or a profane history. In this get-together we talk about "The Interface of the Cultural Identity and Development", and, therefore, we should remember that this interface is the man. 'Interface' is the essence of man.

> What a strange elixir is Man, he is a compound of the animal and the angel, moving towards the former makes him lower than the animals and by moving towards the latter he can surpass the angels.
>
> (Sadi, 13th century)

Therefore, the ontological basis of man's problem lies in the fact that he is the interface between light and darkness, and also the left (wrong) and the right dimensions of Being as well as the East and the West; and that, the solution to this problem is the reconciliation of the two. Thus, if we accept that the onslaught of the army of the left (wrong) dimension of Being and the happening of profane history is something entirely human, and if we accept that the happening of the sacred history and the realization of the right dimension of Being is also human to the same degree, the reconciliation between the two necessitates the fact that man should not merely be the symbol of one of the two dimensions of his existence but he should emerge as the universality of his exterior and interior dimensions — a status which puts the left (wrong) dimension of the human existence at the service of his enlightened and sacred dimension, the status of spirituality in which the rules of heavens are extended to the present world. This new kind of spirituality, which is quite different from the purely Eastern spirituality, is called the station of *Jamoljam*, i.e., the United Union, or *Itlaq*, i.e., absoluteness, or *Farg-i-badal-jam*, i.e., dispersion after Union. This kind of spirituality is beyond East and West. It is neither Eastern nor Western but it is Westernized East and Easternized West. With this sort of spirituality a new epoch has emerged.

But are we in a position to undergo such a transformation? Can we cease our existence in this earthly life and be reborn in a spiritual life and thereafter live in absolute timelessness and return to the world and technology, and build our relationship with technology on the basis of this new sort of life? Is it possible entirely to bring the left (wrong) dimension of our existence to the service of the high and right dimension of our existence? Do we have the power to eliminate the gap between the earthly-life and the after-life and make the earthly-life identified with the after-life? As human beings, are we united with the spiritual station of the *Jamoljam* : the United Union? Are we that unique person "whose both hands are Right?"

Obviously the answer to all these questions is negative. Why, it is because achieving this ideal requires cessation of the earthly life and a new birth. As the holy Prophet suggested the solution is *Maut towa Kabl Aan Tmewo towa*, i.e,"Let your Ego die, before you enter the realm of death" which in fact is the elimination of illusions (*Mho-su-hum*) and the collapse of the reign and majesty of the earthly life, culminating in a new sobriety which is based upon the after-life (*Shahu maslum*). Extinction in God (*Fana-Fi Allah*) along with subsistence with God (*Baya-Ballh*) is the solution. In a nutshell the solution lies in sacrifice. Something should be sacrificed to achieve something else. Sacrifice is the remedy and the only possible way of salvation.

The word sacrifice has been derived from the Latin word "Sacrificium" which means "to make holy". By itself, this word does hold religious significance. In the course of its history, which can be traced through several millennia, the idea of sacrifice has undergone many changes, and the basis of this in all its aspects has been "the self-giving of human being to the divinity", without which the external rite has no religious value.

Man has always been experiencing divinity in himself by sacrificing his egoism This cast of mind could only be possible through sacrifice. In many religions this cast of mind had been the ultimate goal. In these religions the spiritual journey of man should amount to absolute extinction which is the end of journey. In the early Hebrew scriptures, however, the idea was expressed that obedience to God's commandments is better than sacrifice. From the beginning, Christianity too emphasized not only the continuance of Cultic sacrifice in the celebration of the Eucharist but also the necessity of a self-surrender that finds external expression in other ways as well; thus, even in the New Testament, prayers, hymns of praise, good work, and especially love of neighbour are described as 'sacrifice'.[4] In Islam too obedience to God's decrees, performance of religious duties, avoiding sins, purification of the self, invocation (*Zikr*) and meditation (*Fikr*) are the ways of achieving salvation. The *Holy Quran* puts it in these words: *Sum Jasnak Ali Saryatin Minal Lamar Fabeyayaaha* "Then we placed you on the path of the Divine Rule, to follow it" or *Mad Falah Min Tajki wa gikrashm Rabi Fashli bil Law-saraun Alyahaladyaya-d-walad Karunn vaki.* "He indeed shall be successful who purifies himself, and invokes the name of his Lord and prays. Nay! you prefer the life of this world, while the hereafter is better and more lasting." Also good deeds and obseervance of religious duties are vehicles to divinity *Jamjeka yadjawaleka Rabbi Falyyamla Amlann Sallayyha.* "Whoever hopes to meet his Lord, he should do good deeds." Therefore, in Semitic religions, sacrifice means observance of religious duties and sacraments, and sacrament itself is the vehicle to self-extinction and annihilation. In other words in Semitic religions sacrifice has given its place to sacrament. But what is the ontological basis of sacrament? How does sacrament come into being? In Semitic religions after self-annihilation and cast of mind and coming to the end of the majesty of the earthly life, and when the reign of time and temporal existence is over, the Prophet returns to the mankind, after his extinction along with subsistence. He returns to time in absolute timelessness, to the status of humanhood to guide his people.

But now he returns free from illusions, knowing how to look at the world and how to treat others. He knows how all human transactions and for that matter all aspects of human livelihood can be reconciled with lasting truth of his own existence and be spiritually oriented. Therefore, he brings a religion, and legislates laws, sets rules and regulations (*Shariah*) and establishes a spiritual society (*Ummah*). Since he attains the status of extinction along with subsistence, he always puts into consideration the harmony between rites and rules, and the lasting truth of his own existence. Therefore obedience to the Prophet and his decrees can result to gradual, and correct orientation. The earthly life focuses on the after-life and on this path, which is called *Siratalmostigeem*, i.e., the Right path voluntary death and self-annihilation is achieved and *Maulawa Fabel An Awtuwa*, i.e., "let your ego die, before you enter the realm of death" would be applicable to the situation.

However, self-annihilation is the solution. Sacrifice is the solution. The illusory being and the chaotic gap between the earthly-life and the after-life must be removed. But if this self-extinction is to be finished here and not followed by sobriety and awareness, the foundation of this world collapses. Therefore, although cessation of the earthly life is the solution, it should be alongside a completely different life to begin. It is being alive, and at the same time being dead. It proceeds through disillusion, along with enlightenment through sobriety and intuition, extinctions side by side with subsistence (*Wa Al Fana Maubaka*). This has resulted in the difference between the sacrifice in this sort of spirituality and the purely Eastern spirituality. In the Eastern form of sacrifice the earthly-life suddenly collapses and the spiritual traveller reaches the status of salvation. In this sort of sacrifice the traveller sacrifices the left (wrong) dimension of his existence entirely and reaches the angelic status. But in the sacrifice of the status of *Jamoljam*, that is, United Union, disillusionment and the collapse of the majesty and sovereignty of the earthly-life is not sudden. It is gradual, and along with bringing the left (wrong) dimension under training. The spirituality of the status of *Jamoljam* is the bringing together oneself between spiritual attraction and treatment, between compulsion and free will, between unity (oneness) and plurality and between dispersion and union.

Jabes bistam Khayal Ku Tu sitam Ta Sharman
Tu Amadjhi jhi Rafta man Ahista-Ahista

So much I imagined of your Lovely face that I became you from head to toe. Little by little, You moved in and piece by piece Me faded away.

In purely Eastern spirituality sacrifice negates the majesty of the earthly-life and ends the illusions and traveller will never return to the world. But in the sacrifice of the status of *Jamoljam*, while the traveller gradually does away with the illusions and by piecemeal, eliminates the majesty of this world, he also reaches sobriety and subsistence with God. It is for this reason that in this sort of spirituality divine legislation Tashri and attention to worldly affairs and establishment of a spiritual society has come to be possible. The purely Eastern spirituality is going to the heavens; whereas Spirituality of the status of *Jamoljam*, is bringing the heavens to the earth and taking the earth to the heavens. It is the status of *Katayadih ymeen* "His hands are both Right". It is the status of *Jawal Feena*, "one who has two spiritual eyes with one of which he can see the earthly-life and with the other the after-life; and can bring the two together". It is the status of universal inclusion. The rules and regulations of this sort of spirituality refer to both worldly affairs as well as the inner self, the heart, and spirituality. That is why, this station is the station of universal unconcealedness and the universality of the interior and the exterior dimensions of human existence. The *Holy Quran* describes this station in these words: *HuwaAwwal Awaala Akir wa Jahir wa Babin* "He is the First and the Last and the Manifest and the concealed Essence." (*Holy Quran* 57:3)

Today the bringing together of spirituality with technology, and the bringing together of spirituality with Western culture and development calls for such a spirituality Therefore, spirituality is always historic and has historicity. In this sort of spirituality, sacrifice comes about by observance of the religious duties and sacraments and obedience to the Perfect Man (*Insani-Kamil*). (That is why the words sacrifice, sacred, sacrament, sanctify and saint are all from the same root). By observance of duties and sacrament the earthly dimension of human existence is trained while it is retained and its dependent technology which is the result of turning towards this earthly life becomes sanctified. In this way the earthly dimension of human existence becomes divine and technology, which is not inherently holy and is basically chaotic and advancing towards the earthly life and commensurate with the left (wrong) dimension of the human existence, is enlightened by the Eastern dimension of the human existence and comes to be at the service of the East. But such a transformation takes place only in those spiritual beings (*Auliya*), whose spirituality is that of the status of *Jamoljam*, those who have achieved authenticity By following such men and by obeying their do's and don't's, we can gradually benefit from their authenticity and be a true orientation towards technology and build a correct relationship with it. We can, therefore, achieve the courage to say 'No' to the left (wrong) dimension for our existence and its dependent technology to be free from its sovereignty and abandon it with our hearts. But this abandonment is not wiping out and negating the technology. It is freeing the heart from its bondage. Not having, it is not the issue; not having any attachment, is the issue. Once the heart is detached from it, its mastery and majesty comes to an end and we build a correct relationship with it. This change is not a sudden orientation. It is something gradual, and is accompanied by the union between the spiritual attraction, along with treating the others, which is the exclusive spirituality of the status of *Jamoljam*. Depending upon the level of spiritual journey, authenticity emerges and man in delivered from the sovereignty of time and the temporal existence and achieves the status of *Varastegi*, (Salvation). With this 'Salvation' we shall once again move towards technology. In this status we are no more the captives of technology; technology is our captive. In this status, the relationship has changed. This time our mind and soul is not after the technology but is after those "spiritual beings, *Aulia*" because of whom the pillars of the earth are erected. In this status, sacrifice is brought about by sacrament; technology is retained, and gradually sanctified, and the earth, free from the present chaotic state, once again becomes the "kind dwelling place" for man.

> *Admi Ra Alam Khaki Nami Aa Eeed ba sab*
> *Aalami Raykar Babayad Shaht Dajnawa Admi*
>
> From this earthly world does not emerge man out of the spiritual essence; A new World has to be created for a new Man to emerge.
> (Hafiz, 14th century)

Today, the issue is not that no one is taking a serious step to save the earth by holding seminars, symposia etc. or the lack of adequate allocation of funds. The main issue is that we are avoiding the confrontation with ourselves. We are lost in ourselves and are captives ourselves. Therefore, how can we save ourselves and the earth? Until and unless we get to the bottom of the problem but remain engaged with superficial issues, we are not in a position to confront the main issue and "Save The Earth" remains merely a slogan. We are worried about the earth because we see our future in danger. We are scared that our happiness may come to an end and, therefore, we talk about "saving the earth" and joining "the friends of the earth". We want to save the earth to guarantee our future projects, so that we are in a position to exploit and destroy it further. But the only way to save the earth necessitates obedience to spiritual beings (*Aulia*), the observance of religious duties (sacrament) and treading the spiritual path, thereby sanctifying the left (wrong) dimension of our existence and its dependent technology. The whole issue depends upon the fact that we have to confront ourselves and it is only in this case that the earth and us can be delivered from the sovereignty of the left (wrong) dimension of our own existence.

> *Magar ba roi Ralorae ya mawrani*
> *Bahija jah Dgarka rabrnami Aeed*
>
> Perchance, by (the blessing of) the heart-adoring face of our Beloved (our desire will be fulfilled); if not in any way (to accomplishment), another work cometh not. (Hafiz, 14th century)

Notes

1. Aletheia, which in Greek means truth, is made of two parts, "letheia" which means cover and the prefix "A" corresponding to "un" in English. Hence, literally Aletheia means "uncover", "unhiddenness".
2. Cf. Martin Heidegger, *Basic Writing*, "The Question concerning Technology", Translated by David Farrel, London. 1979, p. 293.
3. Meibodi's *Commentary on Divan-i-Maula Ali-Ibn-e Abi Talib*, Lithography, p. 32.
4. Cf. *The Encyclopaedia of Religion*, Edited by Mircea Eliade, volume 12, "Sacrifice".

16

Culture and Technology

The Cultural Aspect of Technology

Fatemeh Farahani

Today in many developing countries insufficient progress in science and technology is considered to be the chief reason for general backwardness; on the contrary, many in the industrially advanced societies hold unfettered technological progress as the roots of all social ills.

Is it really possible that all social and political upheavals of the past decades are the byproduct of thoughtless advance in technology? Does it make sense to think of technology as an 'inhumane force' that has somehow managed to throw 'human relations' into disorder and chaos.

Are we faced with a kind of technological determinism that places man and society in a particular direction with no discernible horizon? Or is it after all possible that technology is independent, neutral and free of any values, whose benefits and faults are chiefly by the use to which it is put by man?

Is it possible for traditional societies to import technology and then try to weave it into their own cultural fabric? Does technology cause alienation? Or is it, as an Iranian thinker has put it, a necessary evil equally harmful in presence as in absence?

Finally, how are we equipped, the people of the Third World, to cope with the great power that technology is? And of course a host of other questions that are fashioned ever anew with respect to technology.

The friction between technological development and the preservation of cultural values, in particular and the influence of the former upon the course of social and cultural changes have been a great source of controversy, the consideration of which is obviously beyond this assignment. Our main objective here is to discuss the cultural aspect of technology and the effect it has had on the cultural identity of the Third World.

Today, human life is an industrial life. In this life which is governed by technical relations, all products are interrelated and interdependent, where the purchase of a product commits one to the purchase of another. Technology advances constantly and rapidly; what has been useful and favoured one day runs out of style next day.

The Evolutionists introduced technology as the major component of culture and put the other components at second place holding that all the components of culture are affected by technology. In this regard Leslie White has introduced the most important theory on technological determinism. According to him not only technology determines the direction of cultural development, but it also determines the need for building social foundation.[1] In fact technological determinism assumes that technological innovation is the driving force behind social change imposing its own logic on the social actors and their relations.

Parsons believed that technology is a kind of capability on the part of the organization for a more effective control and necessary change in the physical environment in favour of human needs and demands.[2]

And A. Reddy wrote, "Science and technology carry the genetic codes of communities where they have been produced".[3] Therefore technology is a product of the Western industrialized communities which owe their present position to the attempt made by their ancestors within certain traditional culture patterns. The industrial communities have been organized on the basis of rational management and advancement of science and technology. Therefore any discussion concerning development ultimately leads to the question of science and technology and any discussion concerning these two leads to the question of development. Unfortunately, the sociological dimensions of development, specially the link between culture and development and technology, and technology and culture have not been properly considered. This negligence has led to the conclusion that development is merely synonymous to economic change. Whereas development is in fact a complicated and multi-dimensional process which includes social, political and cultural spheres.

In order to bring about deep economic and social changes and promotion of the living standard as well as filling the gap between themselves and the developed countries, the developing countries are in need of science and technology, and development has become an important factor for industrial and economic progress. But science and technology have not been created and developed in isolation and introduction of any new technology is a cultural phenomenon, directly affecting the cultural values and the behaviour of communities.

Besides, technology is not by itself the basis of progress and development though today the communities which consume more and exhaust nature are considered more advanced and more humanistic. In the public mind, too, development is a synonym for the culture, social and economic, of the developed countries, the owners of technology.

But development by itself is a historical change, that is, the communities move and transit from one historical stage to another. In fact preparing the community for development is a historical necessity, depending on time and place. The pattern of development policy-making in each country is peculiar to that country, but the laws of development are general and comprehensive. Therefore the transfer of technology can be effective in the progress and development of orient communities only when they are in harmony with the social and cultural conditions of such communities.

So, claiming that with mere transfer of technology the Third World will easily develop is an optimistic idea. Since the transfer of technology is a question of establishing a rational balance between world culture and national or endogenous culture. Cultural development is the process of self-sufficiency which, at a macro level, is fulfilled by the community itself and, at a micro level, by the individuals and groups. On this same basis it is directly the result of endogenous cultural creativities against prevalent methods of the transfer of science and technology.

Development is the seed which should be sown in the soil of a country, and should grow there. It is not a sapling which may be brought from one place and transplanted in another place. However, external communication, especially technological devices, will have influence in the growth of this seed.

Aspects of Technology

The peculiarity of our era is generalization and similarity of desires and dreams. The mass culture is the shape of the culture in our age. Any kind of production or any kind of technology, as it is introduced to the market, will change shape and undergo numerous changes from one side of the world to the other. A notion has been prevalent that technology is basically immoral, i.e., what is beyond values and the means which can be equally used for either good or evil purposes. However, is technology really culturally impartial? If one looks at technology as a machine and the principle of work the response will be positive, but if one looks at the minute details of human activities which take place in line with the use of technology the answer will be negative. Technology appears as a part of life and not something separate from it. Arnold Pacey in his book entitled the *Culture of Technology* has considered three different aspects for technology:[4]

1. The organizational aspect, consisting of the activity of designers, engineers, consumers and labour unions.
2. The technical aspect which is a limited concept of technology, that is to say, knowledge, skill and know-how, tolls and machines.
3. The cultural aspect means goals, values and moral rules, belief in progress, affecting the creativity of designers.

He believed that people use technology in its wide-scale concept and sometimes with its limited meaning. When technology is presented in a more limited way, the cultural values and the organizational factors related to it assume for it the shape of an alien factor. In this case technology is known in its complete technical aspects, but in its broad concept it should be considered equal to practicality. In this way it is not impartial and has direct and indirect impacts on values, traditions and the environment.

Therefore, since we know that cultural values are a determining factor in the choice and impact of technology and the latter actually transforms cultural values, how can technology and culture as independent systems be co-ordinated?

Technology is a means for change in the environment in order to make it compatible with necessary and inevitable human needs; and culture is also man's compatibility with the environment around him and the relation he establishes with it. A direct relation exists between culture and technology and both of these affect the other in a sequential manner. In advanced societies — which are the birth place of technology, it is attempted that social and cultural organization be put in line with technological development.

Ladriere by referring to the vast place occupied by science and technology in the life of modern societies wrote: "the problem that arises is how cultures can accommodate them without going astray, how they can at one and the same time satisfy the requirement in regard to roots and having ultimate aims, and giving science and technology the full recognition due to them." We are faced with two questions: on the one hand we must consider under what conditions science and technology can be integrated into a culture without destroying its inner harmony, and on the other hand we must examine what is meant by the unity of a culture in the circumstances of the world today, epitomized as these are by science, technology and their attendant economic and political phenomena.[5]

In developing countries especially in traditional societies the situation is considerably more complicated, because technology will be made an alien entity which appears as an independent system in the face of existing cultural systems.

As we know, culture determines the way in which individuals identify and recognize one another within their own social sphere of action and the traditional cultures and value systems on them constitute the factor for social harmony, and give a special cultural identity to the members of a community which, in itself, is one of the needs for endogenous development. In the compulsory process of social evolution and change which emanates from the introduction of values and models of external behaviour inspired by the advent of foreign technologies the cultural system in their entirety are attacked upon. Therefore, the main risk lies in the endangering of cultural identity which is rooted in the tradition of nations and in the issue of preservation of cultural pluralism for the entire human community. For example, the development of communication technology, the ability to record and transmit sounds and images over any distance, and the easy reproduction of these on a large scale, have changed the face of contemporary culture. Mr. Amadou-Mathar M. Bow, in his opening address at the conference on cultural policies in Latin America and the Carribbean (Bogota 1978) clearly highlighted the interrelation between culture and communication. He stated, "the mass media. . . are not culturally neutral." They reflect the thinking, the idea, the values, in short the vision of the world of those who use them when they serve as the channel for transmitting to given region value systems or ways of life which are foreign to the people of that region and cannot be prevented in the end from wiping out the specific values of those people, thus becoming even if unintentionally, instruments of cultural alienation. Other feature of technology is the structuration of social consumption patterns and introduction of a consumer logic into the developing countries.[6]

Much has been said about the impact of technology on the educational systems of the Third World and also on the aesthetic values. We emphasized mainly on negative cultural aspects of technology. But we live in a world which is reliant on technology where the motivating power of national development constitutes that technology. Although it is recognized that technical devices have been designed in response to the determined cultural needs and their compatibility with the goals of another culture requires great endeavour.

We know that Third World countries are faced with two major crises in the selection of technology :

1. Importation of technology has not brought desirable results.
2. Countries have not succeeded in developing the technologies in conformity with their needs and cultural values.

Main reason for these two crises originates from the fact that promotion of technology in these countries was not an endogenous activity but the vast and uncontrolled diffusion of technical implements. Basically the Third World have three options in the face of modern technologies:

1. Passive posture or total acceptance of technologies without paying any attention to their own endogenous environment.
2. Tendency on relinquishment that is a total dismissal of any type of technology, and
3. Selection of those technologies which have greater conformity with the socio-cultural and economic conditions of those countries.

Selection of an appropriate technology emanates from this same third option. Even though the goal of an appropriate technology is to maximize, the opportunities (positive effects), and to minimize their harms (negative effects). Generally speaking, it is not the inherent nature of a technology but the proportion of the link which that technology is to have with the environment where it is to be used, that becomes meaningful.

In our country too, similar to many Third World countries there exist certain problems which, on account of historical background and continuation, have emerged in the form of a tradition. For instance, we quote here some cases to show as to how our country, by making proper and positive use of technology, has succeeded in bringing about a fundamental change in the ways of the people's thinking and mentality:

1. Large-scale use of the media technology in order to generalize literacy among the people, and to bring about a change in the educational system.
2. Use of modern technology such as video cassettes to promote family planning in rural areas.
3. Use of long-range television pictures for promoting health care in villages.
4. Use of media and communication technologies for creating understanding among different ethnic groups.

Special attention has also been devoted to the significance of technology, selection of an appropriate technology, and its transfer within the framework of an industrial model. In this case, a section entitled land processing "has been set up at the Planning and Budget Ministry with the following two major goals": Determination of the capacity of various sectors in the country, and specification of an appropriate industrial and economic model. Simultaneous with it general criteria have been set for the contracts in connection with the transfer of technology. A commission has been formed to enforce this legislation. Its main objectives stipulate that the commission will make its best efforts to prevent the import of alien and non-essential technologies in the country, and endeavour to realize this task through the self-sufficiency cells. Much stress is being laid on the role of research and enquiry as the main factor for the attainment of an endogenous technology. Currently more than 60 institutions are engaged in cultural, scientific, social and economic researches throughout the country.

Iran, in its capacity as a pioneer of science in history, and a country which is going through a transitional phase and had gone through eight major political events over the past eight decades, views technology as a positive device in the service of humanity and intellectual development.

Culturally speaking, technology is neither evil nor disastrous, rather it is a means that, if used properly, could bring up the welfare of human beings. By deploying the laser technology we may help cure the eye of a child in a village. However, laser could be used to guide a bomb. We can use satellites for education and intellectual and cultural progress of human beings or we can use them as a means to spread the destructive cultural and ideological patterns. Therefore, if we accept the idea which says, "technology is a means in the service of a superior objective that is the better recognition of nature and a more suitable utilization of nature, and safeguarding the cultural identity as a factor for the solidarity and a requisite for the survival of nation", we have to know that the best technology is not the most modern technology.

Technique produces the need. And Man's thirst could not be satiated. Therefore our culture necessitates evasion of extremes (to abstain from extravagance) in using the natural resources.

The appropriate deployment of technology should be acquired so that we would not be afflicted with its negative outcome.

By depending on the people's innate abilities and capacities we should acquire more share in creating and spreading technology.

Safeguarding the cultural authenticity and identity does not mean to go away from the current of technology and/or return to the past and to experience what was already experienced by others, rather it is to go away from the atmosphere of slogans, to harmonize ourselves, and accept the realities of the present world. Protection of cultural identity and reinforcing it are of vital importance. Similarly, technology constitutes the reality of time. Our goal must be to protect our cultural identity by using the gifts of technology and not sacrifice the former for the sake of the latter or ignore the benefits of technology.

Notes

1. Leslie White, *The Evolution of Culture*, N.Y. 1959.
2. Talcott Parsons, *Societies*, Engle Wood, N.J. Prentice Hall, 1966, p. 150.
3. *La Culture, Clef de Development*, UNESCO, 1983, p. 105.
4. Arnold Pacey, *The Culture of Technology*, Basil Blackwell, 1983, pp. 8-12.
5. Jean Ladrier, *The Challenge Presented to Culture*, UNESCO, 1977, p. 147.
6. *Inter-governmental Conference on Cultural Policies in Latin America and Caribbean*, Bogota, 10-20 January 1978, p. 72.

17

Civilizations and Settlement Societies

Cultural Development and Identity at the End of Twentieth Century

Ravindra K. Jain

This paper deals with an unstated premise of the twentieth century paradigm for cultural development. This premise is that civilizations are the legitimate teleology of cultural development and that settlement societies like the plantation societies formed from the eighteenth century onwards ought to be considered as resting on the peripheries of developmental process. On the face of it, there is nothing wrong in this premise: in our quest for authenticity and ennobling ideals of human development, we do of course look upon civilizations as the pinnacle. But the reality of the politicization of culture introduces a kind of historical distortion in the myth of civilization. I need not dwell at length on the nature of this distortion which is manifest in our own country at this time and historical conjuncture in the *Mandir-Masjid* dispute. In this dispute the civilizational myth of Ram has been hijacked for extremely parochial and violent ends. I plead, therefore, for a reversal of analytical perspectives between civilizations and settlement societies at the end of the twentieth century.

The paper is divided in three parts. Part one deals with the problematic of culture where India is considered as a civilization. Part two considers the East Indian culture in Trinidad and Tobago which is an example of a settlement society in a Caribbean context. Finally, in part three, I look upon civilizations and settlement societies in the dialectic between the 'self' and the 'other'.

THE PROBLEMATIC OF CULTURE : INDIA AS A CIVILIZATION

Perspective

It is best to locate the problematic of culture in India—'Unity in diversity', to put it briefly — in the framework of the kind of plural society that obtains in this land. Here the Furnivallian concept of plural society, which is characterized by (a) culturally incongruous and mutually incompatible socio-cultural sections, (b) having inter-relationships only of the market place, and (c) all kept together as a functioning whole by the exercise of a superordinate power, is clearly inapplicable. We shall be wrong to postulate at the start that the Indian unity lacks a common will. It will be argued that the Furnivallian paradigm applies only to 'settlement societies' and not to civilizations.

The Civilizational Synthesis of Culture

Here we might take a lead from the anthropological conceptualizations of unity in diversity in India, and posit the existence of a Great Tradition and several little traditions. The civilizational process in Indian history can then be traced as a continuous and sustained interaction between the Great Tradition and little traditions. Whereas this resolution to the problematic of culture takes us part of the way to understanding the dynamics of the Indian civilizational process, it has two shortcomings:

(a) There is a tendency to put greater value and hegemony on the centralizing classical traditions and a commensurate under-playing of the regional and local (decentralizing) significance of the little traditions.

(b) The civilizational process tends to marginalize the problems of culture that are encountered in building the Indian nation (especially in the last two hundred years) and the Indian state (especially during the post-Independence period of last forty to fifty years).

The Decentralized Paradigm of Unity in Diversity

Here we must recall, (a) the issues raised in the process of nation-building in India, especially during the nationalist struggle, and (b) the cultural problems in the functioning of a federal state structure in India. As soon as we focus on the dominant thrust of the above problem areas two cultural problems, namely, clash and diversity of religion with its twin faces of communalism and the partition of the country into India and Pakistan, and the formation of linguistic states in India as the solution to centralization/decentralization dilemma come to the fore. In other words the decentralized paradigm of unity in diversity forces us to look closely at religion and language as forces of present discord and potential unity in the problematic of the Indian culture.

Religion and Language

Crisis and creativity in Indian culture: As regards the potential of Indian religions not only for cultural diversity but for the potential unification of the heritage of the country, one type of solution was suggested by the Nehruvian secularism which, with some modification, was enshrined in our Constitution as *Sarva-dharma-sambhava* or the coexistence of all religions in the eyes of the state. A glaring inadequacy in the **implementation** of this policy has been that the appearance (ritualism) rather than the reality (spiritualism) of religious diversity in India has been encouraged and sponsored by the state. This has led to the unhealthy phenomenon of a tie-up between religion and politics such that the *status quoist* and recondite aspects of religious tradition (cf. the *Mandir-Masjid* issue) have gained prominence and, in the name of religion and creed, vote banks have been created. What is needed for disentangling religion from politics is a

(a) philosophical acceptance fundamentally of the individual rather than collective freedom of religious faith and worship.

(b) following from (a), the distinguishing of spiritual from the merely ritualistic aspects of religion, and

(c) following from (a) and (b) the recognition by both the state and the voluntary agencies that religion is not only a force for cultural persistence and *status quo* but also for change and liberation. An accent on mediaeval *bhakti* tradition of India which still powerfully influences the weaker sections of society and the incorporation and welcoming of such tendencies as liberation theology in Christianity are signs in this direction. It has been rightly pointed out that a fundamental tenet of all spiritual quest for change is the mutual respect between various religions.

This brings me to the second focal aspect of culture, namely language which is seen primarily as a factor for fissiparous rather than synthesising currents in Indian society. Here it must be emphasized that a diversity of mother tongues spoken by the Indian population is a source of tremendous strength rather than weakness. The preservation of mother tongues not only makes the problem of spreading literacy much easier (cf. in Kerala); as in the biological world the ecologists have come to value the diversity and preservation of multi-form species, as students of culture we should value the preservation of linguistic and cultural diversity. A culturally homogeneous world will be an unbearably boring place to live in. It only needs a moment's reflection to appreciate how richly the diverse written and unwritten languages of the country have contributed to our cultural heritage. The experiment carried out by the *Bharatiya Jnanapitha* is a point in that direction.

Finally, we shall try to show that diverse languages far from creating tendencies for disunity will merge into a common stream. Our argument rests on the fundamental cultural discovery that Indian languages, though they may be syntactically diverse, are semantically similar. They furnish an exciting proof of the unity in diversity that is the Indian culture.

I have often been asked as to what I think of 'national integration' — what is the import of what I have said for this acute problem? I think that the whole question of 'national integration' is abstruse, primarily because of its monopolization in a politicized universe of discourse. Not the least difficult is the fact — in that political perspective — that the very idea of nation is a Western import. I think in a decentralized framework, such as I am pleading for, one may strive for the 'culturalization' of the idea of national integration.

THE EAST INDIAN CULTURE IN A CARIBBEAN CONTEXT CRISIS AND CREATIVITY IN A 'SETTLEMENT SOCIETY'

A. I now wish to come back to the paradigm of settlement societies about which I had spoken earlier. It would be seen at once that the whole exercise would be self-defeating, and I shall be undoing what I said in my critique of the great tradition — little traditions construct — were I to impose the hegemonic framework or meta-narrative of civilizations on our understanding of settlement societies. The logical drift of my argument on the other hand is to derive the principle of 'becoming' —

creativity out of a crisis — from the consideration of a settlement society, namely the Indian community settled in Trinidad and Tobago since the mid-nineteenth century.

B. The outstanding feature for a theory of socio-cultural change which I discern in this society is inter-culturation — the real give and take of cultures which has been the bedrock of composite culture in this society. Let us make no mistake. Even here the bedrock of inter-culturation has been overlaid by models of plural society and acculturation but as I propose to show these are hegemonic ideologies very largely consciously propagated by the political processes of colonial rule. They represent the politicization of culture as against the culturalization of politics that I am going to explore through a probe into the processes of inter-culturation in Trinidad and Tobago.

C. The process of inter-culturation is symmetrical and based on reciprocity. Before the entry of the Indian element into the population of Trinidad and Tobago in 1845 it had been going on in terms of creolization, a synthesis between the earlier Spanish, French and British cultures on the one hand and the culture of the West African blacks (original slaves) on the other. A unique Caribbean culture had been fostered, including a distinct type of language — the Creole.

The Indian element entered this scene as indentured labourers. Much has been written about the interaction between Creoles and Indians from a politico-economic angle, specially the competition for jobs, the predominance of Indians in the economy and of the blacks in politics, and mutual suspicion and antagonism between the two ethnic groups. What the plural society and acculturation to the Anglo-Saxon norm-models have completely covered up is the process of inter-culturation between the 'kirwal' and the 'coolies' — both being at the same lowest rung of the racially structured stratification in this society. From the Indian side, there were new cultural developments as regards the racial interpretation of caste, dress, food habits, language etc. And on the other side, the elements of folk culture, for example, Tassa Drumming, Gadka (playing with sticks) and participation in Hoesay (Moharram) by the blacks or Africans are evidenced. That the process of inter-culturation by its very nature was reciprocal can be illustrated by many examples. To give a single instance, in Trinidad today, what they call the *pilau* is considered to be a Creole dish and the *roti* and Indian one. If we examine the cultural roots of these two items of the cuisine, we find that in fact *pilau*, both in its preparation and name, is Indian and the *roti*, though Indian in nature, is typically prepared in a creole manner with no counterpart anywhere in India; This example clearly shows that the process of inter-culturation was largely unconscious, for if someone today points out to a Trinidadian actual origins of the items of cuisine mentioned above, his statements would be greeted with utter puzzlement.

D. However, neither culture got absorbed into the other and hence cultural pluralism was retained. Yet, the mutual influence of Creole norms over Indian elements and *vice-versa* is there to see even today. For example, there were three models of cultural change in historical succession — the Christian, the Indian great tradition and Westernization for the East Indian community in Trinidad. And we find examples for each of these models in a very clear manner even today.

For a variety of reasons — of which we need not go into the details — the early Catholic and Anglican Churches in Trinidad had neither the motivation nor any success in proselytizing East Indians. A common reason given was that the Indian was merely a bird of passage and that any time and effort spent on converting him was a waste since we would necessarily revert to his heathenish ways back in India. It fell to the lot of the Canadian Presbyterian Church to successfully initiate and sustain the process of evangelization among the East Indians. The instrument used was education and the form that guaranteed its success was Indianization. The history of Presbyterian Indian education dates back to March 23, 1868 when Dr. John Morton began to teach Kunjah's three little children at his door and as the numbers increased he took them to the Church. Within the next decade scores of primary schools for Indian children were opened by the Presbyterian missionaries, and they made sustained efforts to introduce Secondary education in the opening decades of the present century. To the extent that the products of this educational stream provided the initial core of the educated East Indian middle class — the elite — the specific contribution of the Canadian Presbyterian Mission has to be recognized. The auspices was typically 'white' and in that sense colonial. To this day many informants confess that though they were originally Hindus, they got their children baptized and gave them Christian names in order to reap the material benefits of education! In so much as this was an imposed mode of adaptation, the early Christian influence was an example of acculturation.

However, the point I wish to emphasize is that though this was overtly a process of acculturation, it was founded on the bedrock of inter-culturation. The initial success of the Canadian Presbyterian missionary effort was based on the fact — well documented — that they spared no effort to indigenize the Church for the East Indians. Hindi and Bhojpuri were adopted as the media for preaching and the services in the congregation were deliberately modelled after the 'folk' patterns of the immigrants. Not only the singing of *bhajans* (devotional songs) and *kirtans* (musical offering to the deity) retained, but the musical instruments were also the ones brought over from India by the immigrants. Thus, with the early Christian influence on the East Indian group, we are in the twilight zone — so to speak — between acculturation and inter-culturation. And typically, it was a reciprocal process. The Christian pattern of sitting in congregations on wooden benches (with shoes on), the notion of a pulpit, a *pandit* almost like a parish-priest, 'God-fatherhood' and a Sunday service in Hindu temples etc. are just visible marks, to this day, of how much syncretism has taken place between Hinduism and Christianity in the Caribbean context.

The so-called Hindu revival, forming an integral part of what Professor K. N. Sharma has called 'reinstitutionalization' (1871-1930), has got to be placed in the above context of historical succession for its cultural symbolism to be properly understood. There can be little doubt that with a large number of Indians leaving the barracks and forming their own villages at the end of the indenture contract, Hindu temples and Muslim mosques appeared and there was an urge to find Hindu *pandits* and Muslim *Kazis* for the performance of life-cycle rituals. Initially, this posed a problem. Although some Brahmans did immigrate to the Caribbean it is a well-known fact that not all Brahmans in India are *pandits* or well-versed in the task of performing priestly roles. It is on record that sometimes local Brahmans were instructed in the task of performing religious rites by old women. When these *pandits* conducted the East Indian sacramental marriage rituals — the form still known as 'bamboo marriage' — neither they themselves not the others for whose benefit the ceremonies were being conducted, could explain the symbolism and meaning of these rituals. No wonder, therefore, that the Hindu sacramental wedding, already unrecognized as a legitimate union by law, came to be derived by the East Indians and the creoles alike as a makeshift arrangement, no better and no worse than the 'common law' unions of the other groups. The point we wish to highlight, is the fact that in Trinidad (for example) the folk or village forms of Hindu institutions existed divorced from the great tradition which gave the former legitimacy and acceptability in traditional terms. The solution which the Hindus in Trinidad gradually found was through the expedient importing *pandits* from India (and the Muslim, their *Kazis*) who could train a battery of local priestly officials. While historians (Jha) and some sociologists (e.g. Sharma) have recorded the process of formation of Indian associations, revealingly called 'pressure groups', like the East

Indian National Congress of Couva and the Indian League of Tunapuna around 1910, the social and cultural characteristics and aims of this movement have not yet evolved the scrutiny that they deserve. Here I can attempt only a bare outline of the sociological feature of this movement but it deserves in-depth study.

I have already observed the initiative taken by the Presbyterian Church towards the evangelization and educational upliftment of the East Indians. All evidence points to the fact that it had the support and blessings of the colonial authority. Paradoxically enough, the East Indian leaders of the movement for reinstitutionalization were typically the members of a newly emergent middle class who — though in some measure spearheading Hindu revival — were at the same time deeply imbued by the Christian and colonial ethos which had given birth to it. Indeed, it is no exaggeration to say that what these East Indian leaders were aiming at was a recognition of Hindu marriages in exactly the same terms as the already legally recognized Christian marriage in Trinidad. Given the syncretism between Christianity and Hinduism in the Caribbean setting, it is no wonder that the cultural form in which the reinstitutionalization of Indian way of life was proposed and effected was strikingly different from India and had specifically Trinidadian features. For one thing, the *pandits* — either imported from India or trained by the newly-acquired Indian ones constituted a distinct 'sub-class' of the newly emergent middle class of East Indians. Far from the usual Indian model in which the Brahman *pandit* though ritually and spiritually 'higher' than the other castes is materially of a low and dependent status, in this case the *pandits* of Trinidad had at once status, wealth and power in the community. One is not trying to make a value judgement here, but the 'difference' is worth remarking. A Brahman *pandit*, who in 'off-work' hours drinks scotch, may even eat non-vegetarian food, drives a car and sends his children to foreign schools and universities is an entirely different creature from his Indian counterpart — even in modern India.

A word needs to be said about the growth of 'denominational' Hinduism (and Islam) in Trinidad during the next phase, that of the 'emergence of distinct forms' (1931-50). Here too, I believe, that the Christianization process referred to earlier casts its shadow. The manner in which the Hindu Sanatan Dharma Mahasabha and the Arya Samaj formed themselves and got recognition both from the colonial authority and their followers — and the manner in which a variety of small bodies like the Divine Life Society, the Hindu Seva Sangth etc., continue today to proliferate, strongly suggest that we have here a re-enactment, **in cultural terms**, of the process whereby various Christian denominational sects were introduced and vied with each other for following and support during the nineteenth century and even earlier. I do not wish to open up, on this occasion, the fascinating subject of relationship between religion and politics in contemporary community of East Indians in Trinidad, but in so much as it touches on the cultural manifestations of adherence, alliance and rivalry this is an 'embedded' process which has everything to do with the constituted social and economic processes of Trinidad and the Caribbean and hardly anything to do with India. Indeed the 'Indian location' of this process may have an instrumental use for 'embedded' politics as in the famous imputation by the late Dr. Eric Williams quoting Nehru that the Sanatan Dharma Hindu Sabha (which he deliberately or otherwise confused with the arch-reactionary Hindu Mahasabha of India) was the epitome of reaction and conservatism (cf. Ryan, 1974). The point simply is that the various Hindu bodies in Trinidad are either the carry-over of folk forms inherited from the immigrant past (e.g., Kabirpanth, Sieunaraine, etc.). or they are political 'pressure groups' in a community which faces an acute identity-crisis. The latest manifestation of a typically middle-class religious movement — perhaps as yet not jelled into a pressure-group — is the Sai Baba cult. It is another good example of a cultural import from India, typically reinterpreted in terms of a syncretist and plural Trinidadian reality.

While considering the non-religious or secular acculturation of the East Indians with reference to the 'traditional' Indian model, one should centrally take into account what may be called the 'neo-traditional' forms. The most important of these, beginning in the 1930s was the impact of Indian movies, spreading out eventually to video-cassettes, records of Indian music and lavish receptions accorded to visiting star actors and actresses of Indian movies. The reason for calling this a 'neo-traditional' process of acculturation is the fact that the themes, characterizations, and the entire depiction of Indian culture in these forms is shot through and through with fantasy and the constraints of growing commercialism. It is indeed a travesty of modern culture in the Trinidadian context when the dress and adornment of brides in Indian movies is duplicated in the actual marriage ceremonies of East Indian men and women, or when the highly sexy and culturally inauthentic dances shown in the popular Hindi movies are performed as though they were specimens of authentic Indian culture. And all this is enacted without an understanding of the meaning of the words of the songs and dialogues because Hindi has all but died for the young generation of East Indians. I realize that in his bitterness towards these imitational forms from India, V. S. Naipaul has called the Indian culture in Trinidad and other Caribbean countries as the culture of 'mimic men'. Fortunately I do not share his anger, but looking at this process objectively one is reminded of an earlier phase of creolization in Caribbean society when many of the European culture forms in the slave society were simply 'imitated'. Indeed, Braithwaite has discussed 'imitation' as a prominent feature of the inter-culturation process in plantation societies of the Caribbean. A similar tendency in respect of contemporary East Indians is exhibited in creating 'duplicates', such as a Trinidadian Mohammad Rafi, rather than throwing up artistes of their own. But in making this broad generalization I am not wholly correct. There are, at the same time, schools of classical Indian dancing, classes like those of Bharatiya Vidya Sansthan where classical Indian music is systematically taught and artistes like Mungal Patessar who have taken to playing sitar in the genuine Indian tradition. My contention, however, is about the kind of Indian 'neo-culture' which is attracting the majority of the younger generation. It is a highly 'processed' Indian tradition which finds great popularity in Trinidad.

This brings me to the third major process of acculturation, namely, 'Westernization' which corresponds to what Professor K. N. Sharma has called the phase of 'destabilization' (1951-83). I do not think there is any big need to dwell on this aspect at great length. Its manifestations are constantly being evaluated as either negative or, exceptionally, as positive, in the debates in contemporary Caribbean in the press, on television, and in many associational and group discussions.

E. The important element in the inter-culturation between blacks and the Indians was a philosophy of 'we agree to disagree'. There were instrumental uses too of cultural differences for political purposes and there was quite a bit of bickering and mutually unfavourable stereotypes. But this became politically significant only when incitement was provided by extraneous factors or, in other words, when there was politicization of culture. By and large, there has been harmony, tolerance, peaceful coexistence and an attitude to 'live and let live'. Cultural pluralism is a marked characteristic of this society. In Trinidad and Tobago — in contrast to Fiji for example — the two major ethnic groups, Indians and Africans, lived in close interaction while at the same time preserving their cultural distinctiveness. Indeed, as Chandra Jayawardena has pointed out, Indian ethnicity is more 'public' in Trinidad, whereas in Fiji it is more 'private', since their relative isolation from ethnic Fijians has called for little display of symbols of difference. The *jhandis* on Indian houses in Trinidad and Guyana are one such public symbolic manifestation of cultural difference.

F. It is interesting to note what a black scholar, historian-cum-poet of the Caribbean, Edward Braithwaite has to say about the modernization of the East Indian group:

> . . . .following the post-indenture emancipation and urbanization, has come a new Indian development, stemming from the cultural dispositions (of) **selective creolization**. Here, the Indian relates his own notion of cultural norms to the master-culture of Euro-America, and selects/adapts in order to **modernize**. The Afro-Saxon 'imitates' not modernizes, because, unlike the Indian, he has no core culture to adapt from. (p. 54)

I feel that this is an over-optimistic appraisal of the East Indian culture in Trinidad today. As I have already pointed out there are certain pseudo neo-traditional and imitative aspects in this culture. Also, sometimes use is made of their culture by the Indians as a stick to beat the creoles with. However, the creativity of the settlement society — a culture in 'becoming' — is very marked. You may read it as flexibility or the capacity for syncretism. At the same time the way tradition of a civilization continues to haunt its modernization is very conspicuous.

G. This, then, is the lesson from our comparison. In this post-modernist, post-Marxist and post-structuralist intellectual ambience we have learnt that politico-economy and culture are the two faces of day-to-day living and that understanding consists not in reducing one to the other but in realizing their juxtaposition.

This brief comparative experiment shows how we may proceed from the dominant paradigm of the politicization of culture to a culturization of politics in the understanding of plural society and cultural change.

CIVILIZATIONS AND SETTLEMENT SOCITIES IN THE DIALECTIC BETWEEN 'SELF' AND THE 'OTHER'

In a paper published in 1986 (The East Indian Culture in a Cribbean Context: Crises and Creativity, I suggested an anthropological distinction to be made between civilizations and settlement societies. While civilizations have had a continuous history of cultural development for a millennium or more, the settlement societies were formed only after the European contact with certain islands or plantation societies throughout the world. In historiography and anthropological writings, civilizations seem to have been taken as the ideal of culture and the settlement societies are treated on the peripheries of cultural development. But, the concept of civilizations besides being hegemonic also lacks a politico-economic dimension, as for example in the case of studies of Indian civilization according to a 'great tradition' and 'little traditions' interaction. On the other hand, whenever politico-economic dimensions and hegemony are considered in the context of civilizational encounter between Europe and the colonized people, there is always (in contemporary writing) an anti-colonial bias.

In this paper I have taken up the case of settlement societies, specially Trinidad and Tobago, as an example of responses to colonialist expansion. I emphasize in this discussion the cultural frame of the politico-economic expansion. This enables comparisons between, diverse responses by the colonized to European colonialisms. For example, in Trinidad and Tobago, there was a succession of Spanish, French and British colonialist influence. The exploration between self and the other in such settlement societies can be done from the Third World or the 'south' point of view.

Such a comparison throws up the cultural process of 'creolization' in these settlement societies which, I believe, has a lesson to drive home for the valorized civilizations in anthropological and historical literature. The creation of a Creole culture in situations such as those of Trinidad and Tobago and Mauritius shows the process of 'becoming' rather than 'being'. Such a process is relevant to an appreciation of modernity and post-modernity even in the world of civilizations like those in India, China or parts of Africa as well as Europe. In other words, I wish to emphasize in this paper a reversal of points of view, viz., the relevance which settlement societies have in cultural terms for the ongoing processes of socio-cultural change in a civilizational country like India.

References

Braithwaite, Edward, 1974. *Contradictory Omens: Cultural Diversity and Integration in the Caribbean*, Mona, Jamaica.

Clifford, James, 1988. *The Predicament of Culture*, Cambridge, Mass.: Harvard University Press.

Drummond, Lee, 1980. "The Cultural Continuum: A Theory of Intersystems", In *Man*, 15, pp. 352-74.

Furnivall, J.S., 1948. *Colonial Policy and Practice: A Comparative Study of Burma and Netherlands India*. New York: New York University Press.

Jain, R.K., 1986. "The East Indian Culture in a Caribbean Context: Crisis and Creativity", In *India International Centre Quarterly*, 13(2), pp. 153-64.

Jha, J.C., 1974-75. "Indian Pressure Groups in Trinidad, 1897-1921", In *Quarterly Review of Historical Studies*, 14, pp. 138-56.

Marriott, McKim, 1955. "Little Communities in an Indigenous Civilization", In McKim Marriott (ed.), *Village India: Studies in the Little Community*. Chicago: The University of Chicago Press.

Sharma, K.N. (n.d.). *Changing forms of East Indian Marriage and Family in the Caribbean*, Mimeographed.

Singer, Milton, 1972. "The Social Organization of Indian Civilization", In *When a Great Tradition Modernizes*, London: The Pall Mall Press, pp. 250-71.

18

Cultural Preconditions for Development

Tradition and Modernity Reconsidered in the Light of Post-modernism

Dawa Norbu

Most theorists of both modernization and revolution had previously assumed the replacement of tradition by modernity as development progresses (e.g., see Lerner 1958, Stalin 1975). In such a preconceived theory of development, tradition has no function to perform; it is, in fact, considered an obstacle to modernization. However, from the perspective of the late twentieth century, it is clear that neither revolution had completely destroyed tradition as amply evident in post-Communist societies nor modernization has entirely replaced tradition as richly evident in the newly industrializing Countries (NICs). In fact, in the latter cases, tradition has been an invisible maid-servant of industrial revolution. This raises the possibilities of harnessing cultural resources from great traditions for doable development in other parts of the Third World. Thus, we may shift our view of the tradition as an obstacle to modernization to a tradition as a labyrinth of development.

In this paper I examine the various positive functions that tradition has so far played in the process of development and modernization in several Asian societies since Independence. In order to do so I venture to enumerate some of the basic imperatives of industrial development and demonstrate how such requirements might be met by the congruent structures of tradition. This means we must consider not only state intervention in the economy but also social sources of productivity which owe their origins to a great tradition.

Cultural Sources of Productivity and Imperatives of Industrialization

We have already encountered some troublesome but necessary terms which call for some explanations. By **tradition** I refer to a literate culture usually based on a world religion; and **modernization** means rationalization of means to given ends as applied to economy, society and polity. Often I use a broader term, **development** to include both economic and social changes associated with industrialization. By doable development I mean possible basic (not excessive) industrial development that is people-oriented, ecology-friendly and congruent with cultural patterns.

Previous writers postulated certain necessary preconditions or prerequisites without which presumably no modernization could take place. But the historical fact is that modernization "could, and did, in fact, occur because human ingenuity discovered a number of ways to substitute for the missing and allegedly necessary prerequisites" (Gerschenkron 1966: 257). Being an economic historian, Alexander Gerschenkron understandably did not dabble with cultural factors. I would argue that the possibilities of "human ingenuity" to discover a number of ways to substitute for the missing prerequisites are greater where there is a great tradition which implies at least a literate culture. We shall later demonstrate how the Eurocentric ideal-type prerequisites of industrial development may be and have been substituted by cultural resources of a great tradition.

Outside the Western orbit successful industrialization and modernization have taken place in societies which have had traditionally high literate cultures, such as Japan and NICs. In most of these societies there existed — and still continue to exist — two great traditions, Confucianism and Buddhism, both of which have enriched and increased the possibilities of human ingenuity for centuries. At any rate such traditions propagated and promoted high literate cultures which have made the tasks of modernization much easier.

If the Buddho-Confucian culture — areas as cases of successful industrialization appear to be an exercise in retrospective determinism, we may turn to pre-literate societies which might falsify our argument. Up-to-date we don't see any case of successful industrialization and modernization taking place in societies that have traditionally been preliterate. Greater parts of Africa, Oceania and Asian tribal areas are cases in point. No great industrial nation has ever emerged out of a preliterate culture and fragmented social structure.[1] One of the reasons may be that such societies' engagement with any of the world religions is rather short and shallow, such as they characteristically lack most cultural preconditions for modernization. They are too fragmented along tribal lines to enjoy sustained political stability. Their minds are not used to play with ideas that literate cultures encourage. Nor are they used to large-scale **organized** activity that encourages self-discipline and work culture. However, that does not mean that preliterate societies cannot modernize. They can and do modernize such as African societies but with much more difficulty than a literate society. The reason may be that they typically lack cultural resources which most world religions have endowed their followers over the ages.

The preceding illustrative evidences might then suggest that the scope for various substitutions for the Western historical experience of industrialization may be greater where there is a great tradition and what it (tradition) sociologically implies. The central question is not really whether what perceived to be 'prerequisites' of modernization are present in non-Western societies. Rather it is whether the functional equivalents of industrial imperatives of development are present or absent in given cultures. That will determine the relative success or failure to develop in any sustained way. Any sociology of development in the Third World must ask more relevant questions than rush out to programme neat solutions. Does a given community have historical experiences of similar nature and functions that industrial civilization demands today? Can we find enough substitutions for the technical imperatives of industrial development from the existing cultural resources of a given tradition? Is there a literate culture that makes transition to modern education system easy? And so on. Our intention is to examine whether cultural resources of a great tradition are congruent with the industrial imperatives of doable development.

While looking for functional equivalents of prerequisites that modernization supposedly necessitates, we realize the importance of **adaptability** that has historically come out of a given community's exposure to, and experience of, multiple traditions such as the Buddho-Confucian culture illustrates. In a sense it boils down to the question of whether a given society have had in its history enough experience of thinking and doing certain things methodically (no matter how non-rational in economic sense) whose structure and functions, though not their scale, are objectively or functionally similar to the tasks and challenges of modernization. For the transition from tradition to modernity, if there is such a thing, entails a great structural adjustment, but not a revolution.

My discussion might sound like an attempt to elevate commonsense sociology to the level of academic discourse. However, the fact is that historical experiences of a complex nature have made critical differences to the ways in which a community faces that structural adjustment even in the West. In the late 1940s Harold Pedersen compared the rate of adoption of farm ideas by Danish and Polish farmers in Wisconsin (USA). The Polish farmers came from subsistence farming background whereas the Danish farmers were accustomed to producing for a world food market. "The cultural values of the Danish farmers facilitated the adoption of new ideas whereas the norms of Polish community perpetuated the *status quo*" (Rogers 1962: 59).

The natural history of industrial development suggests certain pre-conditions for primary development such as cultural adaptability, political stability, organizational discipline, work culture etc., and certain other prerequisites for modernization[2] such as literacy, rationality, entrepreneurship, innovation and so on. I shall try to argue that most of these prerequisites for development and modernization may be functionally inherent within the structure and **praxis** of a world religion. The more a society has been exposed to multiple and complex cultures, the better are its chances for successful modernization.

One of the first problems that confronts any attempt at industrial development is how to train a relatively disciplined labour force out of the agrarian population. A study of economic history verifies the fact that peasants of Europe, North America, Australia and Japan did migrate "from farm to factory, from village to city, they introduced new techniques and new products, they saved their money and acquired new skills when opportunity arose, they accepted — sooner or later — new agricultural techniques and new organizations" (Higgins 1977: 107). Similar trends are observable in several Latin American countries, Taiwan, South Korea, China, India, Malaysia, Singapore, Hong Kong and Indonesia. Such basic modernization of agrarian population is, in no small measure, facilitated by the great or little traditions in which peasants or farmers are embedded, which sensatizes us to draw our attention to the fairly favourable psychological conditions that religion had unintentionally created in society prior to the modern era.

Not all world religions are equally open to economic changes. The **adaptability** of a religious tradition may be measured by two criteria; whether its sacred texts are open to translation and interpretation. Islam and Catholicism, for example, did not until recently allow any translation of their canonical texts which had to be read in their original languages, Arabic and Latin. Nor do they, especially Islam, sanction new interpretations of the *Koran* and the *Old Testament*. Where tradition has inbuilt hostility to modernization, modernization revolutions were imposed from above by certain charismatic leaders such as Kamel Attartuk, Nasser and Sukarno in Turkey, Egypt and Indonesia respectively. This was not the case with Buddhism, Confucianism or Hinduism. In fact Kingsley Davis comments on the relative openness of the Hindu tradition to economic changes: "One trait of Hinduism that presumably permits, if it does not favour, economic changes as its syncretic, non-dogmatic, and rather tolerant character" (Singh, 1978: 165).

While the non-dogmatic and open-ended character of a tradition does ease the problems of modernization, especially in the initial stages, the same tradition must be able to maintain social order. **Political stability** is one of the basic conditions for sustained development. Such a stability stems from shared value system emanating usually from religion in most traditional societies. The value system engenders social consensus and makes political stability possible. A well-ordered society is as important a consideration as economic resources or labour before the consideration of any investment company.

Since modernization is essentially a vocational civilization, it presupposes **discipline** and **work culture**. Freedom may be one of the blessings of a modern society; yet paradoxically discipline is required in any modern setting, school, college, university, office, factory, mines, plantations all of which operate on the basis of routinization and regulation. That is why traditional learned classes such as Brahmins, Mandarins, Sumarois have made easy transition to modern professions. That is why also the nineteenth-century factory owners in the Western societies made sure that their workers went to church regularly. Religion is among other things a great discipline, which is not imposed from above but internalized from below.

Closely associated with self-discipline is work culture, both of which owe their origins to religion. Following Max Weber's theory of "Protestant work ethic", many scholars have tried to find similar analogies in Asian industrializing countries (Bellah 1965). The critical question is whether a world religion orients its followers into an activist interpretation of 'salvation' or not. If not originally, then has it experienced in its religious history a Protestant type reformation? Buddhism gives an activist interpretation of *karma* which makes Buddhists work hard for their enlightenment. Herein lie the seeds of work culture. Similarly, Confucian tradition emphasizes personal self-cultivation as the central goal of its followers. The Mahatma Gandhi and other Indian religious reformers tried to give an activist reinterpretation to the notion of *Dharma*: "Work is Worship". Clifford Geertz describes how Javanese entrepreneurs in the 1950s resemble New England Puritan and Dutch Calvanist reformists; religious, serious petty businessmen who believed in the virtue of hard honest work and saving (Geertz 1963: 28-81). Similar are the cases with Marwaris and Jains whose religiosity, thrift and business acumen are well-known in India. It is also interesting to note that the most successful business ventures in Dharamsala belong to ex-lamas; also Bhutan's first and largest business company (Tashi Commercial Corporation) was started and is run by an ex-lama.

It is, therefore, understandable why the deeply religious background of certain social classes, has lent itself to be quite congruent with the dictates of modern entrepreneurship: business ethics, discipline and work culture. Apart from the ability to plan far ahead of time, business ethics is equally important. In most traditional societies, the relations between a merchant and his or her customers were often once-over transactions; there was no need to maintain a scrupulous attitude toward the buyer. Hence, in several European languages trade meant cheating and deception (Gerschenkron 1966: 248). In contrast modern enterprises and entrepreneurship do not encourage such practices; they practice business ethics in their long-term interest. The stronger the reputation of a company, the larger is its market share.

We have explained some general ways by which religion, however unintended from its original scheme of other-worldly things, have contributed towards laying the foundations of industrial development. We may now consider some finer legacies of a great tradition which have action consequences to modernization, such as high literacy, rationality and innovation.

Connections between literate culture and modernity are obvious, but often ignored in development literature. Industry runs on oil but modernity operates on the basis of literacy as a minimum requirement. Whatever might have been the original purpose behind the invention of various writing-systems, it is a historical fact that religious propagation necessitated large-scale usage of such writing-systems in the late ancient and early medieval periods. In due course high literate cultures flourished in societies where world religions had penetrated. And where there is a culture of learning it is easier to make the transition to modern education system. This is where the transformation of priests into professionals begins. The

Jha community in Bihar is a good example. Jhas are high-caste Brahmins previously noted for their Sanskrit learning, in recognition of which a Moghul ruler conferred upon them the title of *Jha* (derivative of *Upadhya* in Sanskrit, meaning 'scholar' in Persian). This culture of learning facilitated the Jha community to make quick and easy transition to modern education and professionals.[3] Nor is this an isolated case. Anil Seal (1968: 118) records that vast majority of first Indian professionals to emerge by 1887 were of Brahmanic background, having graduated from the universities of Calcutta, Bombay and Madras.

Modern education system is essentially designed to train manpower to man various specialized sectors of the modern economy. As such its main tenets are scientific and rational, though value inculcation in education is being increasingly realized. But rationality which is the soul of modernization, is not alien to some world religions such as Buddhism and Confucianism. If modernization is defined as the rationalization of means to given ends, the end means that strategic thinking is apparent in most religious systems. But the departure for such religions has theologically, though not sociologically, been the ends for which rational means are deployed but they are not economic, as they are characteristically other-worldly. That is why modern Indian thinkers such as Gandhi (Iyer 1986: 238-320) critiqued modernization as the misuse of reason which is meant for a higher purpose.

Finally, in order to maintain a competitive edge in the world market, producers must have a **sense of perfection**, that is rigid quality control over their products. Among the world religions perhaps Buddhism may be said to have inculcated and encouraged a greater sense of perfection among its advanced practitioners in their ceaseless quest for enlightenment. The semi-empirical orientation of Confucian tradition and its emphasis on personal self-cultivation as the end and essence of life — also may encourage a sense of perfection. Where there is a cultured sense of perfection such as Japan there is more evidence of advanced modernization, excelling in international competition.

Modernization Mediated by Culture

We have discussed some ways in which religion has facilitated or accelerated the process of modernization in industrializing Asian societies. Such a discourse assumes continual interaction between tradition and modernity over a long period of time under the conditions of industrial development. So what is the relationship between tradition and modernity in the age of post-modernism? What is the fate of tradition in the age of globalization of economy and modernization of industry? What have been the consequences of the continual interaction between tradition and modernity to the evolving nature of each? We have perhaps raised some questions than we can answer; they are intended to point the direction towards which the rest of the discussion will be addressed.

Early Asian responses to modernity are similar. They all cherished their traditions but thought modernization was an economic and political necessity. In so doing, they tended to treat tradition and modernity as autonomous entities with no possibilities of interaction between the two sets. The Chinese scholar officials in the nineteenth century perhaps gave the clearest expression of this thesis: preserving tradition while modernizing, Chang Chih-tung (1837-1909) argued traditional Chinese learning would constitute *ti* (essence/value), and Western learning *vung* (utility). (Levenson 1958: 60) Translated into our idiom, this means that Confucian tradition would continue to be the sources of value system, and modernization for material gains.

Jamal al-Din al-Afghani (1839-97) and his pupil Muhammad Abduh (1849-1905) argued that modernization was useful and necessary in order to preserve and defend Islamic culture and civilization in the modern world. (Tibi 1981: 65) The rationale for modernization from the early Arab perspective was not for its own sake but power and plenty that modernity promised which would be used in the defence of tradition.

The central message of Bengal Renaissance in the nineteenth century, though more complex than those in China or Arab countries, was similar. That is why a contemporary Indian sociologist characterizes modernity as "instrumental values". (Singh 1978: 35) That is, modernity has no intrinsic values, which presumably emanate from tradition, except its powerful utility. In other words early Asian modernists identified the place of modernity: the factory, not the temple or family.

In contrast to the early Asian views of tradition and modernity as autonomous realms, a number of influential post-war Western theorists of modernization swang to the other extreme. They emphasized "the importance of cultural change as a part and precondition of economic development" (Singer 1977: 3). In their view "cultural resistance to change" was a definite obstacle to modernization. Thus, they advocated a wholesale modernization of society, economy and polity, including modernization of religion (Singer 1966: 55-67), social relations (Smelser 1966:

110-21) and man (Inkles 1966: 138-50). In short, modernization was seen as "a unilinear evolutionary process whose growth would bring all societies to a level of cultural homogeneity washing their original cultural identities" (Singh 1978: 24). Nowhere in the Third World do we see such a prediction coming true after nearly half a century of development.

To be sure there have been more cautious scholars who did not observe the simple replacement of tradition by modernity, but they are few in number. Reinhard Bendix (1969: 210) saw Germany's and Japan's industrializations as "characterized by a symbiosis between tradition and modernity that was tension-ridden but enduring". Lloyd and Susanne Rudolph (1967: 12) wrote about "the modernity of tradition and its correlate, that modernity incorporates traditional aspects".

Seen from such a perspective, tradition and modernity are misplaced polarities. This is a good corrective to the orthodox Western paradigm of modernity which bulldozed tradition as an obstacle to an all-encompassing modernization. But neither Bendix nor Rudolphs tried to show the precise relationship between tradition and modernity that might have evolved in the course of development. Nor did they indicate which of the two idea-systems was an ascendant one, which might have induced more changes in the other. They observed the symbiotic and continual nature of tradition and modernity, a great corrective to the Eurocentric theory of modernization but quite vague.

On the other hand the early Asian visions of modernization still enjoy a great deal of attraction in the Third World. For the pioneer neo-traditionalists in China, India and the Middle East reasoned that it was possible to modernize while preserving tradition. They envisaged modernization to be purely a technical process, meaning industrialization which, they assumed, would have no impact on tradition. But is such a clinical separation of tradition from modernization possible? It might indeed be desirable from the point of those who embark upon modernization in traditional societies because their cultural or national identities are bound up with one religious tradition or the other. However, our paper as a whole argues that such a clinical separation of tradition and modernity is ahistorical and asociological. It may be highly desirable but practically impossible for the simple reason that modernization does not occur in a vacuum. It takes place in society which makes the interaction between tradition and modernity inevitable.

Our interaction hypothesis should specify the critical variable. There is little doubt that modernity is the ascendant idea-system because its rationalizing logic is rooted in the modern state power structure and national economy, whereas tradition is a psycho-cultural phenomena essentially rooted in society. This explains the economic appeal of modernity and at the same time the tenacity of tradition. Neither can replace the other. Nor is there much need to replace tradition by modernity. Religious tradition has played a positive role in the course of development, especially during the early critical stages in several Asian societies. Such experiences show that although tradition and modernity are two contrasting idea-systems, their potential conflict may be diffused and their differing roles transformed into complimentary ones through skilful political management.

Development induces continual interaction between tradition and modernity, generating creative tension between the two sets. Even though modernity is the ascendant idea-system, it can neither replace nor erase tradition completely. Modernization only compels tradition to reformulate its ideas and to redefine its functions in the light of modernity. Thus, what is implicit in tradition is made explicit; more systematic what is random. In other words, tradition makes a structural adjustment, not a total transformation during the process of modernization. The only tentative generalization we can make at the present state of our knowledge is this: Modernization is a relatively universal process but **mediated** by specific cultures. Different cultures have responded differently to the challenges of modernization. That mediation shows the specific ways to industrialization as well as the manners in which the functions of tradition are reoriented both for its own survival and in the service of development, and how traditional ideas are reformulated.

Culturetology is usually associated with conservatism with no theory of social change. Our study of culture in relation to modernization and nationalism in the Third World (Norbu 1992: 223) reveals three distinct ways in which social change is possible: (a) exigencial necessity, (b) instrumental utility, and (c) elective affinity. These are the typical ways by which different cultures have accepted modernity to varying degrees, causing considerable social change in their wake.

To be sure the initial reaction of tradition to modernity in Asian societies was one of fear, suspicion and hostility. This was so because modernity appeared to pose challenges to authority structures which are closely bound up with tradition as the sole legitimation mechanism. But once the sheer utility and benefits of industrialization were demonstrated by authorities, limited modernization programmes in Chinese, Arab and Indian societies were accepted and embarked upon in the nineteenth century. To be sure early reformers like Raja Rammohun

Roy (1772-1833) in India, Lin Tse-hsu (1785-1850) in China, Jamal al-Din al-Afghani (1839-97) in the Middle East had to advocate modernization in the name of tradition as absolutely necessary in order to defend traditional value systems and authority structures on the face of European imperialism. This was the case of **exigencial necessity** by which modernization began in leading Asian societies. Such programmes were initially confined to a limited modernization of armed forces due to intense threat perceptions. (Blunt 1907: 482; Teng and Fairbank 1970: 28-30)

Secondly, **instrumental utility** that drives societies towards industrialization includes science and technology that can produce power, plenty and progress. As we have noted earlier, it was this sheer utility of modernization that attracted the early Asian modernists to modernity. This appeal and attraction still continues to hold true in the Third World. There is today hardly any country in world that does not want to embrace science and technology for their sheer utility, even though many have serious reservations about 'modernizing' the superstructures of their societies. Whether they can in practice maintain a clinical separation of science and technology from society, insulating the social consequences of industrialization — or not remains problematic. There may be an element of truth in Marxian theory; Marx argued that once you introduce changes in the economic base, such changes in turn will bring about changes in the superstructure. The remaining Marxist-Leninist regimes and others are today faced with this dilemma.

Elective affinity refers to the way in which the members of a society easily accept those changes or apparently new ideas which have echoed in their past experiences. Work culture which modern society demands and which was present in Buddho-Confucian societies — is an example. A number of other religious callings which have been reoriented to fit the imperatives of modern enterprises may belong to this category of social change. We can cite more examples but our point should be clear. These are the three principal ways by which culture has absorbed or accepted several aspects of modernity. They suggest that modernization is not a wholesale Westernization but a deliberate and discriminating process by which a given culture absorbs new techniques and ideas on the ground of exigencial necessity, elective affinity and instrumental utility.

Our essay is a theoretical exercise with practical intent. In conclusion, therefore, we may ask what are the implications of our exploration into the tradition — modernity debate in the age of post-modernism. If most of what we have argued in this essay is correct, then it is high time to realize that tradition need not be an obstacle to development. In fact, high literate culture may provide favourable conditions, if not one of the preconditions, for development and modernization. Most of the great traditions may be considered a significant part of the human resources to be skilfully utilized in the process of development, and not an obstacle to be destroyed.[4] If that proposition is somewhat convincing, then development planners and practitioners need to study not only economic viability or feasibility of a development programme but its cultural conditions for successful implementation. And the relevant key question to be asked is this: Are the major components of a proposed development programme congruent with certain aspects of a culture concerned? If not, discourage (but not destroy) those inhibiting aspects of a culture. If yes, encourage such traits of a culture that facilitate or accelerate the process of modernization. Japan's industrialization, in particular, shows the ingeneous ways by which Japanese entrepreneurs made skilful use of their society's traditional social structure and value system in the course of industrial development. The strong sense of **group loyalty** that feudal society had fostered over the ages has been transformed into loyalty to the company one works for through lifelong employment. The importance of the family as a natural and venerable social institution that Confucian tradition had always emphasized has been transformed into an efficient unit of industrial production. If we go by the orthodox tenets of modernization, feudal loyalty and the extended family are anathema to modernity.

We end this paper with some disclaimers and clarifications, which might make the limited purpose of our discourse clear. We have tried to demonstrate how and why religion-induced culture might have provided some of the necessary favourable cultural preconditions for development in most of the industrializing Asian societies. That is, the behaviour-orienting values and ideas of Buddhism, Confucianism and Hinduism have over the centuries dug deep psychological and ethical grooves (habits) along which the initial wheels of industrialization found it easier to run. This assumption is verified by illustrative evidences from East, Southeast and South Asia.

Our focus, therefore has been on the role of tradition in economic development but this does not mean we rule out other competing explanations. For example the role of the state in Korean, Taiwanese, Singaporian and even Japanese economic development is quite obvious and worthy of being considered as a competing explanation. Or the favourable US policy, both defence and economic, towards East Asian countries except China. We have not discussed such explanations because they have already received enough scholarly attention. Our purpose has been to delineate the role of culture in development as a plausible explanation for the relatively successful cases of industrialization in Asia and to re-examine some of the earlier assumptions about tradition/modernity debate.

Notes

1. Such remarks might smack of cultural chauvinism, which in fact goes against the grain of my personal philosophy. However, such reasoning flows from the logic of my analysis. My argument implies that it is not race *per se* but high literate culture that basically shapes one's ability to function in the modern world.
2. In this context I give slightly differentiated meanings to **development** and **modernization**. Development refers to primary industrialization, whereas modernization here and elsewhere means to update and further improve the means of production, following the current usage.
3. The Jha example is particularly instructive, because otherwise Bihar **is** believed to be one of the educationally most backward states of the Indian union.
4. Apart from their ideological objections, one aspect of the main rationale behind Communists' destruction of traditional culture is their view that tradition is an obstacle to progress and modernity. A similar view is shared by early liberal social scientists but their means differ from the Marxists'.

   Liberals advocate cultural change as a precondition for modernization, whereas Leninist regimes sought to destroy culture as happened in Russia and China.

References

Bellah, Robert N. (ed.), 1965. *Religion and Progress in Modern Asia.* New York: The Free Press.

Bendix, Reinhard, 1989. *Nation-Building and Citizenship.* New Delhi: Eastern Wiley.

Blunt, Wilfred Acainen, 1907. *Secret History of the English Occupation of Egypt.* London: Macmillan.

Ceertz, Clifford, 1963. *Peddlers and Princes.* Chicago: University of Chicago Press.

Cerschenkron, Alexander, 1966. "The Modernization of Entrepreneurship", In Myron Weiner. (ed.) *Modernization.* New York: Basic Books.

Higgins, Benjamin 1977. "Economic Development and Cultural Change: Seamless Web or

Patchwork Quilt?", In Manning Nasha. (ed.) *Essays on Economic Development and Cultural Change, Economic Development and Cultural Change*, vol. 25, Supplement, 1977.

Inkles, Alex, 1966. "The Modernization of Man", In Myron Weiner, (ed.) *Modernization*. New York: Basic Books.

Iyer, Raghavan (ed.), 1986. *The Moral and Political Writings of Mahatma Gandhi*, vol. 1, Oxford: Clarendon Press.

Lerner, Daniel, 1958. *The Passing of Traditional Society*. Glencoe, Ill.: The Free Press.

Levenson, Joseph R., 1958. *Confucian China and its Modern Fate*. Berkeley: University of California Press.

Norbu, Dawa, 1992. *Culture and the Politics of Third World Nationalism*. London and New York: Routledge.

Rogers, Everett M., 1962. *Diffusion of Innovations*. New York: The Free Press.

Rudolph, Lloyd I. and Rudolph, Susanne Hoeber 1967. *The Modernity of Tradition*. Chicago: University of Chicago Press.

Seal, Anil, 1968. *The Emergence of Indian Nationalism*. Cambridge: Cambridge University Press.

Singh, Yogendra, 1978. *Essays on Modernization*. New Delhi: Manohar.

Singer, H. W., 1977. "Reflections of Sociological Aspects of Economic Growth Based on the Work of Bert Hoselitz", In Hanning, Nash. (ed.) *Essays on Economic Development and Cultural Change, Economic Development and Cultural Change*, vol. 25, Supplement.

Singer, Milton, 1966. "The Modernization of Religious Beliefs", In Myron Weiner (ed.) *Modernization* New York: Basic Books.

Smelser, Neil J., 1966. "Modernization of Social Relations", In Myron Weiner (ed.) *Modernization*. New York: Basic Books.

Stalin, Joseph, 1975. *Marxism and the National-Colonial Question*. San Francisco Proletarian Publishers.

Teng, Su-yu and Fairbank, John K., 1970. *China's Response to the West*. New York: Athenuem.

Tibi, Bassam, 1981. *Arab Nationalism*. London: Macmillan.

19

Cultural Identity and Development Process in Thailand

Wit Wisadavet

The conflict between cultural identity and development in our society does not seem to me a big problem. It can be said in general that there is no ethnic minority in Thailand. There are a considerable number of Chinese in our country but most, if not all of them, have been culturalized into the mainstream. The member minority group in Thailand is Thai Muslim, most of whom live in the South. There is very little conflict between Thai Buddhists and Thai Muslims. Our country, it can be said, is quite homogeneous, and consequently cultural identity does not pose a big problem.

The pillars of Thai cultural identity are the institution of monarchy and the religion of Buddhism. The institution of monarchy has been in Thai society for more than 700 years, without any interruption. The king has been much respected, loved, and revered. In the time of crisis he is the one who would come down to solve the problem. The king is indeed the symbol of Thai identity.

As for Buddhism we have accepted it as a way of life for almost 800 years. It is a force that culturally binds the hearts and the thoughts of the Thai people together. Some of us even equate Thai-nees with Buddhism.

Buddhism is one of the most open-minded religions. According to the teaching in the *Kalamasutta*, a Buddhist does not accept anything merely because it is logical, said in the scripture or even taught by his teacher. Think for yourself and then try it in practice. If it is good then accept it. By its principle of no-self (*anatta*), it teaches us not to have a strong attachment to things. Everything is changing. There is no Being — only Becoming. Do not believe in permanence or identity. This may be the reason why Thais are quite flexible and pragmatic.

We Thais are not so conscious about self-identity. Perhaps this is because we are so pragmatic or because we are so certain about our identity. We never despise foreign culture or civilization. In the older time we accepted Indian culture, such as religion, literature, language and so on. But we modify them a little and make them our own. We adapt ourselves to them and we adopt them to ourselves.

In the modern time we have introduced Western culture into our society. We believe that science, technology and other things from the West can help develop our nation. The majority of the Thai people do not have a negative attitude towards Westernization. Of course some, mostly intellectuals, do. Their criticism, it seems to me, does not receive much attention. The majority want to follow the West in the technological process and the capitalistic way of development. To many there is little or no conflict between development in such a way and cultural identity.

The problem is not the conflict between identity and development. Of course there are some who complain about this. But for the majority the problem is two-fold. Firstly the material progress is advancing so fast that it creates social problems like morality, selfishness, drug addiction and so on. Secondly, many complain that the economic development of this kind makes richer the rich and poorer the poor. What they call for is not the coming back to self-identity, but solving these two problems.

According to Buddhism, wealth in itself is not something to be despised. A man who gets rich in a morally acceptable way and is generous can be a good Buddhist. The ultimate aim of life is to live well. To live well means to have a balance between material well-being and peace of mind. But culture is not an end in itself. It is a means. Culture and everything else change all the time. This must be accepted. We have to admit, however, that culture is rooted in the heart of man and, therefore, plays a role in making life richer.

When there rises a conflict between culture and development we should take the middle way. Cultural identity is a good thing, and material well-being is also a good thing. To a certain extent we have to sacrifice the one for the other. But we should not sacrifice all of the one for the other. We must not be too romantic to think that we can keep our culture unchanged. We must not be too serious to think that material progress is the only good thing for life.

20

Freedom to Grow and Growing into One

Baidyanath Saraswati

Gandhi, the Greatest Need of the Time

This essay follows the footsteps of Mahatma Gandhi. It is written for those who are in sympathy with the spirit. That spirit is different from the one which blows about modern civilization.

This is not a theoretical paper. It is concerned with problems of human freedom and growth. It touches the context of modern civilization and tries to break the monopoly of 'development' ideology. It reflects India's cultural identity without indulging in a general theory. It prepares the ground for a *swadesi* model of growth, bringing into focus the insight of that great genial master and mahatma*

Such a model of growth is not easy to realize. *Swadesi* in today's world is a practical impossibility The problem is something like that of the fabled lion who having been brought about in the company of goats found it impossible to feel that he was a lion. But, then, to make *swadesi* operative is to make oneself free from the mental state of helplessness.

---

* The following pages contain long and large quotations, all from D.G. Tendulkar's monumental work, *Mahatma*. Words like *swaraj*, *swadesi*, *samabhava*, *aparigraha*, etc. are used precisely in the Gandhian sense.

Technolatry, the Modern Paranoia

Gandhiji wrote his famous 30,000-word book, *Hind Swaraj*, or *Indian Home Rule*, in 1909. The questions there dealt with have great relevance today, not only for India, but for the whole humanity. A ten-point summary of this *Gita* of the Kali Age, the modern age of darkness, is pertinent.

(1) There is no impassable barrier between East and West.

(2) There is no such thing as Western or European civilization, but there is a modern civilization which is purely material.

(3) The people of Europe, before they were touched by modern civilization, had much in common with the people of the East.

(4) It is not the British people who are ruling India, but it is modern civilization, through its very invention which has been claimed to be a triumph of civilization.

(5) Bombay, Calcutta, and the other cities of India are the real plague-spots.

(6) East and West can really meet when the West has thrown over board modern civilization, almost in its entirety. They can also seemingly meet when East has also adopted modern civilization, but that meeting would be an armed truce.

(7) It is impertinence for any man or anybody of men to begin or to contemplate reform of the whole world. To attempt to do so by means of highly artificial and speedy locomotion, is to attempt the impossible.

(8) Increase of material comforts, it may be generally laid down, does not in any way whatsoever conduce to moral growth.

(9) India's salvation consists in unlearning what she has learnt during the past fifty years or so.

(10) There was true wisdom in the sages of old having so regulated society as to limit the material conditions of the people. Therein lies salvation. People live long under such conditions in comparative peace, much greater than Europe has enjoyed after having taken up modern activity, and I feel that every

> enlightened man may, if he chooses, learn this truth and act according to it.

Gandhiji was not an ivory-tower intellectual; he was a practical idealist. *Hind Swaraj* is not a concept book; it deals with practical questions in an original way. The fact that it is a product of his experiment with truth imparts it a certain universality that makes it all-time relevant.

Gandhiji severely condemned the railways, telegraphs, telephones, hospitals, lawyers, doctors and such others. He was unconcerned whether such a gigantic reformation that he was suggesting can be brought about to people who find their satisfaction from the mad rush of his time. He held the view that all of us who think likewise have to take the necessary step, and the rest, if we are in the right, must follow. "The theory is there; our practice will have to approach it as much as possible", he said.

What Gandhiji said at the turn of this century is self-evident by the close of the century. It is already apparent to the world that technologically advanced countries are obsessed by the demons of commercial selfishness. The fault is not of men but of the system.

The modern system of knowledge is based on the presupposition that man himself is at the centre of his own history and civilization. Today man's greatest glory is described in terms of science and technology by virtue of which the modern man has achieved near complete conquest of nature. But, ironically, science, which prides itself in being autotelic, is controlled by technology and man, who boasts his conquest of nature, is reduced to a level of consumer.

Modern system tends to be holistic and universalistic. In determining the normative nature of 'development' its thrust is clearly toward uniformization, homogenization and globalization. It is unconcerned with the fact that there are other systems of knowledge and other models of growth. Taking itself as a universal frame of reference, it declares all other rationalities and all other world-views false. It claims that technologically-controlled economics and science-supported aspirations alone constitute the true model of 'development'. In its own final analysis the modern system is infallible and the cosmologically-designed and morally-ordered pre-industrial societies are backward. The upshot is plain: all cultures must be reduced to a single pattern to practice technolatry to fall in line with the modern paranoic civilization.

Spinning Wheel, The Universal Pancea

Technolatry has an inherent faith that only in a technologically advanced society can the higher possibilities of man be fully realized. Unfortunately many eminent people of our time are wedded to this belief.

Tagore did not like Gandhiji's command "Spin and Weave". He asked: "Is this the gospel of a new creative age? If large machinery constitutes a danger for the West, will not the small machines constitute a greater danger for us?"

Tagore's noble word, evoked firm reply from Gandhiji. On October 13, 1921, he wrote in *Young India*:

> To a people famishing and idle, the only acceptable forms in which God can dare appear is work and promise of food as wages. God created man to work for his good, and said that those who ate without work were thieves. Eighty per cent of India are compulsorily thieves half the year. Is it any wonder if India has become one vast prison? Hunger is the argument that is driving India to the spinning wheel. The call of the spinning wheel is the noblest of all. Because it is the call of love. And love is swaraj. Swaraj has no meaning for the millions, if they do not know how to employ their enforced idleness. The attainment of this swaraj is possible within a short time, and it is so possible only by the revival of the spinning wheel.
>
> I do want growth, I do want self-determination, I do want freedom, but I want all these for the soul. I doubt if the steel age is an advance upon the flint age. I am indifferent. It is the evolution of the soul to which the intellect and all our faculties have to be devoted. I have no difficulty in imagining the possibility of a man armoured after the modern style making some lasting and new discovery for mankind, but I have less difficulty in imagining the possibility of a man having nothing but a bit of flint and a nail for lighting his path or his matchlock ever singing new hymns of praise and delivering to an aching world a message of peace and goodwill upon earth. A plea for the spinning wheel is a plea for recognizing the dignity of labour.
>
> I claim that in losing the spinning wheel we lost our left lung. We are, therefore, suffering from galloping consumption. The restoration of the wheel arrests the progress of the fell disease. There are certain

> things which all must do in all climes. There are certain things which all must do in certain climes. The spinning wheel is the thing which all must turn in the Indian clime for the transition stage at any rate and the vast majority must for all time.
>
> It was over love of foreign cloth that ousted the wheel from its position of dignity. Therefore, I consider it a sin to wear foreign cloth. I must confess that I do not draw a sharp or any distinction between economics and ethics. Economics that hurt the moral well-being of an individual or a nation are immoral and, therefore, sinful. Thus the economics that permit one country to prey upon another are immoral. It is sinful to buy and use articles made by sweated labour. It is sinful to eat the American wheat and let my neighbour the grain dealer starve for want of custom.
>
> My modesty has prevented me from declaring from the house top that the message of non-cooperation, non-violence and swadeshi is a message to the world. It must fall flat, if it does not bear fruit in the soil where it has been delivered.
>
> We must refuse to be lifted off our feet. A drowning man cannot save others, we must try to save ourselves. Indian nationalism is not exclusive, nor aggressive, nor destructive. India must learn to live before she can aspire to die for humanity. The mice which helplessly find themselves between the cat's teeth, acquire no merit from their enforced sacrifice.

May folk songs of pre-Independence India revolve around the spinning wheel. The metaphor can reach metaphysical heights, or can be plainly plaintive such as

My spinning wheel is multi-coloured
Inlaid with nails of gold,
O mother, I think of you
Whenever I see my spinning wheel
Burfi (sweets) sells in bazar;
Oh, bring me a small spinning wheel
That I may spin my cotton rolls of sorrow.
Two pieces of cloth are stiched into one,
Though we sulk and fume without,

Within we two are one
Flowers in garden bloom,
But hard are those to find
Who honour till the end of the ties of love.

This song aptly voice, the pangs of a prisoner of modern civilization, of a hanging *trisanku*, or of a fleeing Shiva unnerved by his own boon to Bhasmasur.

Swaraj, My Birth Right

At Gandhiji's call I seek *purna swaraj*, complete self rule. I march with time with my 'spinning wheel'. I respond to varying conditions and yet remain changeless within. I wish to grow in my own style, with reverence for all other lifestyles.

If God has created me in his own image I want to remain true to that self. My relationship to the universe, to all my fellow beings and to human society is derived from my relationship to God. I do not want this relationship to be controlled by Satan.

If my body is made up of earth, water, air, fire and sky, I want to grow freely in that beautiful order of the cosmos. My temporal existence is derived from and nourished by these elements of Nature. I do not want this human-cosmic relation to sever for any good.

As God's man I am empowered to grow in a normal way. Constant growth is the law of life. As a cosmic being I have the right to live on earth, to bask in the radiant light and warmth of the sun, to be purified by the holy waters and to move and breathe fearlessly.

I do not want to live a whole life at one time. I want to be born again and again to be nourished in the womb of the Mother Earth.

I do not want to live on 'bread alone'. I want to work for my food. I want to live the 'bread of life'. I trust the God's promise of food, *vasordhara*, the cosmic circulation of never-ending food.

I do not want to impersonate and replace God by the *maya* (demiurgic image) of creativity. I want to create with the powers of Cosmic Intelligence, the divine wisdom. I do not want to be the victim of my own creation.

I want *swaraj* in organizing the entire way of my life. 'Swaraj is my birth right'.

Knowing the cosmic principle of One into Two into Many, I cannot be egocentric, or ethnocentric. Having made my own world as 'open space' I move up to grow into one.

As a self apart from the otherselves, I perform a cosmic act of union in terms of marriage, family, kinship and all such forms of human relation. I do experience the totality of the species with my own colour, caste and clan.

As a citizen of the earth I relate with all, without losing my self-identity. As a citizen of the heaven I get fully integrated with the ultimate, the One.

My human identity is enveloped by five sheaths or envelops: *anandamaya kosa* (beatific envelope), *vigyanmaya kosa* (noetic or intellectual envelope), *manomaya kosa* (mental envelope), *pranamaya kosa* (vital envelope) and *annamaya kosa* (vegetative envelope). These are hierarchical orders, the first and the highest is the beatific envelope. It is in this order of hierarchy that I wish to grow as a universal self.

I hold on to my *swadesi* world-view, without being disrespectful to other world-views.

I seek not to impose my ideas on others. Nor do I brook the spirit of superiority and dominance of destructive forces.

Swadesi, My Religion

Swaraj is loftier than God. The attainment of *swaraj* is closely linked with the advancement of *swadesi*. If *swaraj* is the deity, *swadesi* is the prayer. I cannot think of one without the other.

To get rid of economic and intellectual slavery I look upon *swadesi* as a rule of life.

Gandhiji gave a clarion call to boycott foreign goods and foreign system of education, saying:

> It is inconsistent with truth to use articles about which, or about whose makers, there is a possibility of deception.
>
> Swadeshi is that spirit in us which restricts us to the use and service of our immediate surroundings to the exclusion of the more remote.
>
> I think of swadeshi not as a boycott movement undertaken by way of revenge. I conceive it as a religious principle to be followed by all.

> There is a verse in the Gita which, freely rendered, means: masses follow the classes. It is easy to undo the evil if the thinking portion of the community were to take the swadeshi vow, even though it may for a time cause considerable inconvenience.
>
> It has often been urged that India cannot adopt swadeshi in the economic life at any rate. Those who advance this objection do not look upon swadeshi as a rule of life. With them it is a more patriotic effort not to be made if it involved any self-denial. Swadeshi, as defined here, is a religious discipline to be undergone in utter disregard of the physical discomfort it may cause to individuals. Under its spell the deprivation of a pin or needle, because these are not manufactured in India, need cause no terror. A swadeshi will learn to do without hundreds of things which today he considers necessary. Moreover, those who dismiss swadeshi from their minds by arguing the impossible, forget that swadeshi, after all, is a goal to be reached by steady effort. Swadeshi is the only doctrine consistent with the law of humility and love.

My prayer, then, is: Let a thousand flowers blossom. Let every culture grow with the joy of fearlessness. Let it discover its own roots. Let it also discover a spiritual link, an unbreakable relationship with other cultures. Let it hasten slowly. Let it condemn technology. Let it reject modern technological thinking. Let it refuse measuring poverty in terms of technologically controlled economics. Let it refrain from making a fetish of literacy. Let it denounce secularism, resist tyranny. Let it protect itself from exploitation and fight in the open an honourable battle. Let it arm itself with the weapons of non-cooperation and non-violence, Let it learn to rule itself. Let it follow the ideal of democratic *swaraj*. Let the democracy of fear be replaced by the kingdom of God. Let every culture be firmly rooted in its *swadharma*, harbouring no ill-will for other religions.

For the realization of such blossoming, let a thousand *swadesi* models operate. Let each model be self-organizing, self-sustaining and self-perpetuating. Let each nation determine priorities in the development programme, according to its own resources and world-views.

To evolve a *swadesi* model a *pancaseela*-programme must begin:

(1) Redefining 'development' as a human project concerned with

the fulfilment of higher human values, rather than a technologically controlled one-point affluence-serving programme,

(2) Rethinking universality in terms of the cosmological principle of "One into Two into Many", rather than the sociological pickle of "uniformization and homogenization",

(3) Restrengthening swadeshi with the eternal rule of life,

(4) Resanctifying human creativity and interpersonal relationship, and

(5) Rededicating oneself to the law of moral advancement with the minimum material.

The *swadesi* model of growth does not preclude a normal global interaction. It is an open system built on a dynamic principle of *swaraj*, freedom of culture, *sambhava*, equability of culture, and *aparigraha*, non-possession, all of which presuppose a change of heart, a change of attitude.

To conclude, I turn to Gandhiji: "I do not want my house to be walled in all sides and my windows to be stuffed. I want the cultures of all land to be blown about my house as freely as possible. But I refuse to be blown off my feet by any. I refuse to live in other people's houses as an interloper, a beggar or a slave" (*Young India*, June 1, 1921).

21

Taming Structural Transformation

The Significance of Community Resolve of Mavalibhata

B. D. Sharma

The people's struggle against authoritarian state and insidious money-power has taken a new turn on October 10, 1992 at Mavalibhata in Bastar, Madhya Pradesh. The foundation stone of a giant steel plant laid just four days back by the Chief Minister — the symbol of state power and the first epitaph of the onward march of the neo-colonial imperialist Axis in the remote tribal areas of our country — was reduced to rubble quietly by the simple people of that village and thrown away with utter contempt which it richly deserved. The Community's command over its habitat was reaffirmed with exemplary equanimity in open defiance of the rising tide of the new world order all set to engulf the same.

Ironically at about the same time the government at the Centre — the final authority for protection and welfare of the tribal people — was making empty noises about a comprehensive rehabilitation policy — its umpteenth performance during the last 44 years without any qualms for the fact that demonic development had already claimed some 15 per cent of the tribal people as its victims even as the Constitution stood still all through and remained a mute witness to the violation of the most scarce of the sacred human rights, the right to life with dignity. In fact the idea of mere rehabilitation as a benign and acceptable proposition was dead the moment community staked its natural claim for ownership of industries which may be set up in its territory. It is amusing that while making that ritualistic statement the paper kings did not realise that they had already surrendered their right to do so, when they accepted privatization and globalization as guiding principles for managing the national economy, a position totally unacceptable to the people though. In fact, the State is guilty of betrayal to a sacred contract and the great trust reposed in it by the people while adopting the Constitution.

The people of Mavalibhata in Bastar in a significant move decided to stand up against the State. They have given their verdict — the State has transgressed the limits of its authorization. They have given a new formulation concerning the structure of industrial enterprises not only in tribal areas but in the country as a whole. It is being welcomed by ordinary village people and also the working classes everywhere. The Mavalibhata Declaration which may become a landmark, *inter alia*, maintains —

> Only those enterprises will be allowed to be established in our respective areas which agree to accept community control over them. This provision will not be against money, but will be in lieu of the real contribution of the community, by way of cooperation and consent for use of those resources by the enterprise over which it has enjoyed full control through the ages and which have provided the community and its members with sustenance in all aspects of their life. Other partners in the enterprise will be those who may invest capital and all categories of workers.

The Real Nature of Industrialization

The process of industrialization and its implications for the ordinary people by now are well-known even in India where we are still in an early phase of industrialization. A big industry is set up in a resource-rich area ostensible for its development. A few persons with money-bags and their retinue march in like prize-cocks with bright tails. The local people are at the receiving end, sullen and apprehensive about their future. Some of them are directly displaced as their lands are taken over. Many times more are gradually squeezed out in a ruthless struggle, with no rules of game even as a guide. Small, usually token, monetary compensation is doled out to some with no relationship with the real value of those assets since land is not an article of free trade there. The whole process is plagued with manipulation, cuts, frauds in a milieu of open loot. What reaches the man in the end is frittered away in no time. The grand promise of a new era of prosperity and even just employment proves illusory. Employment at best turns out to be casual wage drudgery. The proud farmer and the care-free tribal are forced to join the long queues of destitute job-seekers. Want of 'wanted' skills and fear of people with roots who could become unmanageable or even revolt at some turn, militate against their regular engagement.

And after the industry is established, a new devastation-wave sets in assuming numerous forms. Gases poison the air; flying ash darkens the sky settling ubiquitously on trees, plants, crops outside and vital organs within; chemicals and sediments spread out and get mixed in earth around and pollute streams, tanks and even wells. Consequently fields turn barren, water is rendered unusable even for nistar, life itself becomes hazardous. And what remains by way of their cultural tradition and social identity is ravaged by gangsters of all descriptions swarming the area.

The area may develop but the son of soil is pushed to the margin. Resources are depleted and drained leaving behind desolate land. The new lords could not care less about this holocaust, the price of their shares continues to soar high in the magic market. They are all well-guarded by quotable quotes — 'is this not a necessary concomitant of industrialization and legitimate price of development which someone has to pay'? Pleading and plaints are received with studied equanimity and arrogant unconcern from pedestals well-kempt, well-protected and declared "out of bounds" Everything turns upside down — the sons of the soil and erstwhile masters crawl and supplicate in the new Regime while neo-lords consolidate their hold absolute and divine.

The transformation from agriculture to industry in the West with a similar trauma-potential in course of time proved to be a benign turbulence at the top as a global phenomenon. The respective national economies attained new heights after each of them acquired a colonial underworld. The colonies served as sinks for all that was hazardous, sinful or was deemed to be not-so-desirable. Now the very same style of transformation has been accepted for the Third World countries by their leaders without making its implications explicit, guided largely by their self-interest. The process by its very nature is creating a great divide and conditions of internal colonialism in every country including our own. The tribal area with rich resources and simple people is a special target of neo-colonial forces, the people there do not enjoy even the protection of the common law. In many other areas the process is the same though its intensity is not that severe. Rich agricultural lands are being devoured and entire farming communities are being rendered resourceless and destitutes. Chota Nagpur in Bihar, Chhattisgarh in Madhya Pradesh and Koraput in Orissa are just a few examples where the area has developed but the original inhabitants have no space even to stand on. They can be found perching precariously near some *nala* in a nearby town or pulling *rikshaws* on its streets, serving the 'Greater Nation of bigger brothers'. The community resources are literally transformed into luxuriant private estates, high value shares of industries claiming phenomenal growth held mostly by urbanite manipulators of the economic system. And the dazzle of development bewitches the onlooker as modern *minars* sore high in the ocean-blue sky and shining 'five stars' punctuate pervading darkness around.

Conflict with National Goals

This process of structural transformation is clearly against the schema of change envisaged in our Constitution. The state is committed to establish an egalitarian social order. In particular, while measures were to be taken for rooting out all inequitous and exploitative elements of the traditional economy, efforts were to be made for not allowing similar elements to get entrenched in the new economic structure built around modern industry. Accordingly, the Constitution enjoined on the state the duty to adopt certain basic principles in making the laws—the Directive Principles — for it is the law which can make the intent of Constitution real and concrete.

The most important Constitutional injunction in this case is that the state shall strive to promote the welfare of the people. Welfare itself has not been left to be interpreted at will, it is qualified by a categorical statement by securing and protecting, as effectively as it may, a social order in which justice social, economic and political shall inform all institutions of national life. Nor was this considered as an easy walk-over even for the new ebullient nation. The state had to **strive** to achieve this goal. The founding fathers were clear that free market economy could not be trusted, money could not be allowed to become the sole arbiter in all aspects of community life which had been the motto all through of the capitalistic world of old masters. Therefore, sufficient space was created for state action. The state was obliged (Article 39) to direct its policy, *inter alia*, towards

(i) securing for every citizen the right to an adequate means of livelihood,

(ii) ensuring that the ownership and control of **material resources of the community** are so distributed as best to subserve the common good, and

(iii) managing the **economic system** in such a way that its operation does not result in concentration of **wealth and means of production** to common detriment.

It was in persuance of these objectives that a **mixed economy** was sought to be created. The public sector was assigned a dominant role in the modern industrial sector with private sector as a junior partner. Certain vital items such as command and ownership of resources were taken out of the operation of free market. Nevertheless the directive principles, which showed the path clear and straight, were not made legally enforceable. The reason was simple. The operation of a policy, of necessity, has to be through appropriate legislative and concomitant administrative measures. The pace of change cannot be a matter of wish, but is governed by a variety of elements not always amenable to simple commands. Nevertheless the direction was clear. In particular, any action of the state-legislative or administrative, including studied non-action in vital matters which goes against the spirit of these provisions, is violative of the Constitution.

The Great Manipulation Game

However, there were insidious counter-currents from the very beginning. Equity was ominously relegated to a subsidiary position in the mistaken belief that once there was development, the benefits would gradually spread out and trickle down. But that was not to be. On the contrary, in that feigned fond hope concentration of economic power was allowed, even though it was against the basic grain of the Constitution. Superficial efforts to counter it proved counter-productive. They led to centralization of administrative and political authority, which was glibly misused. This ambivalence had disastrous effect on the public sector whose performance can be said to have been excellent looking to the pioneering task in an unchartered setting and also the serious handicaps under which it was obliged to function. Most of those who were responsible for promoting and building it up, used it for personal gains and many in key positions worked against it. The promoters mostly were not committed even to the idea of public sector. On the other hand with growing inequality, corruption and manipulation, the elite market at the top expanded phenomenally while ordinary people were denied even bare essentials. The private sector operating in softer areas, aided and abetted by multinationals gained on all counts, though as a deviant, and distorted the economy beyond recognition. Policy-makers ostensibly made Herculean efforts for keeping the criminals under check and the aberrant economy on the track. But half-baked and insincere measures increased the malady rather than curing the same. In fact, the disease remained undiagnosed and that too on purpose.

In this ambivalent phase of socialist claims and deceptive designs vested interests gradually consolidated their position. Even reasonable restraints on market and money power were removed or made ineffective negating the general and even specific provisions of the Constitution. The economy was therefore allowed to run down in the name of liberalization, modernization, *et al.* incurring heavy debt, internal and external. And the vested interests struck, and struck hard at that, as soon as they captured vantage points in terms of persons, institutions and the system itself. All sins were piled against the idealist egalitarian goals, overzealous concerns for human rights, indolence and inefficiency of the public sector, in fact all that the nation had so far stood for. And the pseudo-radicals of that socialist era lost no time to join the contrived chorus, casting off egalitarian cloaks of many colours. A so-called new economic policy has been thrust on the unsuspecting nation under slogans of efficiency, liberalization, globalization and what not.

The most nefarious aspect of this ambivalent phase of intellectual dishonesty was that not many dared or even cared to touch the question of inequity inherent in the structural transformation from agricultural economy to industrial economy. This was so largely because the articulate and the ruling elite got accommodated in the emerging modern sector which cornered all the gains of development and proceeds of continued expropriation from the rural economy and the tribal region. Some ideological under-pinning even amongst the progressives as also the radicals was also responsible for ignoring this issue. The farmer was deemed to represent a decadent system, which had to go, and expropriation from the rural economy had to be justified for capital formation, modernization and advancement. The primitive tribal, according to this view, in any case has no place in the new system. It is a pity that the resultant inequitous deal remained shrouded in the haze created by welfare activities of the state and operations of the ubiquitous public sector. The people were confused as the system adopted the easy path and treacherous method of cooperation of a few such as exceptionally talented, vocal, influential people, persons showing leadership potential and mischief-makers, and dangling of carrot before the rest.

The three vital issues in this structural transformation are

(i) the nature of control over and ownership of natural resources,

(ii) generation of surpluses and claims thereon, and

(iii) entitlement of ordinary people and workers in the emerging system.

It is a matter of national shame that the colonial legacy of denial of human rights to the innocent people not only continued after Independence but it got reinforced. The legal and institutional frame built on altogether different premises of an imperial regime was not changed or not even adapted even after the adoption of the Constitution. The vital issue of community claim over natural resources and citizen's right to use them for their sustenance was pushed into background as the state assumed the responsibility of development through planning. The state was deemed to represent the community and, *ex hypothesis*, to serve the same. Accordingly public sector was created with an aura of idealism. But the behaviour of enterprises in this sector in practice was no different from that of capitalists on any of the three counts. This has been sought to be rationalized on a variety of pretexts — efficiency, competition and such like. The result is that the fact that community is the real owner, nay, even the idea that the community can have a claim over the natural resources has been ignored and forgotten.

This position is in a way the continuation of the global piracy of community resources by the erstwhile colonial powers. The early loot was later camouflaged under the theology of capitalistic order in which capital was ordained as the high priest of development. The real productive forces were pushed into background. Everything was made money-convertible. And the rulers armed with authority of creating money developed the dubious game of manipulating the same. Accordingly natural resources could be easily taken over or purchased like any other commodity in a free market. The distinction between right to use the resources and their ownership got obliterated *de facto* and even *de jure* in the bewildering maze of usage, contract, rules and laws.

The expropriation of community resources in our country has continued in the age-old colonial style after Independence, only the destination of its proceeds and the beneficiary groups have changed. Accordingly these resources are being siphoned off through a variety of institutional devices and pooled in numerous forms such as inflated share values and corporate and private assets. It is this unabashed loot and transfer which is at the base of what are paraded as high growth industries where dividends of hundred per cent and more are not exceptions any more. In the rat race of emerging elite, open loot is legitimatized and daring dacoity glamourized:

The Real Face of New Economic Policy

The new economic policy has put a seal of approval on this incongruous situation. The capitalistic neo-colonial onslaught through this policy has three objectives — (i) usurpation of natural resources, (ii) exploitation of plentiful manpower, and (iii) creation of a captive market for its merchandise. The nefarious game is being played under the garb of removing all hurdles from the path of development and establishing a free market which has acquired a divine aura after the disintegration of the Soviet Union. Privatization and globalization are now passwords for anything and everything. The globalization trap-theory amounts to a virtual surrender of the sovereign national claim to create a society of our dreams and accept a subservient role in the community of nations **as per** the dictat of the Rich. Privatization is a surrender of community claims and general welfare concerns of an egalitarian society. These two processes admirably complement each other and ominously converge on the three-point objective of the Axis.

The command over natural resources can be simply purchased with no constraints of any description. As logic of free market and modernization of technology unfolds and opportunities for human labour shrink, people will be thrown out of the system. Surplus labour with no opportunity and no regulations even as a guide will float around. This background will provide the best possible situation for exploitation in all forms, child and female labour and sex included. As inequality grows, the nation of the affluent at the top including the labour-aristocracy as its appendage, which are essentially an extension of Western economies, will be best suited to dump anything unwanted under label, 'Phoren'. The ruling elite will thus accept the role of an agent of the neo-colonials and the history of landlord-stranglehold under direct British Rule will repeat, albeit with a new idiom, a new frame and a new East India Company after just three centuries.

The inequity of structural transformation in this context is bound to be accentuated and acquire many new dimensions. All areas in the country have been thrown open for all sorts of ventures — big and small, basic and superficial, serious and superciliously speculative. Money of any colour and technology of any genre with their angle-like halo are being given red-carpet treatment. The worst affected and also the main target of this new annexation is the resource-rich tribal area which even under the benign Constitutional dispensation has been badly mauled. The simple logic of special Constitutional safeguards for the tribal people under the fifth and the sixth schedules are so pervasive and radical that they have been termed as 'Constitution within Constitution'. The executive has been bestowed with unlimited power even to 'legislate'. There is specific mention for making regulations for such simple but vital matters as money-lending, trading and transfer of land. Yet 'rogues' — brown, yellow and white — are being let loose under the new economic policy without even an allusion to possible checks against imminent depredation which they will surely indulge in.

The First Assault Effectively Countered

The first spectacular display of the new game plan was slated for Madhya Pradesh. The Government proudly announced its decision to invite private parties to establish three steel plants and four super-thermal projects in the extensive resource-rich regions of the State. Open market was to be the sole guide in all matters. Therefore, even the routine processes of the by-gone era were not gone through. These processes no doubt did not serve much purpose but at least held the state formally responsible for many possible actions such as rational choice about their location as also certain preventive measures such as choice of technology, measures against health hazards, environmental degradation and human misery. The new schema is essentially designed as a 'free for all' game ironically under the patronage of the state. So best 'site-value' locations were chosen not caring even for the best agricultural land (*Nagarnar*) and heavy population concentration (*Mavalibhata*) in this otherwise sparsely populated area with more than 70 per cent under the so-called forest. Everyone was to gain except the simple tribal who was still not really out of the stone age.

But the people on the other side in the proposed location of the first steel plant (Mavalibhata) proved to be of a different mettle. They are not prepared to accept a servile status and humiliation of serving others about which they have come to know personally and through word of mouth from areas already afflicted. Money has no value in their paradigm. 'Even a truck load of notes would not burn through a winter night' runs their simple logic. Consequently *katenge, par katege nahin* was their natural response and a firm resolve from the Day-One after the word about the location of steel plant reached them even as a rumour. This was the natural and transparent rustic expression of the community's claim over its habitat otherwise lost in the bewildering complexity of the modern world. This was perhaps also the proverbial last straw in the deteriorating situation in the tribal areas where discontent has been simmering and internal pressure has been building up for quite some time. Perhaps time has already changed even though the rulers have obstinately refused to take due note of it, being obsessed by the beautiful make-believe world of what has been termed as 'development'.

And a New Lead

This confrontation in Mavalibhata provided an opportunity for serious deliberation over basic issues involved in the modernizing process by the people facing similar onslaughts in many other places. The state has no power under the Constitution to grant virtual sovereign claims to individuals or corporate bodies. And allowing foreign bodies/multinationals to move in the grand style of rulers is not only abominable but the surrender of national sovereignty itself. Here it must be noted that the basic and the natural claim over all resources — natural and man-made — is that of the community. Community is the real living entity while state is an abstraction. The rationale and legitimacy of state control over resources are derived from a 'social contract' and its role in promoting the welfare of the community. It is unfortunate that this aspect was ignored even by state-run public sector enterprises which behaved like a capitalist, albiet amenable to governmental directions and advice. This neglect was responsible for the confusion in which capitalists-institutions and individuals merrily acquired virtual ownership of resources after payment of compensation to individuals and lease money to the State. With the advent of the new economic policy, the formal limitations imposed on the acquisition of land and use of resources by individuals / corporate bodies have become redundant — making it possible for those with money to acquire virtual absolute ownership.

The claim of capital, that is, people with money, to the central place in the economy conceded in the historical setting of the colonial capitalist era, stands thoroughly debunked in the present state of our economy. Capital formation is no longer a function of abstinence from current consumption. Afterall all those who claim to make savings do so from highly inflated and inequitous entitlements perfected insidiously, unearned incomes and ill-gotten money. Moreover there are innumerable devices in vogue for manipulating capital formation through invisible sectral transfers such as erosion of due entitlements of real workers through depressed wages and contrived prices of primary produce, creation of money by the state, simple underhand deals of individuals and such like. Harshad Mehta episode has finally exploded the 'sacrifice myth' and shattered the legitimacy of capitalist control on any segment of national economy. The call for privatization with a free license to the private sector to acquire control over national resources and dismantling the public sector in the name of capital mobilization are a big fraud for the nation.

The moot question is, can we afford to accept the logic of free-market and the power of money in such vital matters as command over an area and its resources, ownership of means of production and labour relations? The dice in that case, *ex hypothesis*, is heavily loaded against the ordinary people in general and the primary producer in particular. The production of goods has a physical limit. They have to be exchanged with money which serves as a severe constraint on their entitlements. Persons commanding money suffer no such handicap particularly in the age of created and manipulated money. Moreover even otherwise, with the growing inequality under the spell of an inequitous order, the relative strength of the urban and organized has greatly increased. And the entry of dollar, with welcome arches at every corner, has made the two sides incomparable. People with money (dollar) bags from Bombay and Delhi can acquire anything which can be purchased with money. In the free market economy which is being thrust on simple people, the former are destined to be the new lords of all they survey, human forms included, particularly in backward tribal areas where money is still counted 'pairing with pebbles', the revolutionary mathematical invention of a primitive age.

The avalanche of money-power which will subsume community resources and enslave the worker, cannot be checked as long as the current logic of money and market reigns supreme. This logic must be rejected and money power immunised in all vital sectors of national life. The command over community resources is one such sector-community resources which cannot be deemed to be money-convertible. That is also a Constitutional Directive.

The capitalist can have only a limited claim subject always to the suzerainty of the community at large. The state holds that right in trust after the adoption of the Constitution by the people a 'civil contract', solemnised through the declaration — 'We, the people of India, having solemnly resolved to constitute India. . . adopt, enact and give to ourselves. . .' It is subject to clear limitations laid down in the Directive Principles and other provisions of the Constitution.

When the state fails or ignores the vital conditions of that contract of acquiesces their violation, the community has a right, as also the responsibility to defend its natural rights against any intrusion. With the acceptance of privatization and globalization as guiding principles the state has formally absolved itself of the grave responsibility and is not standing by the people, nay, have betrayed them. Therefore so far as the people are concerned the state is 'withering away'. The people cannot afford either to wait for the unfolding of the great historical process and eventual withering away of the state, or to witness helplessly the grand feast of vultures arrayed by promiscuous rulers of the state. It is ironically the primitive man (like Russians instead of Germans in the earlier context), who is determined to drive away those vultures with just a 'sling and pebbles' in both his hands. The wheel of history is moving on. Now that the community has appeared on the scene, state has no *locus standi* to speak or to act on its behalf. 'Mavalibhata Declaration' is thus a resolute assertion of that natural and unalienable right of the people by the people for the people.

Implications of Community Assertion

The prepositions of Mavalibhata Declaration are simple and unequivocal. The people reject the anti-people and undemocratic laws on the statute book. They have brushed aside with contempt the demonic claim of money to omnipotence by simply opting out of the market so far as their land is concerned and by making the command over their territory non-negotiable. Accordingly the people of Mavalibhata 'have resolved to defend their right to life and not to move out of their villages'. This is firm and final. But the question here is not of Mavalibhata alone. The spectre is haunting many others throughout the country. The process however is extremely severe in the tribal areas which will be engulfed by it sooner than later. It is clear from the string of surrender deeds being authenticated by the government one after another in quick succession, ostensibly to meet the national crisis and in the name of so-called development.

The story of the earlier surrender cannot be allowed to repeat itself. The Mavalibhata Declaration is a call for a renewed struggle particularly by the tribal people who have been subject to worst ignominy and inequitous deal. It stands 'for creating an alternative equitable order by suitably changing the law and, if necessary, also by amending the Constitution'. The new system will comprise two tiers at the mass-roots. The *gaon sabha* will be fully responsible for managing all affairs of the village. The second tier of regional councils will have adequate legislative and executive powers. The present dependence on remote authorities on matters vital for a life with dignity of ordinary people should end and a firm foundation of the new order should be laid.

In this Regime, the process of development, and its content will be decided by the people. Accordingly the community as the natural owner of resources calls on the people with capital and also necessary skills to join them if they so wish, in a new process of sustainable development with equity. It could include industries and even a steel mill, provided they satisfy certain basic norms. The ownership issue, however, is clearly non-negotiable. The community which commands the habitat shall be the owner of any venture taken up in the area, albeit with a reasonable share for other participants therein as well.

The only formal expression of this central theme in the present system can be in the form of majority shareholding in favour of the local community. This shareholding shall be in due recognition of community's command over resources and in a way can be said to be, in lieu of allowing the use of those resources, a real tangible contribution. This formulation will not in any way affect the claims of individuals and of groups who may be affected directly or indirectly such as through denial of access to those resources or otherwise after the establishment of industry. In fact, since the community will be the owner and all affected people, by definition, are members of that community, they will be the decision-makers. Their claims will become the first charge on the system. No one will be required to pay the price of development. All those dislocated and otherwise affected will automatically get absorbed in the new system, with suitable preparation where necessary, as distinguished and honourable members.

Sustainable Development with Equity

No longer will issues like pollution of air and water, destruction of fauna and flora, denudation of agricultural land and such like will be the prerogatives of an abstraction called limited company whose prime objective is profit and sole criterion of success is the quotation on the stock-market. Sustainable and non-destructive development will be the first concern of the community. It cannot afford to leave behind the legacy of ugly holes and parched earth for successor generations. The diseconomics of industrial development, which today are being thrust as costs of development on an unsuspecting people and indulgent nature, will become an integral part of company account. Any rise in share-index will reflect the honest gains of industrial activity rather than representing proceeds of expropriation of natural resources. The state as representative of the larger community can continue to claim a share as royalty. But the virtual loot of resources by those who command money through high dividends on shares and appreciation of their value must end. Those contributing capital will have a claim not as indolent *jagirdars* but as partners in an honest venture with reasonable reward built in for their entreprenurial skills as well. In particular what is taken out of an area shall flow back to the community in the form of money-entitlements which could be and should be used to maintain and improve the social, economic and ecological status of the habitat.

Once the basic principles are accepted, details of the model can be worked out. For example, the community claiming ownership over a small industry could comprise village-communities in a small area. In the case of a large enterprise like a steel plant it may comprise people of a bigger region, say, a block, a tehsil, or even a district. But the relevant region should not be too restrictive such as the directly affected villages, or too large which may become yet another abstraction like state beyond the understanding and effective control of the ordinary people. The natural basic unit of informal social interaction, humanised economic transactions and participative democracy is a habitation complex in a village and *mohalla* in a town. Therefore these units can be deemed to be the building blocks of the 'community' of the region. The share-entitlements in this case will naturally be in the name of concerned *gaon/mohalla sabhas*, making them all co-partners in the great adventure of real development.

The working classes have a legitimate claim for a share in industry. Hitherto worker's participation has remained merely an idea of a wish. Moreover, only these workers who are directly engaged in industry have claimed some attention in this regard. The legitimate claims of those engaged in production of raw materials such as bamboo-cutters in paper-industry and mine workers supplying ore to a steel mill have been ignored. All workers associated with an industry should be partners in ownership and should hold a proportion of equity-shares therein.

A New Alliance in the Making

The simple propositions outlined above are just logical corollaries of the basic premises set in the Constitution for establishing a new social order. They may appear to be too drastic today because the nation has moved far away from the egalitarian goal and socialism itself has become a dirty word. Moreover a variety of vested interests have appeared and acquired total control over the economic as also the political system. Therefore the neo-colonial capitalist Axis looming large in the national scene cannot be expected to beat an easy retreat. Nor can we expect the gilded vultures to get scared at the very sight of the tribal with his sling.

The vested interests have been operating treacherously. The manipulation game in an area begins even before an industry is set up. The local people become the first target of that manipulation with breaking of the community as its prime objective. They are not given even the 'subject' status in the new empire. They are excluded, exhumed and flushed out consciously and otherwise. And people with good links, appropriate skills and opposite demeanour are inducted, induced or allowed to move in from outside for creating a congenial new world. Within this reference even the public sector did not make much difference except for a relatively better deal for those directly employed. The basic model in either case was the same. The unwholesome and inequitous differentiation amongst workers engaged in different segments of the national economy has driven a wedge within the working classes. There is a great divide between the organized and the unorganized sectors. They are two different worlds altogether with different norms, different entitlements and different perspectives. There is a wide twilight zone in between no doubt. It is crowded by restless people, the organized-unorganized, bewitched by dreams of a promised land above and haunted by the spectre of an abominable underworld below. We have a fragmented and fractured working class. Consequently their struggles have not only lacked a focus but have been, not infrequently, at cross purposes as well. For example, the struggles of organized sector workers against capitalists have remained exclusive urban phenomena with sectoral interests in the fore. The community at large and the rural people in particular have stood apart, unconcerned, alienated and deprived. Within the rural sector even farmers with soiled hands and agricultural labourers, totally broke and badly bruised, have not realized that both are victims of the same system, mercilessly exploited through depressed wages and trifled prices. The middle classes in the tertiary sector have remained satisfied with crumbs which they got in the vile game of expropriation making all sorts of noises, sadly only for a larger crumb.

This scene is changing fast with unbelievable speed. After devastating the rural economy the main target of the new Axis is the middle class including workers in the organized sector. This class has become much too large to serve the elite objective as the funnel and also the instrument of expropriation. Moreover this class has itself become a vested interest and also dysfunctional. That it needs to be pruned is universally accepted with no one to defend it. Therefore, a process of so-called rationalization has been started whose main target ironically is the working class which needs to be protected, with some qualifications, so as to serve as a strong foundation of the modern sector of new economy. Management skills are on ascendency now. The advances in technology are being used to break this class to push it to the other side, may be into the twilight zone for the time being. The upper crust, comprising mostly managers of the system, will admirably serve as agents of capital and as virtual extention of the Western economy, with the dubious status of *pratilomi* (offsprings of higher caste women and lower caste men) though. The remaining will get reclaimed by the amorphous mass below — the subject people of the new Regime.

The call for struggle in Mavalibhata Declaration is qualitatively different. It is the community, which has been ignored, despised and broken, it is ordinary people — farmers, workers, artisans and tribals — who have been trampled on relentlessly and mercilessly and who are getting ready for leading the revolt. They are no longer prepared to accept the current ownership concept of industry or its revised version of control through management structures. The choice before the workers, of all hues with all their faults and fractures, is clear. They must close their ranks, align with the community to which they belong and accept the place of honour designated for them in the new schema. The capitalist also will have no choice but to accept the reality. If he fails to do so he will be totally isolated. The borrowed, nay, contrived glory cannot last forever. He must accept the role in keeping with the modest contribution which money makes as a junior 'four-anna' partner and participate in the exhilarating march towards sustainable development with equity under the benign and wise leadership of the community. Or else, he will be swept away in the torrential currents of the new history of the working classes in the making.

What the people may gain in terms of economic benefits and welfare is no doubt important. But, the real issues are those of national honour, dignity of the people and identity of the community. The people have resolved not to allow their primacy slip by and make their honour negotiable in the new scheme of structural transformation and retrieve the same where damage has already been done. The rulers shall not be allowed to proceed further with bartering away the suzerainty which has been mischievously planned under deceptive titles, deeds and forms. These paper titles will have no force on the ground firmly held by the people. The alliance of farmers, workers, artisans, tribals, that is, the community comprising working classes, is formidable with the capitalists and their agents standing isolated on the other side. The new alliance is destined to create a new world order based on equality, justice and fraternity.

Annexure
Mavalibhata Declaration of People's Right

We, the people of Mavalibhata*, Mardum and Nagarnar areas, and representatives of people's organisations all over the country have assembled this day, December 5, 1992, at Mavalibhata, Bastar, M.P. We reviewed the situation arising from the arbitrary decision of the State Government to permit and facilitate establishment of a big steel plant in private sector and, that too, with foreign collaboration at Mavalibhata. We have also deliberated in depth on its immediate and long term effects at different levels. The State Government, as also the local administration, showed no concern for the people's rights and their aspirations. That was not all. The Chief Minister went ahead and laid the foundation stone on October 6, 1992, without waiting for the completion of legal processes necessary for setting up such industrial projects.

The people of Mavalibhata area were up in arms against the project ever since they had heard the rumours about its possible establishment. This area falls within *Dandami* tribal territory. The community is almost totally free from outside influence. Land is their only source of livelihood. The level of fomal education is insignificant. The *Dandamis* are known for their valour, self-esteem and unrestrained emotional responses. This open attack in the form of a foundation stone on their basic right — right to life with dignity — could not be tolerated.

Their reaction was simple, sharp and swift. The foundation stone was broken. The approach roads to their villages were barricated. That foundation stone in their perception was a challenge to their very existence thrown by the entire

---

* Mavalibhata is located about 35 kms from Jagdalpur on way to Bailadila in Bastar, M.P. Like countless other tribal habitations it was also lost on its small world. Education is almost nil notwithstanding the existence of a school for years. Neither they understand the *farsi* (the colloquial term for unintelligible tongue of others and a corrupt form of the term Persian) of others, nor others can understand their *koitur* (*Gondi*). A few, however, have smattering of Hindi. So even though they are living close to an important highway, they are leading a happy life behind the impregnable wall of language.

Dandami by nature is volatile, simple and joy-logging. They have no peer in social solidarity. After the harvest, bands of *Dandami* youth start moving out for *shikar* to distant hills and forests with *pej* (rice-liquid) in gourd and bow-and-arrow in their hands. No one can dare cross their route. It is *Dandami* youth who have the sacred duty of pulling the great-grand chariot of Goddess Danteshwari, the ruling deity of Bastar, during *Dussera* festival in Jagdalpur. →

outside world. And the stone barriers were the silent answer of the community with a counter-challenge "let us see, who dares to come and occupy our ancestral and sacred lands?". They also resolved '*katenge par hatenge nahin*' (we will get killed but we will not move out).

The government did not give due regard to the spirit of this natural response of the people. No one cared to ponder over its real meaning. It was simple affirmation of their right to life with dignity. Instead, it was taken as an affront to the supreme authority of the omnipotent state. The ruling party, in collusion with administration, made a callous attempt to silence the dissident voice through Goebbelian mis-information and resorting to medieval techniques of incitement and mob-violence.

← One evening of December 1991, everything appeared to have changed for this small village. Mavalibhata and five neighbouring villages (Burungpal, Durram, Patharli Uduwa and Katakanda) were caught in a whirl. The government officials told them that a steel plant with an investment of rupees four thousand crores will be established there. About five thousand acres of land will be acquired for that purpose. All the five villages will have to move out. The people were shaken by the unanswered questions — 'where will we go?' The government's reply was dry — 'you will get compensation. You can go wherever you can find land'. Their silent reaction was 'what will we do with money? Our deities, sacred places, *gata-kalk* (burial stones), all that we can call ours is here'. 'Why not establish the plant, where government wants us to go?' was their simple logic.

But no one listened to them. The government remained unmoved. On October 6, 1992 the Chief Minister laid the foundation stone under heavy police *bandobast*. The elite of the district and the state was jubilant. All political parties of 'right' and 'left' were overwhelmed by the grand procession of development in Bastar.

But in the deep dark shadow at the centre of that flurry of hope and joy, the approach roads to their villages were dug, stone walls were erected by *Dandami Marias*. . . . Let's see who dares to come on our sacred land — *katenge par hatenge nahin* (we will get killed but not move!). . . . *Ami Dandami* (We are *Dandamis*).

The signal of *Bhumkal* (Revolt) is clear and categorical. It is not only a declaration of community's right over resources, but a resolve to die for the same.

The Mavalibhata Declaration of human rights is before you — may be a precursor of an epoch-making *BHUMKAL*.

The Jagadalpur episode* was just the last ugly glimpse of that nefarious conspiracy.

The people of Mavalibhata and Nagarnar had placed before the local administration their 'Resolve' (Appendix 1 and Appendix 2) and also certain important questions (Appendix 3) about the State's Constitutional responsibility for safeguarding the rights and interests of the tribal peóple, on October 15, 1992. The government has maintained studied silence on these issues. Moreover, the state is unrelenting, unmindful of the severe and universal condemnation of Jagadalpur-episode. But Mavalibhata people's resolve remains unshaken, nay, it is assuming tidal dimension with spontaneous response all around. The people are standing firm like a rock. Thus, there is a state of uneasy peace in the area as the shadow of implicit confrontation is deepening. It may turn into a serious crisis if the State continues to ignore the voice of reason, insists on going ahead without taking the people in confidence and without following the well-established processes in consonance with the State's policy, laws and the Constitution.

This confrontation at Mavalibhata is not an unusual or unique event for the tribal areas. The process of encroachment on tribal resources in the name of development by the state and also others has been continuing for a long time. But so far there was some concern, some realisation of injustice as well. If nothing else, at least some paper provisions were made to counter its ill effects. But now perceptions are changing. The power-brokers are openly asserting that the grand procession of development cannot be stopped simply because a handful people may not agree to move out. 'The work in Bastar will continue even if lakhs, what to speak of thousands, are displaced', thus spake the District Magistrate. Thus the Mavalibhata crisis is just an advance signal of the new catastrophe. This confrontation is an inevitable consequence of the open entry of unbridled market

---

* A large crowd of about a thousand people in thirteen motor-vehicles reached Patharli Uruwa in search of Dr. B.D. Sharma who dared to tell and also warn the outside world about the resolve of the people of Mavalibhata. On not finding him there, the returning convoy intercepted him on the high way as he was proceeding in the opposite direction back to the village from Jagdalpur alone on the pillion of a motor cycle. He was thrashed, but protected from the murderous assault of the excited crowd, and was rushed to Jagdalpur bundled in a jeep with cinema-style chase of others in vehicles not convinced about sparing him. In the safety of the town, he was stripped and paraded on the streets of that town, where he served as District Magistrate two decades back, in a bid to demonstrate to the world the fate which awaits for those daring to oppose development. The entire town witnessed that act of retribution benumbed with shock while the entire administration including police remained an amused silent spectator!

forces in the so-called backward but resource-rich tribal areas.

A new alignment of national and international forces is now being forged. The most terrible form of this alignment is on the rise in tribal areas. Here, on the one side are the simple tribal people. Their numerical strength is small. But they are imbued with high sense of dignity, self-reliance and strong tradition of community life. On the other side is the new power-axis of neocolonial capitalist forces. The irony is that the all powerful state itself, which has the Constitutional responsibility of protecting the tribal people, has assumed the role of promoter and protector of that Axis. Thus the people, particularly the tribal people, are now facing a demonic challenge. Their very identity is at stake. And in this confusion, all values and traditions, that we as a nation can be proud of, have also got staked.

Thus, our country is passing through a very delicate phase in its history. Mavalibhata is the first victim of this International Combine. If it succeeds here, devastation of other areas will be a matter of time only. This horrendous situation in the tribal and also other areas calls for closing of ranks by all progressive forces. The sharp reaction and rustic reply of the people of Mavalibhata to the anti-people and fascist ways of the state have become the symbol of a people's struggle. Mobilisation of utmost support for this struggle is a must now. In the context of issues raised in Mavalibhata, we once again resolve that :

> We will intensify our struggles for basic changes in the institutional structure, national laws and for establishment of a new order in which the people will enjoy undisputed rights over resources, they will be partner in development, everyone will have a place of honour in the new economy and the right to life with dignity of every citizen will be non-violable.

Nation

In contravention of the general and the specific Constitutional provisions against unlimited expansion and unregulated sovereignty by private and State entities over the resources of the community, whose aim was creation of an egalitarian order, the government has virtually rewritten the Constitution in the garb of a new economic policy. The new policy is giving rise to extreme concentration of economic and political powers and authoritarian fascist regimes. In fact, the government has abrogated its responsibility for equitable and sustainable development and to ensure judicious use of natural resources. It has thrown them open for rapacious exploitation by the new global Axis. It has shown no concern even for the fact that these resources after all are people's sacred trust.

We are not prepared to accept this position. We hereby resolve and declare that :

> Only those enterprises will be allowed to be established in our respective areas which agree to accept coomunity control over them. Under this arrangement, there will be a provision for majority shares in the name of local community. This provision will not be against money but will be in lieu of the real contribution of the community by way of cooperation and consent for use of those resources by the enterprise, over which it has enjoyed full control through the ages and which have provided the community and its members with sustenance in all aspects of their life. Other partners in the enterprise will be those who may invest capital and all categories of workers.
>
> This form of shareholding by the community will not compromise in any way the claims of the displaced and the affected individuals for compensation and honourable resettlement.
>
> In the context of this claim on behalf of the people, we will prevent further privatisation of public sector enterprises. In case it becomes necessary to change the structure of an enterprise, the government should accept this claim of the community and hand it over to them as its rightful owner.

Tribal areas

After Independence, on the one hand, traditional self-governing institutions of tribal people have been totally ignored. On the other hand, exotic laws and institutions have been indiscriminately superimposed. During this phase, the Governors did not discharge their Constitutional responsibility to adapt the formal system in accordance with the needs of tribal system for which full powers had been bestowed on them under the Fifth Schedule of the Constitution. Consequently, entire communities are deemed as law-breakers; traditional institutions have collapsed and ordinary tribals are facing worst forms of destitution. We therefore, resolve that —

> We will struggle for ending the anti-people and inhuman situation in

the tribal areas and for creating and alternative equitable order by suitably changing the law and, if necessary, also by amending the Consitution. In the new system, (i) the *gaon sabha* (village assembly) will be fully responsible for all affairs of the village and villages will function as self-governing units of participatory democracy; (ii) Regional Councils will be established for larger tribal tracts. They will be endowed with legislative and executive powers. The jurisdiction of these Regional Councils, wherever necessary, may cut across the present administrative boundaries.

Bastar and Mavalibhata

Dandakaranya is endowed with rich natural resources. Private capital and multinationals are making a concerted bid to enter these areas in utter disregard of the Constitutional safeguards and legal provisions. The state is allowing open entry, nay, is welcoming large industries with no concern for its own policies, guidelines and also human rights and people's welfare. We strongly condemn this open attack on the interests of the ordinary people, particularly the tribal people.

We also note that the tribal habitats are extensive and the life of the people depends on the natural resources of the entire habitat. The irony is that the *de juro* command of the tribal people has been generally circumscribed to a small part thereof. The remaining area (70% in Bastar) is formally termed as the so-called 'forest', which may or may not have tree cover. Thus, the people have to make do with a limited area. It includes *abadi*, agriculture and *nistar*. In this situation, if land is assigned from the limited area used by the people for industry and other institutions, the condition of people depending on it is bound to deteriorate.

It may be further noted that the level of education is very low in tribal communities and the modern skills are almost non-existent. Thus the people are not prepared for participation with dignity in modern economic activities.

There is no justification for acquisition of tribal lands in this critical phase in the history of tribal communities. Similarly diversion of so-called government land, which is being used by the tribal people for a variety of other purposes, is not proper. In this situation all new activities in tribal areas should be taken up, wherever necessary, on the so-called 'forest' land. But concurrently, action should also be taken for enriching the so-called forest with people's participation as partners.

In this situation we resolve and declare that —

> The people of Mavalibhata today are faced with the question of life and death. The people have resolved to defend their right to life and not to move out of their village. All of us are fully with people in this struggle. If the vested interests or administration resort to oppressive measures against them, we will stand by the people of Mavalibhata and together give a befitting reply to the intruders.

Democratic Norms and Human Rights

We condemn the anti-people and fascist actions by the government and the administration to silence the voice of dissence and to evict the tribal people from their ancestral homes and habitat. Honest adherence to democratic norms and full regard for human rights in dealing with the people are essential. We expect that political leaders and officials will change their behaviour and fulfil their responsibilities as public servants. So far as the issue of use of natural resources is concerned no family, as a rule, can be deprived of its right over the resources on which it may be depending on for its living (i) without prior willing consent of the family and the community; and (ii) without providing to the family in advance an honourable alternative means of livelihood acceptable to it.

All those laws which are not in consonance with these basic premises are unacceptable to us. So long as the State does not establish an equitable order, the people have full right to defend themselves their right to life with dignity. We accordingly resolve that —

> We will intensify our struggle for changing the anti-people laws and for establishment of the most fundamental of all rights, the right to life with dignity, and take the struggle to its logical end. We call upon all progressive forces in the country to extend all possible support, physical and financial, to this crucial struggle in Bastar for upholding of people's rights.

Appendix 1
The Resolve of Mavalibhata People

The State Government has extended an invitation to industrialists for establishing large industries based on local resources. It was in pursuance of this policy that S.M. Dichem has been offered thousands of acres of land in Mavalibhata region and the foundation stone of a steel plant was laid on October 6, 1982. The Chief Minister also declared that two more plants will be started very soon. There has been some talk of a steel plant in Nagarnar area for quite some time. There is no information about other industries and their likely location so far. Some smaller industrial units have come up in recent years on Jagdalpur-Dantewara highway.

We, the people of Mavalibhata, Nagarnar and surrounding areas, are extremely concerned about the policy of utilisation of resources in our area adopted by the government and the governmental attitude and behaviour towards the people. There is anger about the same. The public opinion had been treated with contempt while establishing industries on Jagdalpur-Dantewara Road. The people are destined to be ruined. The government has paid no attention to these aspects. Foundation stone has been laid in Mavalibhata without any prior intimation of significance. There was no dialogue with the people about their future. A bolt from the blue has struck the people. It appears that some processes are on under the cover of secrecy about the other steel plant, in spite of the stiff opposition by the people of Nagarnar. They may face a similar catastrophe any day all of a sudden.

We want to forewarn the government that the policy and the premises of the government about the use of natural resources are totally unacceptable to the people here. All natural resources including land-water-forest, from which we have been making a living for ages, belong to us. We have the natural right to use the same. This right has also been enshrined in our Constitution. The government has no right — Constitutional or moral — to take away our resources. It is obligatory on the state to obtain willing consent of the people depending on them for their living and also the community before putting those resources to any alternative use.

A vast majority of people living in this region belong to scheduled tribes. The levels of education even after 45 years of Independence is negligible. Our life is totally dependent on land and forest. All those lawas are unacceptable to us under which the government can acquire our land after payment of compensation and can remove us from our villages without even asking us. The Constitution has placed the responsibility of protecting us on the Central and State Governments, the Governor and the

President. We are sorry that the State Government has not discharged this responsibility. On the contrary, it has no qualms in dispossessing us from our resources, even our homes and herths, that too using those laws that are unconstitutional and violative of human rights. We are pressurized through hidden threats that we may have to move out either in this simple way or through other methods. We reject this hidden threat. If such pressures continue, the people's reaction may become unrestrained. The responsibility for any consequences will be that of the government.

We people have decided that Mother-Earth is not a saleable commodity. Any talk of compensation is unacceptable to us. Service of the industrialist is slavery which is against our honour. It is clear to us that once we move out of our homes and herths, nothing but destitution will be our fate. Therefore we are not prepared to leave our land and our village at any cost '*katenge par hatenge nahin*' (we will get killed but not move out) is our resolve. We are prepared to sacrifice all that is ours, our life itself, for defending our basic human right, the right to life with dignity.

The question now facing us is of life-and-death. We are not prepared for any negotiations, or even a dialogue of any sort in this regard with the government or anyone else. No one is authorised on our behalf for any dialogue with government notwithstanding his office or status — *Patel* or *manjhi*, *sarpanch* or M.L.A., M.P. or Minister. We will also expect that no official visiting our village will even broach the issue. Let no one dare to attempt misleading our simple people.

We also wish to forewarn all enterprises through you that they should not make any schemes on the strength of any promise or even formal orders of the government. *Gram Swaraj* has been promulgated in our villages in keeping with the spirit of our Constitution. Our resources cannot be put to any alternative use without the consent of our village- community. If any work is done in disregard of people's will, the consequences may be drastic, whose responsibility will be theirs — simple and unequivocal.

Ami Jadkati, Ami Dandami!
(We are root-cutters, We Dandamis)
Gaon Amcho, Raj Amcho!!
(Village is our, Raj is Ours)
Ni Deun Kau Apan Jeeuu !!!
(We will not surrender our life to anyone)

Nate-na-Raj Andolan
(Village Rule Movement)

Appendix 2
Tribal People's Resolve for people-Oriented Development
(Bharat Jan Andolan)

Warning against Loot of Resources in Tribal Areas!

Call for People-oriented (Janwadi) Development!!

The Tribal Areas are developing but tribal communities are being pauperised !!!

We are being evicted overnight from those resources — Water-forest-land-ages — in the name of development in some places, branding us an encroachers at others and in exchange of useless 'pauper' elsewhere. Every attempt of ours for self-defence is deemed to be violation of law and may even be branded as REVOLT. It is crushed mercilessly.

Big 'empires' are being established, but there is no place for us therein because —

- We are not educated,
- When educated, we lack technical skills,
- Even when we have technical skills, we lack desired qualifications?

In other words, our place is in the crowd of casual labourers, domestic servants. If we run away and seek shelter in our forest, what we find is *dafedar* (forest-guard) with a *lathi*. Now they are wielding even guns. The slums of towns — old and new — is our final destiny.

This destiny we reject outright. Those laws and governmental system are unacceptable to us, under whose aegies all that is ours is being snatched away and those who can claim nothing become masters. Our position is simple —

- natural resources are ours, no one can take away that right,
- if these resources are to be used for some other purposes, our prior permission will have to be obtained
- before our resources are otherwise utilised, an alternative arrangement for our living will have to be made which is honourable and acceptable to us
- tribal community shall be the owner of all new enterprises.

The government has paid no heed to these issues. Some twenty out of every hundred tribals in M.P. have already got displaced. But the government even does not know who they were, what are they doing and where they have gone? Before proceeding further full and satisfactory arrangement should be made for them all.

We are not prepared to accept this logic of *developmentwalas* that someone will have to bear the cost of development. It is a duty of the State that those who are expected to make sacrifice for development are assured of a reasonable share in the benefits.

Therefore we reject the current policy of development. We also hope that henceforth the state shall arrange its affairs in accordance with our resolve. All citizens should be co-partners in this development without any discrimination.

Our Resolve

1. We will not allow any work to proceed until all those who have fallen victims of development so far have been suitably provided for.
2. The local tribal community should have not less than 51 per cent share-holding in all industries located in tribal areas so that the community has full control on the direction of development and people's advancement is central in development.
3. The labourers engaged in supply of raw material to an industry should have the same status as that of industrial workers. The labour as a whole should have one-fourth shareholding in the concerned enterprise.
4. The responsibility for capital, technology and management should be of the government through public sector enterprises. If the government is unable to do so, the private enterprise may be allowed. But the capitalist should not have more than 24 per cent shareholding.
5. As far as possible, only small industries should be established in tribal areas, so that the local people themselves can manage the same. As far as possible, cooperatives should be organised for this purpose.
6. Equal share in favour of tribal land owner should be ensured even in small enterprises established on that land.
7. At least 50 per cent of houses in new residential colonies coming up in tribal areas should be reserved for the local tribal people.

These basic principles can serve as the foundation of people-oriented development in tribal areas.

Appendix 3

Some Open Questions about New Industrial Policy and Steel Plants

1. How many people in all will be uprooted by the steel plant? In the beginning land in the tribal areas is acquired only from some (that is, thousands) persons, but later on hundreds of villages and *lakhs* of people face devastation. What will be the zone of influence of this steel-plant and how many villages will be destroyed?
2. Why the planning frame earlier adopted for Malajkhand Project in Balaghat has not been adopted and enforced for Bastar projects? While clearing the Malajkhand Copper Project the Union Government had decided that henceforth before giving clearance to any large industry in tribal areas, a plan for proper placement in the new frame for all persons living in the zone of influence of the concerned project will be prepared. Why such a plan has not been prepared for the proposed industries in Bastar?
3. Why no advance action was taken for preparing the local people to enable them to take advantage of the new industrial activity in accordance with the guidelines of the Central Government? These guidelines were issues as early as 1974 for adoption in the preparation of Integrated Tribal Development Projects. Why no action has been taken thereon?
4. There is a Constitutional duty of the State to take special measures and make special provisions for the scheduled areas for protection against adverse effects of large industries. It was in furtherance of this objective that the Constitution was amended in 1976 and the the entire Bastar district including Jagdalpur was declared as scheduled. Why the government has not made any regulations so far specially under this provision?
5. Why big industries are coming up only around Jagdalpur? When steel plants can run in Bhilai, Vishakhapatnam and even Japan using iron-ore of Bastar, why similar planning is not being done within Baster with a clear objective of balanced development of entire Bastar? What is the sense in steel plants being stuck to existing state highways, national highway or railways? Why are they not being setup in remote forest areas after opening them up by roads and rails? Why the most

populous and the best agricultural region has been selected for steel plants which will destroy lakhs of tribal people?

6. How much employment will be generated? The industrialists claim that latest technology will be used which means that even **robots** can be engaged. There will be no opportunity for the local people of employment except that of manual casual labour that too in the beginning. Why firm figures of employment generation are not being placed before the people?

7. How can we believe that local people will get any benefit? Today the government is not able to ensure flow of benefits to the local people even in its own enterprises. The outsiders are corning everything through various tricks and devices. Then how will the government get that policy of local participation in benefits in case of private enterprise? What law or rules if any have been framed in this regard?

8. Why even in industries based on local resources, the place of tribal is envisaged as that of a labourer, and not is owner? The Commissioner for Scheduled Castes and Scheduled Tribes had made some important recommendations in this regard in 1988. Earlier, the 'Policy formulation Commission' setup soon after the shooting of Pravir Chandra Bhanjdeo, the ruler of Bastar, had also made similar recommendations in 1972. Why this Report has not been published so far? Why have those recommendations not implemented?

9. Why any concessions to industrialists for setting up steel plant? When industries based on iron ore from Bastar are earning huge profit, then the permission to set up a steel plant in Bastar itself is a big concession. In this situation why are we told that concessions are being given because the industrialists have been invited?

10. If the declaration of government about the benefits of industries accruing to Bastar and inhabitants of Bastar is correct, then wny the same principle is not being followed in the case of forests? Why the governments' own declaration of 'master, not labourer' in respect of *tendu* leaves has been falsified?

11. Why is the violation of basic human rights of the tribal people continuing? Many laws particularly those relating to land and forest are inconsistent with the present tribal situation. Under these laws, the Constitutional and human rights of the tribal people are being

openly violated. The Commissioner for Scheduled Castes and Scheduled Tribes had made three major recommendations in this regard in 1986:

(i) No acquisition of tribal land without his consent;

(ii) Provision of alternative means of livelihood acceptable to the concerned person; and

(iii) Legal ban on use of police force in cases of land acquisition.

Why no concrete action has been taken so far? Why the Constitutional and human rights of the tribal people are being still violated?

22

Development Activism

The Importance of Being Voluntary

Bunker Roy

Development, because it concerns people, has to be slow — it cannot be artificially forced in any direction. The process of making people aware of their surroundings, their own strength and finally their own skills to be able to make choices is what development is all about. The dilemma is how to facilitate this process.

In the ultimate analysis it is a question of trust. How much are we willing to trust the people to take their own decisions without influence, without intimidation and without passing judgements on their competence. History has shown we have not trusted enough the people. This is one lesson we shall never learn. In 'we' is included the dominant minority — the literate, the affluent and the powerful who have their interests to protect, and in their grand scheme of things the rural and urban poor have no place.

In other words the first and most formidable obstacle to development today is the Literate Man. The educational system has conditioned him/her to look down on poor rural and urban communities. An illiterate man cannot be intelligent or have any skill to teach. The ways of poor communities in cities and villages have to be primitive and backward and to trust them totally means to treat them as equals which is an impossible expectation today.

The system has made us look down on our own culture, on our own indigenous solutions and institutions and influenced us to mistrust all knowledge and information that originates from those we persist in calling the poor as the backward and the primitive. We must accept there is a fundamental difference between Literacy and Education. Margaret Mead, the anthropologist, once said, "Never let school interfere with your Education".

Another major dilemma is the lack of space for individual growth. In this great desire to help the so-called poor (in material goods but not in spirit) and in the name of development we have encroached on individual space, violated privacy, forced people to think in a certain way and penalized those who have rejected government assistance for good reason. A plethora of schemes from various departments, some duplicating one another, have plagued poorer communities. Generous grants are being handed out and it is nowhere more unseemly than when it comes to procuring family planning cases.

Gifts, bribes, inducements and favours, all being offered by government servants at the village level for family planning cases have reduced this idea to a farce. What is actually being suggested is birth control. The final choice must rest with the women and not with the government as is the case today. It takes time for information to be absorbed. Critical decisions are not influenced by financial year targets nor can the pace be forced.

By far the most serious crisis we face is our lack of self-respect. We should take pride in the way our indigenous institutions and ideas have survived. We should value innovations and make every effort to see that it is replicated because it is low cost, community based and has grown from below. This country has all the answers. The solutions to every problem are well within reach in the boundaries of our own country. Are we prepared to implement them even if the world outside does not understand?

All these are major deficiencies that are not being taken seriously enough. These flaws in the development process are linked to flaws in the human beings implementing the programmes on the field. Till these deficiencies are recognized, funds will continue to be wasted, results will continue to be poor and the poor will remain poor.

Having said this, what can we do as individuals? We can set an example. Action requires a certain belief and faith that one day what you do will bring change. May be it is not what you first wanted to happen. May be its not what others wanted but with every process there is an invisible reaction that manifests itself later. Often we do not have the tools to be able to understand it but, it is noticeable, that it differs all the time.

Tilonia was started with no fixed or long-term plan of action. It grew out of an urgency that had everything to do with my own need and impatience to want to contribute something tangible. I was confident that it should be possible to show compassion and concern directly without intermediaries or levels. It should be possible, I felt, to facilitate action that improved the physical living conditions of people. I had seen far too many people telling others what to do, too many people making promises that were broken, too many individuals who did not believe in the importance of action. This was as important for one's own personal growth and understanding as doing pointless degrees or research in universities.

The fact that many people outside the urban areas were still struggling to live a life of dignity and free from hunger and fear was a matter of great shame to me. I noticed I was taking too many things for granted — basic human needs like drinking water and good schools, inexpensive health services and access to fuel and fodder.

The education I had received was elitist enough to give me blinkers. The mental and physical security I enjoyed made me arrogant. I began to demand for my rights first without considering my duties as a citizen. I was obliged to return, in whatever form or manner, to society what I had received from being born privileged. It was only right and just. The point was how to make the blind see and the deaf listen?

It had to be done by identifying the problems and the human flaws in the development process and doing something about it on the ground. If there is trust, the people will show what is possible and the incredible responsibilities they are prepared to take once they are involved and taken into confidence. If there is no space, then create one. The role of groups like Tilonia is to protect groups from destroying themselves by becoming dependent on government or vested interests.

Give them the space to develop their confidence, create the space to upgrade their skills so that eventually they depend on each other and carve out another space so that they have enough time to try out new ideas, innovate, make mistakes and try again. It is important to stress self-reliance which can be done by reviving old and tested local, self-government institutions, and preserving time-tested cultural traditions that have kept communities together and given them an identity. The use of native skills and local know-how to tackle rural problems should be encouraged instead of bringing in alien ideas, strange people from outside to solve problems.

In the last 17 years of its existence Tilonia has tested many ideas on the ground, explored many myths that people even today are not prepared to accept and proved many points as a result. Strangely enough our problems are somewhat different. Our problems have to do with success. With every simple idea implemented and replicated on the ground we have met envy, jealousy and bitterness. We find no one wants change. Very few want a simple idea that reduces costs to be implemented on the ground.

So long as the solutions are discussed on paper everyone is for it, but as soon as it is put into effect there is resentment and counter-arguments. For instance, the solar electrification for lighting in Ladakh. We have solar-electrified five complete villages in this area, reduced costs, decentralized the power system to the household level and trained illiterate youth to plan, install and maintain the system. It has been working for the last three years. The community of users think it is a miracle. But virtually everyone else is unhappy because it has worked.

Only later we realized that over Pound Sterling one million was being spent every year by the government to reach 200,000 litres of diesel and 200,000 litres of kerosene by road transport. Imagine how many contractors would suffer if the whole region was solar electrified! Generator sets would not be bought, transmission wires would no longer be purchased and wooden poles would not have to be transported by road.

Engineers would be out of jobs, plans for large hydel projects will no longer be considered and the community would no longer be dependent on their patronage. Obviously the files for more villages to be solar electrified are no longer moving and I have been declared public enemy number one. Making a complicated problem look simple and generates its own set of problems.

In real life we face these dilemmas everyday in our personal and professional lives. Who decides what is good or what is bad for the poor? Is it worth fighting on so many fronts? Doubts and fears, ups and downs are all a part of the decision-making process. We may disagree to the roads to take but we must never fear to walk: To standstill is to lose faith.

Traveller there is no path
Paths are made by walking.

Recommendations

MEETING OF EXPERTS
ON
INTERFACE OF CULTURAL IDENTITY AND DEVELOPMENT

Part I. Meeting of Experts

1.1 The experts' meeting was held within the framework of the United Nations World Decade For Cultural Development (1988-1997).

1.2 Participants from Australia, Bangladesh, India, Indonesia, Iran, Mongolia, Nepal, Sri Lanka, Thailand and Turkey attended the meeting, as well as a representative from with World Decade Secretariat (Unesco - Paris), and the Resident Representative for India of the U.N.D.P.

1.3 The experts presented papers which ranged from theoretical issues on cultural identity and development to regional case studies in different field situations.

Part II. Observation

The Meeting,

2.1 **Welcoming** the initiative of the United Nations in launching the "World Decade for Cultural Development" and setting up of "World Commission on Culture and Development", both under the aegis of Unesco,

(a) to promote the cultural dimensions of development with a view to identifying and analysing the ways in which cultural development influences individual and collective well-being; and

(b) to study the implications of the present progressive loss of indigenous knowledge, tradition, language and even entire cultures.

2.2 **Observing** that this initiative had come at an appropriate moment, especially in view of the fact that

(a) development entails transformation of the material base, social structures, value systems and symbolic representation of any community or society, and brings out the creative potential at an individual or collective level;

(b) as such, it amounts to the re-creation of the society that draws on tradition and re-orders it even as it creates while assimilating and adapting any new technology on its own terms;

(c) a society is alive and vibrant only if it has the capacity to be rooted in its own matrix and yet responsive to other cultures; and

(d) development, in the fullest sense, is the development of the human potential in all its economic, material, socio-cultural, and spiritual aspects.

Part III. Recommendation No. 1

3.1 **Calls-upon**

(a) Research Institutions to engage in multi-disciplinary studies of development strategies and programmes in consultation with the representatives of the concerned communities so that the significance of culture as a necessary aspect of development is borne out, especially when there is an external intervention of finance or technology;

(b) National Governments to take cognizance of and reflect the cultural dimension of development in their perspective planning at national, regional and village levels; and

(c) Specialized Agencies of the United Nations System to take the initiative in incorporating cultural parameters in development and to insist on involvement and participation of target groups and communities in the planning process.

Part IV. Recommendation No. 2

4.1 **Recommends** Unesco give support to the organisation of further deliberations on the subject, especially by

(a) experts on culture and ecology and those related to the developmental sectors such as science, technology, rural development, economics, etc.;

(b) representatives of community based and grass roots non-Governmental Organisations working in the field of development programmes such as those of environment, rural development, water resources and those from the fields of education and culture; and

(c) UNESCO, in collaboration with other United Nations Specialized Agencies support a series of pilot studies on cultural identity and regional development.

List of Contributors

Anisuzzaman	Professor of Bengali Dhaka University Dhaka (Bangladesh)
Parthasarathi Banerjee	Scientist NISTADS CISR Dr. K.S. Krishnan Marg New Delhi - 110 012
S. Budhisantoso	Director of Sajarah Dan Nllal Traditional Depdikbud J1. Cilacap 4 Jakarta Pusat (Indonesia)
Francis Childe	Chief Project Coordination and Section World Decade for Cultural Development UNESCO, 7 Place de Fontenoy 75700 Paris (France)
Dilli R. Dahal	Reader Centre for Nepal & Asian Studies Tribhuvan University Kirtipur Kathmandu (Nepal)

Fatemeh Farahani	Director Iranian National Commission for Unesco 1188 Shahid Eslamieh Bldg. Enghelab Felestin Cross Tehran 13158 (Iran)
Olga Gostin	Senier Lecturer Faculty of Aborginal Studies School of Aborginal & Islander Administration University of South Australia Adelaide SA 5001 (Australia)
Bozkurt Güvenc	Former Professor of Anthropology at Hacettepe University Kelebek Sokak 28/4 GOP 06700 Ankara (Turkey)
Ravindra K. Jain	Dean, School of Social Sciences 65, New Campus Jawaharlal Nehru University New Delhi - 110 067
Lachman M. Khubchandani	Director Centre for Communication Studies 270/212, Sind Society Ganeshkhand Road Pune - 411 007
Leah Lui	Policy Resource Officer in Department of Family Services and Aboriginal and Islander Affairs Flat 2, 10 Juluis St. New Farm 4005 Brisbane (Australia)

S.C. Malik	U.G.C. Professor of Anthropology, NMML, New Delhi 5/90 Connaught Circus New Delhi - 110 001
Mrinal Miri	Professor and Head Department of Philosophy North-East Hill University Shillong - 793 003
A.R. Momin	Professor and Head Deptt. of Sociology University of Bombay Bombay - 400 098
Dawa Norbu	Associate Professor School of International Studies Jawaharlal Nehru University New Delhi - 110 067
Y. Otgonbayar	Embassy ofMongolia 34, Golf Links New Delhi - 110 003
Meral Ozbek	Assistant Professor Faculty of Communication University of Ankara Ankara (Turkey)
P.D. Premasiri	Professor of Philosophy and Psychology at the University of Paradeniya C-26, University Park Peradeniya (Sri Lanka)

Mohammed Reza Rikhtegaran	Lecturer in Tehran University Iranian Cultural House 18, Tilak Marg New Delhi
Bunker Roy	Director Social Work and Research Centre Tilonia - 305 816 Madanganj, Dist. Ajmer (Rajasthan)
Baidyanath Saraswati	Research Professor Indira Gandhi National Centre for the Arts Janpath New Delhi - 110 001
B.D. Sharma	Former Commissioner for Scheduled Castes and Scheduled Tribes Village Maralibhata, Post Box 20 Jagdalpur Bastar, Madhya Pradesh
Kapila Vatsyayan	Academic Director Indira Gandhi National Centre for the Arts Janpath New Delhi - 110 001
Wit Wisadavet	Professor Department of Philosophy Faculty of Arts Chulalongkorn University Phyathai Road Bangkok (Thailand)